THE MAN WHO WAS
B. TRAVEN

THE MAN WHO WAS
B. TRAVEN

WILL WYATT

JONATHAN CAPE
THIRTY BEDFORD SQUARE LONDON

First published 1980
Copyright © 1980 by Will Wyatt

Jonathan Cape Ltd, 30 Bedford Square, London WC1

British Library Cataloguing in Publication Data

Wyatt, Will
The man who was B. Traven
1. Traven, B – Biography
2. Authors, German – 20th century – Biography
3. Authors, Mexican – 20th century – Biography
I. Title
813'.5'2   PT3919.T7Z/

ISBN 0–224–01720–9

Printed in Great Britain by
Butler & Tanner Ltd, Frome and London

For Jane, Hannah and Rosalind

Contents

Illustrations

Maps

Genealogy

Acknowledgments

This book is based on a documentary film I produced for BBC Television. I am most grateful to the BBC for providing the resources which enabled me to unravel the secrets of B. Traven, accumulating research material, some of which has served for both film and book.

Making television programmes is a communal activity. I am deeply indebted to the many colleagues who worked on the film and to those who offered aid and advice during the writing of the book. Some of them play a part in the narrative but nowhere have I come near to doing full justice to the weight of their contribution or the stimulus and support of their company. I thank them here.

Of those who pass through the following pages I must single out Robert Robinson who was my full partner in making the film, who first breathed the name B. Traven in my ear and who offered sound advice on the manuscript. Also Jennifer McKay, who began the research and David Turnbull who took over from her. Elaine Thomas and Peter Foges interpreted for me on visits to Germany; Chris Mohr, Mark Caldwell and Mike Roles translated crucial material on other occasions. For secretarial assistance I was fortunate to be aided at various times by Kathy Yvanovitch, Jane Hunt, Helen Murry and, particularly, Janet Crouch, who typed much of the first draft and handled many burdensome arrangements. Others who provided aid, encouragement or useful material were Geoff Botterill, Jane Lush, Denise Smith, John Archer, Iain Johnstone and the ever-helpful staff of the BBC Television Reference Library.

Outside the BBC, I am grateful to the participants who gave willingly of their time and knowledge and tolerated the boredom of being filmed. In particular, I received enormous help and many photographs from Rosa Elena Lujan de Traven Torsvan, who asks me to point out that 'permission to use photographs or quotes from B. Traven's letters in no way indicates my approval or endorsement of the contents, the veracity, ideas or point of view of this book'. I was given much assistance by Michael Baumann, whose continued correspondence has provided many useful leads and challenging questions, and by Herbert and Mina Klein, who kindly showed me material they had denied to others and who have maintained a flow of interest and suggestions. Gabriel Figueroa and Judy Stone were especially generous with their time and assistance. Malu Montes de Oca, Sanora Babb Howe, Lawrence Hill, Robert Goss, Bernard Smith, Paul Kohner, Luis Spota, John Huston, Margarethe Henze and Ernst Feige all provided advice and material, as well as agreeing to be interviewed. Gertraud Fromme, Erna Hamann, Marianne Brabant and the late Gertrude Constabel all gave me lengthy interviews. I am indebted to them all and to the others with whom I corresponded, whose names appear in the text. My thanks also go to Lidia Owczarzak-Biochowisowz and Agnieska Dziedzka in Poland and Heinz Behrends in Germany for their guidance and enthusiasm; to fellow Traven researchers Jonah Raskin and Charles Humphrey for their generous offers of aid; to H.G. Pearson at the Home Office; Joan Moir and Eric Nelson at the British Embassy in Mexico; J.S.L. Pulford of Thames Magistrates Court, several branches of the Metropolitan Police, B.M. Evans at the National Meteorological Archive, Milton Gustafson at the National Archive in Washington, Barbara Ennis at the State Department, Dr Paul Avrich of New York University, D.J. Allerton of Manchester University, Ron Martin at the Registry of Seamen and Shipping in Cardiff, Terry Dinan at Lloyds, Hazel Hunkins-Hallinan, Otto Wendt, Stuart Christie, David Nash, William Fishman, and to the Freedom of Information Act.

I am grateful to Edgar Pässler of the Büchergilde Gutenberg for allowing me to see Traven's letters to Ernst Preczang, to William Koshland for showing me Traven's correspondence with Alfred Knopf, to George McCrossen for permission to quote his letter to Judy Stone, to the *Texas Quarterly* for permission to quote from Charles Miller's article, to Rosa Elena Lujan for permission to quote extensively from *The Death Ship* (Lawrence Hill, New York 1973, and Collier Books, New York 1977) and to the BBC for extracts from filmed interviews.

Other quotes are from the Pocket Book, New York, 1977 edition of *The Treasure of the Sierra Madre*, and the Hill and Wang, New York, editions of *The Cotton-Pickers* (1973), *The Bridge in the Jungle* (1974), *The Rebellion of the Hanged* (1974), *General from the Jungle* (1974) and *The Night Visitor and Other Stories* (1973).

For permission to reproduce photographs, I am grateful to the following: for plate 1, Warner Brothers; 8 and 9, BBC; 10 and 11, Stern; 28, BBC Hulton Picture Library; 44, F. Stoppelman.

Tom Maschler of Jonathan Cape was bold enough to urge me to write this book and tendered invaluable advice when it mattered most; my agent Hilary Rubinstein saved me from embarrassment by his robust criticism and warm encouragement. Topsy Levan produced a beautiful typescript from my messy drafts and put my spelling to rights. As this is my first book, I have scouted the works of others to see how they have handled various matters. For some reason it is customary for male authors to leave the thanks they offer to their wives to the very end of their acknowledgments. Although I have slavishly followed this fashion, I cannot think why it should be so, for without the unflagging support and understanding of my wife there would be no book.

WILL WYATT

London 1980

1 The Mystery

'It is an old rule, only not sufficiently obeyed, but
a good rule: if you do not wish to be lied to, do not
ask questions! The only real defense civilised man
has against anybody who bothers him is to lie. There
would be no lies if there were no questions.'

The Death Ship, B. TRAVEN

The writer who called himself B. Traven is one of the most
mysterious figures of the twentieth century: the *Marie Celeste*
of literature. As that ill-fated vessel was found inexplicably
adrift without a crew, so the alias B. Traven was found only
as a name unoccupied by an identity or even a nationality, for
there has been no certainty as to the country of his birth or of
the language he wrote in. This was no accident. Whoever
Traven was he sought anonymity with the passion other men
devote to the pursuit of power, wealth and fame. While his
stories have sold in their millions around the world, his name
has become synonymous with the unknown and the unknow-
able; his life has been the subject of wild rumour and romantic
legend; his books have been examined for the code which
might answer the questions, 'Who was he?' and 'Why did he
hide?'

When I began my search for Traven it was not with any
serious hope of answering those questions. I knew that many
had taken up the challenge of his secrecy, and that every line
he had written and every clue to his existence had been investigated by reporters and scholars in East Germany, West
Germany, Mexico and the United States. Still no one knew
the origins of the man, no one had plumbed the depths of
his mystery. My aim when I set out was simply to make a

documentary film for television about a great writer whose life
was a mystery which would never be solved.

'The mystery of B. Traven's identity may never be completely
resolved, so successfully did the man hide behind his mask of
pseudonyms ...' was how Donald Chankin began his book
Anonymity and Death,* and he added later, 'it is unlikely at this
late date that any documentary proof of Traven's birth or
original nationality will be found'. That was only in 1975 and
a year later, in his book *B. Traven: An Introduction*, Michael L.
Baumann stated firmly: 'About B. Traven's identity we know
nothing. All statements and reports to the contrary notwith-
standing, the question of who B. Traven really was remains
unanswered.'

The press cuttings on Traven and his entries in biographical
and literary reference works were bewildering. Publicity,
propaganda, lies, guesses, rumours, clues from the books and
the bare facts of publication were connected and reconnected
in a confusing biographical mazurka. The pronouncements
began confidently: 'Some facts are known ...', but the facts
were repetitions of old hearsay or further supposition.

The inventions about him had been so many and so dis-
parate, the facts so few and so difficult to check, that almost
any permutation of ingredients appeared convincing. The only
certainties had been Traven's books themselves: powerful,
riveting tales, some of them apparently autobiographical, and
it was against these works that the speculative identities had
been measured.

So I started work on a film about an insoluble puzzle, but as
my knowledge deepened the story changed and the film
changed; new possibilities appeared, there were questions
others had not asked, investigations they had not made. What
began as an interesting film became almost an obsession as I,
and those working with me, were cast down by false trails and
excited by the magic of discovery. The search took me to
libraries and to docksides, to a prison and to a farmyard, to
royal archives and to the FBI, to Hollywood and to the East
End of London. Slowly, as the clues were ticked off and the

* Details of books cited in the text are to be found in the Select Bibliography, pp. 326–30.

trail switched countries and continents, it dawned that a solution was possible. With luck, with some good sense and with much help, I found my way step by step to the origins of the man who was B. Traven. The luck came in the timing, the sense in asking the simple and obvious questions, and the help from Traven scholars and fans abroad and from colleagues at home. From abroad I received valuable snippets and hints of research, and at home I had the company of sharp and inventive minds with whom to argue the probabilities and plan the next steps. Many of those who helped me will play their part in the course of my narrative but there were many others, infected by the Traven bug, who gave invaluable and timely aid.

What follows, then, is a detective story in which the quarry is the detail of a man's birth and life. It might be argued that the biographical facts of an author's life are of little interest, mere footnotes to the books. They command, it could be said, only antiquarian interest and the attention of pedants. What matters is the work, not the gossip. Certainly Traven would have argued so. But a man's work cannot be separated from his life and an author's books must spring, however transmuted, from his experiences, memories and relationships. The world of the imagination must at some points balance on the material world. In an effort to kick away these supports many people have, like Thomas Hardy, sought to edit their lives for posterity. Hardy wrote his own careful biography in the third person and passed it off as the work of his second wife in order to discourage later biographers from pursuing his secrets. Others, too, have destroyed their own letters and papers. All these efforts may be seen as a decent concern with privacy, or a game with those who follow or, possibly, an admittance that the life and work are closely bound together.

With Traven we have a man who sought not to edit his life but to vanish it. He did not simply have secrets, he was a secret. He intended his work to stand remembered in the known account of time, but for his person he wished only the iniquity of oblivion. He covered the facts of his life with layer upon layer of deception and disguise, inventing histories, names and family. Though he proclaimed that such details as one's birth and nationality were accidents, of no concern or interest, he was bedevilled by the need to hide them.

He was like the king in a fairy tale. In his castle there was one turret which only he could enter; in that turret a room, the key to which he alone possessed; and in that room a chest which only he knew how to open. The contents of that chest were sparing: the simple facts of where he had come from, whose loins had borne him, whose seed had given him life – who he really was. There is no way of knowing if he used to visit that room to gaze upon those contents with pride, curiosity or loathing, or whether he had sealed the door, believing the key to be destroyed, and tried to push the memory of that knowledge from his mind. Whichever was the case, his life was haunted by the irrevocable and binding facts of his birth and family. He was hiding not a treasure but an identity from the world.

The turret has been broached for some time and other enquirers have found the key and entered the room. Now we have found a way to the prize itself, opened up that old sea-chest and seen its contents: for the first time we know who B. Traven actually was. Some mystery will remain and there may still be clauses in the Traven riddle that we have yet to construe. Whatever I have discovered, whatever others may yet discover, every ghost cannot be laid to rest. The strange, elusive and contradictory personality of this great writer is not a mystery which can be entirely magicked away by biographical facts. No simple click can make all things clear. But much speculation about Traven must now move to one side. The reasons for his hiding, the source of his fears and the genesis of his obsessions are all to be found in the man's life. And the full life of this extraordinary man now stands revealed.

A troubling thought must cross anyone's mind at the outset of an investigation into the Traven mystery. Here was a man who denied his parents, denied his country, denied his language and who denied that any of these things mattered. At all costs he did not wish to be tracked down. Should we then try? Do we rob his grave if we defeat him now? I think not. It is beyond our capacity to trouble him; we cannot steal his spirit away even if we uncover much of what he tried to hide, and there is no reason why he should instruct us from the grave as he tried to instruct so many in his life. He has inscribed the runes and it is for us to cast them. After death a man's life belongs to history and to the curious stranger.

Traven's life was long and eventful; if he had written nothing, his adventures, which took him from the stage to a revolution to a prison to a hut in the jungle, would happily bear the telling. But it is his books which demand that B. Traven be honoured and which have prompted the searches for the man behind the name. The best-known of his works, *The Treasure of the Sierra Madre*, was turned into a classic movie, and this and other strong, sweeping stories like *The Death Ship* and *The Bridge in the Jungle*, have inspired disciples of Traven on five continents. The books are about the lives of the underdogs of the world, and they champion the cause of these under-privileged with feeling and with humour. Yet, while Traven longs for the brotherhood of man and despairs of the selfishness of rich and poor alike, he does so in a style that is anarchic rather than socialist, individualistic rather than communal, jaunty rather than solemn. Small wonder that readers have sought to discover something about the man who spoke with so singular and distinctive a voice.

We have our own curiosity and the books to justify our search. And Traven, himself, can surely not complain that we seek him still. In *The Death Ship* he wrote:

An unanswered question flutters about you for the rest of your life. It does not let you sleep: it does not let you think. You feel that the equilibrium of the universe is at stake if you leave a question pending.

Yes, and one such question is: 'Who was B. Traven?'

2 The Beginning

My search for B. Traven started in the summer of 1974 in New York or, to be more truthful, it made a false start then. Certainly that was when I first heard of that inscrutable name and initial. I was producing a television programme about books and writers which ran weekly for much of the year on BBC-2 and which was called 'The Book Programme'. I had started it the previous year and had engaged an old colleague and an avid bookman, Robert Robinson, as the presenter. One of the things I felt the programme had missed during its first winter season was a fuller account of the books and writing coming from the United States, so in July 1974 Robinson and I flew to America for two weeks to film some stories for the autumn programmes.

The trip went well. We spent a day with Joseph Heller whose new novel, *Something Happened* – his first book since *Catch-22* – was about to be published. We flew to Chicago to film Saul Bellow. We visited Peter Benchley, the likeable author of *Jaws*, who had us up to his summer house on an island in Connecticut. We were thus feeling well satisfied already when we came to our last day's filming, a day which was more in the nature of a pilgrimage than mere work, for on July 31st we drove almost the length of Long Island to film an interview with 92-year-old P.G. Wodehouse at his home at Remsenberg. The afternoon was hot, still and sunny, we set up white chairs under the trees in Wodehouse's wooded garden and waited until the great man had finished watching the television soap opera he never missed. He emerged from the house with his wife, treated us like long-lost friends, was full of fun and stories during the

6

filming, and gave us tea and then drinks afterwards. The whole affair went, as he himself might have said, swimmingly.

Thus, as Robinson and I drove back to the city, two inscribed copies of *Psmith* on the back seat, we congratulated ourselves on our luck, skill and charm, and basked in the sense of relief at a mission accomplished. That evening we took a taxi down to Greenwich Village and had dinner at an Italian restaurant to the accompaniment of the drunken conversation of two pink-cheeked college students who were toasting absent friends at a nearby table. 'To John. To Martha. One helluva guy, and one helluva girl who are going to have just one helluva marriage.' (For John and Martha, I gathered, the day of destiny was nigh.) I did not know it but the hour of Traven was also at hand.

We left the restaurant and wandered round the trinket sellers and late-night shops, ending up in a bookshop on 8th Street, where we each picked out a few paperbacks and were about to leave when I heard Robinson exclaim:

'Ah! Ah! B. Traven.'

'Who?'

'B. Traven,' he replied. 'Always meant to read some. Never have.' And he held up a copy of some Traven short stories.

'I don't know anything about him,' I said.

'You must do,' said Robinson. 'He's a mystery man. Supposed to be the President of Mexico, I think. Anyhow he lives in South America, in the jungle or somewhere and no one has ever found out who he is. Now *there's* a story we should do sometime!'

It did sound a good story – jungles, South America, unsolved riddles, 'the writer who never was' and that sort of thing. Robinson added the stories to his pile of paperbacks, but I thought no more about it until the spring of 1977, when another project I was working on fell down. In that same week my eye had been caught by an article in *Time* magazine about B. Traven.

I turned back to the article to read it again, more closely. It was illustrated by two photographs: one was of Humphrey Bogart, Walter Huston and Tim Holt in John Huston's film of Traven's novel, *The Treasure of the Sierra Madre*; the other was of the top half of a man's head as it lay in a silk-lined coffin.

A prominent nose, a large ear, and a bald head with grey hair at the sides were the noticeable features, and the caption read 'Traven in Coffin, 1969'. My first thought was that Robinson had been wrong back in 1974, when he had told me that B. Traven was a mystery and that he was living in South America, for here was a picture of the author showing that it was known who he was and, what's more, that he was dead. The *Time* article itself, however, raised more questions than it answered.

The man in the coffin was a man known variously as Hal Croves and T. Torsvan, once an American, later a naturalised Mexican citizen, who had died in Mexico City in 1969. He had disguised his identity but in latter years had been widely suspected of being the absent and mysterious author B. Traven, a suspicion that his widow had endorsed as a fact. But that was not all. This man who seemed to have three names, Croves, Torsvan and Traven, might well have had a fourth. It was rumoured that he had lived as an anarchist journalist in Munich during the First World War using the name Ret Marut, and under this name had been sentenced to death in that city in 1919. Marut was himself a mystery. No one knew where he had come from, and there were even rumours that he might have been the illegitimate offspring of Kaiser Wilhelm II.

The *Time* article was a review of two new books on Traven, one of which, *The Mystery of B. Traven*, was by Judy Stone, a San Francisco journalist. She had had several interviews with Croves, but the old man had never admitted to her that he was the writer B. Traven. The other book, *B. Traven: An Introduction*, was by Michael L. Baumann, Professor of English at California State University, who evidently connected Ret Marut with the B. Traven books but also raised another spectre – that there might be more than one hand in the writing.

Already I was reeling from the possibilities and confusions. There were four names but how many men? Was there one writer or two, or more? Where did you look for Traven – in Germany, in Mexico or in the United States? Was the man in the coffin Traven and if so where did he come from? What was his nationality? How had this mystery lasted for fifty years and why had it begun? Anyone who has ever looked into the case of Traven will recognise the mixture of bewilderment and fascination – I was already hooked.

The author of the *Time* article also whetted the appetite for Traven's books: 'as curious, as ambiguous and as provocative as the author's life. Not much that is better has been printed – in German or English – since the death of the mystery that was B. Traven.' He believed that the man in the coffin had been Traven but that attempts to track down his life were doomed to failure. 'No matter how these literary sleuths try to run the true B. Traven to earth, his trail ends as it began: a riddle inside an enigma.'

I knew that I had my new film: the story of an insoluble mystery, the search for B. Traven. Before I went ahead I wanted to read one of Traven's books and I chose *The Death Ship*, his first published novel. I am not sure now what I had expected to find. At the back of my mind I think there was a fear that I might be disappointed by the work in spite of being fascinated by the puzzle of the man's life, that *The Death Ship* would be a slightly worthy tale of exploitation, heavily political and a bit dull. If that were to be the case I could still follow the Traven story. But it would be a less satisfying task if the books were of no quality. I need not have worried. *The Death Ship* is a story of exploitation and it has, like all Traven's work, a strong moral theme, but it is also a sweeping legend-like tale full of muscle, opinion and humour.

The story of *The Death Ship* is told by its central character, an easy-going American merchant seaman, Gerard Gales, who arrives back at the dock in Antwerp to find that his ship has departed early, and he has thus been left behind without any possessions, money or papers. Gales's chief problem is that he is unable to prove his identity and without some proof of who he is or of his nationality no one will take responsibility for him and no official will believe what he says. Traven portrays the world's insistence on papers and documents as a bureaucratic obsession, an absurdity. One official even explains to Gales: 'Think it silly or not. I doubt your birth as long as you have no certificate of your birth. The fact that you are sitting in front of me is no proof of your birth. Officially it is no proof.' Gales confronts two American consuls and the police of several countries with his own knowledge of his identity: 'I do not need any papers; I know who I am.' The response of the authorities, however, is to pass the victim from hand to hand and from

country to country, and Gales is powerless, save to reply to the
indignities with jokes, lies and exaggerations. He narrates his
story with a carefree swagger as his odyssey takes him from
Belgium to Holland to France and eventually to Spain, where,
on the spur of the moment, he hops aboard a broken-down
cargo ship to work as a fireman. He has been driven off the
continent of Europe by the unending questions: 'Why are you
here? Where do you come from? What's your name?'

The ship he has joined is the *Yorikke*, the death ship of the
title, a vessel doomed to be sunk at sea so that the owners can
realise its insurance value. Life in the stokehold of this ship is an
almost literal hell with ceaseless heat, backbreaking labour,
foul food and a knowledge that those who sail in the *Yorikke*
have 'vanished from the living'. Gales and his Polish friend,
Stanislav, are shanghaied on to another death ship, *The Empress
of Madagascar*, which sinks in a storm, and the two companions
are marooned on a makeshift raft. The powerful and vision-like
close tells how Stanislav, weak from exposure, swims off after
a dying man's vision of his old ship, the *Yorikke*, while Gales
remains strapped to the raft watching his friend drown.

The book is a song of praise to the individual spirit, above all
to the spirit of the downtrodden and dispossessed. The faceless
and nameless crews of the death ships, men without countries
and without hope, are given heroism and tragic dignity.
Through their work they overcome the horror of their existence; by succeeding in their terrible and exhausting tasks they
achieve a kind of triumph. But when I read the book that first
time it was the early part of Gales's story which aroused my
greatest interest. I knew little enough about Traven and had no
way of knowing how many of Gales's adventures might be
based on the author's own, yet the little I did know – Traven's
hiding, his use of false names, his passion for anonymity – was
reflected here in a work permeated by a concern with identity.
Traven has Gales stow away on a ship; when Gales has to sign
on for his service on the *Yorikke* he used, quite naturally, a
false name; he is beset by demands for his passport, immigration papers, seaman's card. For Traven, even ships seek to hide
their true identity: 'On her hull was her name: *Yorikke*. The
letters were so thin and so washed-off that I got the impression
that she was ashamed to let anybody know her true name.'

I could not guess whether or not this book was in any way a key to Traven, how much he was hiding and how much he was revealing in it. I was struck again and again by the references to disappearing and to non-existence: 'You have no passport. In any civilised country he who has no passport is nobody. He does not exist for us or for anybody else.' Was this something that had happened to Traven or was it an image for what he had tried to *make* happen to himself? Had he been paperless, stateless, nameless and helpless before the world as his sailors were? Or was this merely a way of saying that we are all who we are; not what we are categorised as by others? The more he insisted on this, the more I wished to know what his secret was; the more he relished concealments of every kind, the more I wanted to know why he wished to hide. Already I was trying to guess at what sort of man, or men, I would be dealing with.

The second book of *The Death Ship* begins with the inscription from over the crew's quarters on that doomed vessel. It is laid out on the page like verse and its importance to Traven is unmistakable. It stands forth like a creed, its message black and pessimistic and charged with significance; its tone, heroic, almost triumphant. It reads like an epitaph not just for the faceless crew of *The Death Ship* but for some part of the life of the equally faceless man who was B. Traven.

> He
> Who enters here
> Will no longer have existence;
> His name and soul have vanished
> And are gone for ever.
> Of him there is not left a breath
> In all the vast world.
> He can never return,
> Nor can he ever go onward;
> For where he stands there he must stay.
> No God knows him;
> And unknown will he be in hell.
> He is not day; he is not night.
> He is Nothing and Never.
> He is too great for infinity,
> Too small for a grain of sand,

Which, however small,
Has its place in the universe.
He is what has never been
And never thought.

As soon as I had finished *The Death Ship* I wrote to Aubrey Singer, the Controller of BBC-2, to suggest that I make a film about Traven. He agreed, adding, 'Can you get anywhere near the truth?'

3 The Legend

I had already started work. I sent for copies of the two books reviewed in the *Time* article and started to think about a schedule. Mexico was the home of the Traven mystery, the source of and the setting for the books; I must clearly go there. The United States was where many Traven experts and useful witnesses lived and a visit to them there could easily be combined with a trip to Mexico. What was more, I could shoot one or two stories for 'The Book Programme' in the United States at the same time, thereby squeezing maximum value from the air fares. I still had no idea of the scale of the Traven story and, excited as I was by it, thought I would accumulate a clutch of other programmes or programme items on the same trip. The best arrangement would have been for me to go alone to Mexico and the United States to research and set up the filming and then go back with a film crew. The kitty would not run to this, so instead I would set off with Robinson and piece the story together as we went along, using hired film crews for a day or so here and there. This could be a pleasant, if risky, way of working and there was no alternative.

I decided that we would go in July. This gave me about two and a half months to find out all I could about Traven and set up the filming. I was only working on the story part time, but Jennifer McKay, the researcher on 'The Book Programme', was already intrigued by the project and she began devilling away, making contact with people we might interview, turning up newspaper cuttings and articles, and locating copies of the Traven books.

Traven is not a well-known author in Britain and his books

13

were not easy to find, but this relative scarcity was apparently
not the case in other parts of the world. His work has been
published in more than twenty languages and over 350 editions.
The sales figures of so wide a dissemination are hard to come
by, but in 1967 one journalist, who had delved into the Traven
story, estimated that over twenty-five million copies of his books
had been sold – Russia and Germany being two of the largest
markets. There had even been the murmur of a campaign to
link Traven's name with the Nobel Prize for Literature.

One problem I had from the outset was that I do not speak
or even read German, and this denied me access to those works
of Traven which have not been translated into English and prevented me from reading the fullest book on the author: *B. Traven
– Beiträge zur Biographie*, by the East German scholar, Rolf
Recknagel. I did get extracts from this work translated and
gleaned some useful information from its appendices. More-
over, I soon discovered that most others who had written about
Traven had relied heavily on Recknagel's exhaustive efforts.
With a number of books in English, with some notes translated from Recknagel and with a folder of newspaper and
magazine articles I read myself further into the Traven story.

It was clear that the anonymity of the author had created a
vacuum into which a startling variety of rumours had gusted.
It was anathema to the world of literature, to the world of
journalism, to the world in general that there should be books
without a visible author or a name without a human being,
and some interesting candidates had been canvassed for the role
of mystery writer. Some of these suggestions sounded pre-
posterous and most could quickly be dismissed by simple checking. Others were so vague that they compounded the mystery
rather than clarified it, but there were some guesses, a few,
which might carry within them the seeds of the truth. One or
two rumours were of the species which gave us: 'James Dean
is not really dead but so disfigured that he can never be seen
in public,' and 'Jack Kennedy is kept alive, but only as a
vegetable, on a Greek island.' Taken together, the theories provided a vivid testimony to the frustration and bafflement that
the Traven mystery had induced.

One story was that Traven was none other than the
American writer Jack London, who had not died in 1916 as

everyone had believed, but had mysteriously lived on to produce further books under the new name. Both authors were radicals, both wrote about the lower orders of society, both wrote about Mexico and about the sea and reviewers often compared their works. A second reincarnation theory attributed the Traven *œuvre* to the American satirical journalist and story writer, Ambrose Bierce, another author whose life was brushed by mystery. Bierce, author of *The Devil's Dictionary*, disappeared dramatically into revolutionary Mexico at the end of 1913 and was never seen again. Bierce and Traven shared a sardonic distrust of officials and governments.

There were some less specific reports. One said that Traven was a rogue American millionaire, that he had written so movingly about the poor and dispossessed and railed angrily against the rich and powerful in order to assuage his guilt at amassing a fortune through the labour of his workers. Another story said that Traven was, indeed, an American, not a rich one purging his conscience but a poor black who had fled injustice in the southern states and drifted down into Mexico to take up writing. There were still wilder explanations: Traven was a fugitive Austrian archduke hiding out in Mexico and making his living as a jobbing writer; he was a leper, living in secret in the Chiapas region of southern Mexico, a man so disfigured by the dread disease that his head was permanently bound in bandages. Traven wrote about the Chiapas and he was widely thought to be living there. Thus, at one time the scientist and explorer, Frans Blom, was picked out as the anonymous novelist because he lived in San Cristobal and also wrote about the region.

Scouring Mexico was one technique for Traven seekers, another was playing games with his name. A Yugoslavian newspaper came up with its own home-grown candidate for Travenhood, an illustrator called Franz Traven, who was born in Yugoslavia in 1883 and disappeared during the First World War.

The initial 'B' excited a small mystery of its own. The books were all in the name 'B. Traven' with never a hint as to what the 'B' stood for. I found references to 'Ben', 'Benno', and more commonly 'Bruno' Traven, and the suggestion that the 'B' corresponded to the 'S' in Harry S. Truman; it didn't stand for

anything, it just made the name look right. There were also
several ingenious theories as to where the 'B' had come from.
A man known as Cap'n Bilbo was put forward at one time as
the real Traven and the theory had it that the 'B' was for Bilbo
or the man's real surname, Baruch. Bilbo ran a bar in West
Berlin, but he had knocked about the world as a sailor and had
on one occasion made use of the name B. Traven as his own.
He later admitted that he was not the author, but he did say
that he had once sailed on an old ship which had been sunk
off the coast of Mexico in an insurance swindle. What is more,
he had often told this story in the bars of Mexico City to
German-speaking writers and journalists and he claimed to
remember one man in particular who questioned him closely
about this story and made notes about it. Perhaps, said Bilbo,
this man was Traven and he put the 'B' in front of his name
in recognition of Bilbo's contribution. Even Bilbo did not press
the claims of his Mexico City story too far, backing off to
allow that the 'B' could have been coincidence.

Another inhabitant of the 'B' was one August Bibelje, a
German customs officer turned seaman, who sailed away from
Europe to live on a plantation in Brazil. Bibelje travelled
several times between Europe and South America, wrote some
stories, and was said to have been arrested in Antwerp for being
without documents or money. He was sent funds by his family
and then disappeared. The similarities between Bibelje's adventures and those of Gerard Gales in *The Death Ship* caused a
stir, but the veracity of this story was undermined by its origins.
It appeared to have been made up as a means of extracting
money from Traven's European agent.

The cast list for the part of Traven did not end there. The
chief editor of a leading German publishing house was nomin-
ated. Another shadowy man of letters was pushed forward,
Arthur Breisky, a Czech writer, whose claim was apparently
based on the fact that in 1910 he went to the United States
and there slipped out of sight – although the initial letter of his
surname might not have discouraged his supporters. An altogether more controversial nominee was Adolfo Lopez
Mateos, President of Mexico between 1958 and 1964. Here was
the exciting possibility of a scholar-statesman, a Disraeli of
Latin America, with the energy and talent to manage the great

affairs of his country and write novels at the same time. The rumour started through a family connection. Lopez Mateos's sister, Esperanza, was the Mexican agent and translator for the Traven books until her death in 1951, and for a time in the 1940s the copyright of B. Traven was in her name. Could it be that she was simply covering up for her brother? The rumour achieved such currency that it eventually called for a public denial. When President Lopez Mateos was on a visit to Argentina in 1960 he held a press conference in Buenos Aires. One of the questions was: 'Señor President, what about B. Traven, his existence and personality?' The President replied:

'A legend has been created around B. Traven in Mexico. It has been said that my sister, unfortunately already deceased, was B. Traven, and that she wrote the books, while actually she was his secretary and translator. Also they have said that I was B. Traven. Neither of these two rumours is true. Traven's first book was published when I was five and my sister four. Actually B. Traven exists, he bears that name, he continues to write. My sister only represented him for several years in Mexico, while at the same time she was translating his books into Spanish.'

There were still two theories which sounded distinctly plausible. One had it that there was no such person as B. Traven at all, that it was no use searching for a clue which might reveal the true identity – there was no single identity. It was not a matter of examining the lives and works of writers who had disappeared in the hope that one of them might have made a fatal slip and given the secret away – there was no one secret, B. Traven did not exist. The proposition was that the name B. Traven was a name only, a *nom de plume* used collectively by a group of writers, an umbrella beneath which they could jointly shelter. There were supposed to be five of them in all, living in Honduras: three Germans, a German-Canadian and an American. Names and sketchy biographical details were provided: the American was called MacLean; the Canadian, Theel or Thiel; and the Germans were Brelling, who was supposed to have been mixed up in a duel whilst at Göttingen University, Holthusen, who had been a soldier in Hamburg, and Wollank, who had been a radical in Munich. And the shadowy figure of Ret Marut entered the stage again, for it was said that Wollank had been a colleague of Marut's in Munich and that Marut himself had belonged to this group of writers but had died in 1934 in Honduras, where he was living under a Spanish name. It was a resonant and strangely attractive proposal.

The second of the more credible theories, one held by many Traven scholars, was that he was a poor white American, a Wobbly. A Wobbly was a member of the Industrial Workers of the World, a group of radical labour unions largely made up of itinerant workers. The organisation was founded in 1907 and members acquired the name 'Wobblies' because they were said to go into Chinese restaurants and ask the waiters to say the initials I.W.W., which came out as 'I Wobbleoo Wobbleoo'. Traven's early books had an itinerant American worker as their hero and one of them was called *Der Wobbly* when first published in Germany, so it was natural to imagine the author as just such a man, bumming his way round Mexico in the early years of the century, picking up odd jobs and collecting tales. As well as tallying with the books, this theory was also in accord with hopes of many Traven fans, supplying the kind of man they wanted the writer to be: a handy and independent man, able to look after himself; a worker, self-taught and in touch with the feelings and experiences of the underdogs, and a socialist, politically active and informed. The Wobbly would certainly be a promising member of any short list I might compile – not that there was any hint of a name for him.

With all these aspirants under consideration and with the candidatures of Hal Croves, T. Torsvan and Ret Marut already registered, it was time for me to turn away from the theories and to examine what was known for fact about B. Traven. If there was no man to be seen, then I had to look at the history of the publication of the books. The books and the name had appeared in the world simultaneously, and a history of the one was a history of the other. That history begins in 1925 in Berlin when the literary editor of the socialist daily newspaper *Vorwärts* (*Forward*) received a parcel postmarked Columbus, Tamaulipas, Mexico. It contained the manuscripts in German of a number of short stories. The author's name was B. Traven. *Vorwärts* quickly decided to publish the stories and the serialisation began on June 21st, 1925, under the title *Die Bauwollpflücker* (*The Cotton-Pickers*). There were twenty-two instalments running through until July 16th, and *Vorwärts* proudly announced the arrival of this new author with a claim that he was a man who had known proletarian life in several countries and whose tales came straight from his own experiences. This rang true to the style of *The Cotton-Pickers*. The stories are told in the first person by a young American, called Gerard Gales, who was later to narrate *The Death Ship*, *The Bridge in the Jungle* and the short story, 'The Night Visitor'. He cheerily tells of his efforts to find jobs in Mexico and describes his adventures working in the cotton fields and on oil rigs. There is a bouncy and ironic tone to the stories and they carry the smack of authenticity.

Die Baumwollpflüder.

1]   **Roman von B. Traven.**
Copyright 1925 by B. Traven, Columbus, Tamsulipas, Mexico.

The serialisation caught the eye of Ernst Preczang, one of the editors at a recently formed publishing house and book club of the left, the Büchergilde Gutenberg. Before the instalments had finished running in *Vorwärts*, Preczang made contact with Traven, writing to him, as all correspondents would find they had to, not at an address but through a post-office box number. Preczang complimented the author on his humour and on the freshness and naturalness of his descriptions and he offered to publish *The Cotton-Pickers*, suggesting that Traven might like to add some material to it before it came out as a novel. Preczang said that he would be interested in any other works that Traven had written and assured him that he would not do worse financially with the Büchergilde than with a private capitalist publisher. Preczang said they would print 15,000 copies and he enclosed a couple of the Büchergilde's first books to demonstrate the quality and style of their publications.

I received a copy of this letter and of nearly all the lengthy correspondence between Preczang and Traven from the present-day offices of the Büchergilde Gutenberg in Frankfurt. These letters are an essential starting point on the Traven trail, as they represent the author's first contacts with the outside world, the beginnings of the name, the beginnings of the work and the beginnings of the mystery. The reply that Preczang received to that first approach was an extraordinary, closely typed three-page letter, dated August 5th, 1925 – all in German save for an odd concluding salute of 'Yessir'. It was signed at the bottom with just a handwritten 'T' through the typed signature. All of Traven's correspondence over the years was typed and nearly all of it was unsigned by hand, relying on typed signatures or typed initials. Preczang was one person, perhaps the only one, who did receive letters with a handwritten 'T', and, on one or two occasions, there was even a cramped handwritten signature, but these were never unambiguously clear and if someone had claimed that they were in fact the signatures of a man called, say, Torsvan, not Traven, they would have served that name equally well. Such was the rarity of a Traven signature that on one occasion, I was told, an agent representing Traven's work in Europe lost a long case at law because he was unable to produce for the court an authentic signature of his client's.

But the beginning of that first letter to Preczang was a surprise, too. Traven was on the defensive from the start. In the midst of all the greetings, praise and encouragement in the publisher's letter, Traven's eye had alighted on a brief hint that *The Cotton-Pickers* might be on the short side and that perhaps he would like to fill it out. Like a schoolboy accused of not writing a long-enough essay Traven rattled off an explanation as to why *The Cotton-Pickers* was not longer. They should realise his circumstances: 'I wrote that novel in an Indian hut in the jungle where I had neither table nor chair and had to make a bed from a hammock such as you have never seen, from bits of string tied together.' He had been thirty-five miles from the nearest supplies of pens and paper. He had written on both sides of the paper and when it ran out the novel had to end 'although it should only then have begun'. He had given the manuscript to an Indian to take to the station and send to the United States to be typed. This had cost him all his money, but now he had his own typewriter and some extra money so he would not need to go out to work for a bit. But when he had to work again there would be no more writing, 'work here is something different from in Europe'.

After this defensive fusillade, the letter rambled on. Traven became eager to please, then made categorical demands; he became jumpily protective again, then boastful – it was the letter of a man who had little communication with the outside world and who was uncertain as to how to deal with it. He wanted the Büchergilde to publish his book and he agreed to write a second part to *The Cotton-Pickers*, as Preczang had suggested. He had more stories, some of which were in the hands of other German magazines and publishers, and in his keenness to have his work in print, he carefully itemised them all, suggesting possible collections and trying to choreograph arrangements between Preczang and other publishers. Then came a reprise of his hardship theme. Wagging his finger at Preczang in far-off Berlin, Traven reminded him that he did not just have the usual mental agonies of writing to put up with; for him there were also the physical torments of living in the tropics: 'writing in these countries, when one can't live in a modern hotel, when one has to live in a barrack or hut, is hell. Not only one's brains, but one's bleeding hands and legs and cheeks, stung through and through by mosquitoes and other hellish insects ...' All these things, he told the editor, drove a writer to distraction.

Traven was not so distracted that he did not have a few demands to make. He wanted an advance, he would send Preczang his other stories, but he wanted them back just as soon as they had been read, and he wanted his books printed in Gothic type. Then came a stipulation which clearly carried the force of an order: 'Not a single line from this letter may be published. The letter is purely personal.' Traven was beginning as he meant to continue.

In his own first letter, the editor from the Büchergilde had informed Traven that he was willing to consider publishing travel books and diaries as well as novels and then, not realising that he was attempting to cross the barbed wire, had continued in all innocence to his new author: 'You have obviously experienced a great deal and you have probably taken pictures – what about an illustrated biographical novel?' The answer was simple and to the point: 'Biographical novel? No. Travel

books, diaries about my travels and journeys with photographs?
Yes.' From the first there was to be nothing about the man himself. But let no one think that he was not of interest, far from
it. Traven took up Preczang's remark about his experiences
with a saloon-bar chortle: 'Doubtless I have experienced a
great deal? Twenty volumes the size of the Brockhaus Dictionary
would not be enough to publish even part of it.' Already
Traven was propagating the myth of a stirring and adventurous
past – if it was a myth. He wrote like a man who had
experienced the world, who had travelled, seen places, done
things, handled danger, and, however exaggerated the trum-
peting and however elliptical the hints he let slip, there was
always with Traven the feeling that the truth might not be an
anti-climax, that what he kept hidden might indeed be as
eventful as he liked to suggest.

It was agreed that the Büchergilde Gutenberg would publish
his work and as he still had to complete some extra material
for *The Cotton-Pickers*, the first novel to come out was *The Death
Ship*, published in April 1926. This book was important to
Traven: it was his first published novel and it had a propaganda role on which, as he wrote, much depended: 'it
is important to bring out into the open the business of compulsory passports and visas to see what the effect will be.'
He seemed confident about its success, telling the Büchergilde that they could not have a better advertisement than this
novel and that it would be bound to bring them many
enquiries and even more new members. This may have
been newcomer's bravado, but he was right. In the year the
book was published, the Büchergilde's membership increased
by 11,000 to nearly 28,000 and the publishers believed that
The Death Ship was the chief reason for this. The first edition
was 30,000 and a total of more than 100,000 copies were sold
over the next few years. The book was a rousing success, particularly among those of the left. As one critic wrote: 'I don't
think that any socialist will put this down without feeling
the courage and strength of his class rise up in his heart and
mind.'

The six-year period from 1926, when he burst on to the
German literary scene, until 1931 was a prolific one for Traven,
who published nine books in that time. In 1926, as well as *The

Death Ship, there was *The Wobbly*,* which was *The Cotton-Pickers*, with some new stories about Gerard Gales. In these he was working at a bakery and getting mixed up in a strike; finding a job as a ranch hand; driving cattle and dealing with some bandits – all told in the same happy-go-lucky style as the originals. In the following year came *The Treasure of the Sierra Madre*, a powerful and exciting adventure novel about three Americans who find gold in the Mexican wilderness and whose greed brings disaster. The corruption of the Americans is set against the innocence and nobility of the Indians, a theme which was to recur in Traven's novels.

In 1928 the Büchergilde brought out two more Traven books, again both were set in Mexico. (Apart from *The Death Ship*, all Traven's books until his last, in 1960, were set in that country.) *The Bush* was a collection of short stories, some again told by Gerard Gales, which drew on the lives and legends of the Mexican Indians, notably in a haunting tale, 'The Night Visitor'. *Land of Spring* was the author's only non-fiction work, an account of a journey through the State of Chiapas with observations on the Indians' culture and society, as well as opinions on nearly everything else in Mexico. It was illustrated by sixty-four pages of photographs taken by Traven himself.

The surge of work continued in 1929 with the appearance of *The Bridge in the Jungle*, the last of the books narrated by Gerard Gales. It is the story of the death and funeral of a little Indian boy, who falls from a bridge built by an American oil company and drowns. Through Gales, Traven observes the attitudes of the Americans and the Mexican Indian towards life and death. In the same year came Traven's most wide-ranging novel, *The White Rose*, telling of the efforts of C.C. Collins, president of a huge American oil company, to get hold of the White Rose ranch from the Mexican family who own it; an epic struggle between two cultures. There were no books in 1930, but in 1931 Traven produced *The Carreta* and *Government*, the first two of the six that comprise the Jungle Novels or the Caoba (Mahogany) Cycle. This group of stories, which continued with *The March to Caobaland* (1933), *The Troza* (1936), *The Rebellion of the Hanged* (1936) and *General from the Jungle* (1940), make up a large-scale history of the ox-drivers,

* Later editions of the book reverted to the title of *The Cotton-Pickers*.

the mahogany workers and the forced labourers of south-east Mexico, and of their eventual rebellion against the dictatorship of Porfirio Diaz. The books describe the slavery enforced by debt upon the Mexicans, the cruelty and brutality of the mahogany camps, the corruption of business and industry, and the fatalistic beliefs of the Indians. This series of novels ends with one of the ironic twists which are the very thumbprint of Traven. The small army of rebels who have been living and fighting in the jungle emerge, only to discover that the revolution has been over for sixteen months and that the dictator they have been opposing has long since fled.

Throughout this productive period, which saw the publication of nearly all Traven's work, the author continued to give his publishers no biographical material of any kind. Preczang, not unnaturally, wanted photographs and information with which he could publicise the books and draw attention to the author, but all that was forthcoming was a homily:

> I would like to state very clearly: the biography of a creative person is absolutely unimportant. If that person is not recognisable in his works, then either he is worth nothing or his works are worth nothing. The creative person should therefore have no other biography than his works.

Traven was keen to make sure that his work reached as wide an audience as possible, and particularly that it should find its way to fellow socialists, but he was not prepared to sacrifice even one small part of his privacy in order to achieve this. There was no pleasing him when it came to the matter of saying who he was or who he was not. He did not even like it when the publicity issued by the Büchergilde Gutenberg made some small capital out of his anonymity by saying: 'We know nothing about him.' This, he complained, created the impression that there were secrets about him or, worse still, that he was trying to create a sensation through the pretence of secrets in order to make his books sell better and this was not true. One could forgive Preczang and his colleagues if they ever wondered what on earth the man did want. He certainly had secrets. He was desperate to prevent anyone finding out even the barest and, one would imagine, most harmless facts about himself, and yet he did not like it when people owned up and said they did not know these simple things about him. It was as if the very mention of identity, any identity, threatened him in some way, as if he were irritated by the mundane necessity of having to exist. Indeed, at one time he urged that it was unnecessary to put his or any author's name on the cover of a book, arguing that it only created an expectation or an assumption in the reader's mind, which had nothing to do with the quality or content of the work itself.

He developed variations on this purist line to justify his reticence. His reason for not telling about himself, he wrote once to a Professor Strasser in Switzerland, was to free people, particularly working people, from their belief in authority. Workers should not worship any kind of authority whether it be kings, generals, presidents, ocean fliers – or writers. Again and again he emphasised that everyone was equally important; that being a writer should bring no special attention:

> I feel that I am a worker who like other workers, contributes his share to making mankind advance another step. I feel like a grain of sand out of which the earth is made. My works are important: my person is unimportant ... The typesetter who sets the type for my book is just as important for our culture as I am, and for that reason no one should bother about my person, about the private person I am, any more than he should bother about the person of the typesetter.

I never doubted that Traven believed what he wrote in his correspondence about this; it married with his overt political views and was in keeping with the content of his fiction. All his books celebrate the worth of the individual, especially of the humble, the downtrodden and the persecuted. He casts in heroic mould their struggles to carry out their tasks, to stay true to their origins and simply to survive. But I never felt that this theoretical basis for his anonymity could be the whole explanation. There must be some powerful practical or personal reasons supplying the urge for him to construct his rationale. And it was not so much hypocritical as disingenuous of him to put his hand on his heart and plead that he had no secrets – his whole being was a secret. Perhaps, behind the veil which covered his person, there was an obsession, which he was also trying to conceal.

It was in this climate of his own creation that the myths about Traven sprang up and the rumours were invented. After all, it was pretty well impossible for anyone to deny or disprove anything said about him. The books began to be published in English in the 1930s. In Britain they were translated from the German, but in the United States the publishers received English versions direct from Mexico. The rumours now spread from Europe across the Atlantic and Traven was soon dubbed 'the author nobody knows'. The *New Yorker* said that as far as anyone knew he might be 'an individual or a syndicate, Joan Lovell or The Man in the Iron Mask', and if he were ever photographed the negative would probably refuse to develop. The magazine commended *The Treasure of the Sierra Madre* to its readers as a good adventure story, shot through with a consistent irony and without sentimentality.

So Traven was established as a writer read all round the world, translated by the mid-1930s into fifteen languages, and yet not a soul had met him. The only clue that he volunteered to the Büchergilde was a pair of photographs, which, he said, were of the wooden house in the jungle where he had written his story, 'The Night Visitor'. But the photographs told nothing about Traven himself and the explanation that he sent with them only added to that extravagant version of his hard and primitive existence, which was already in circulation. (Perhaps, also giving rise to the story that he was a disfigured leper.)

I wrote the novel in this bungalow under the most appalling bodily torment. Mosquito plagues during certain hours of the day were so dreadful that I had to bandage my hands and head in order to withstand the attacks of hundreds of thousands of swarming mosquitoes.

Such accounts were all that Traven revealed about himself and, far from diminishing his personal importance, which was his avowed aim, they only inflated the fantasies which surrounded him.

Jaguars and lions would come close to the house from time to time. The house was literally teeming with big scorpions and red spiders as long as a finger. I found many tarantulas as big as a hand underneath the stone rubble at the back of the house. Often vast armies of big ants marched right through the middle of the house in the evenings just before sunset.

In his letters to Preczang, the editor who had discovered and promoted his work, Traven unloaded himself of the agonies and privations of his jungle life. If only half these hardships were true, it is not surprising that he sought some relief from his solitary existence by setting them down in this way. But, as this was the only information he imparted, it was bound to define him as an heroic and tantalising phantom. Even then he was on his guard lest he had let slip too much; lest anyone should try to use the meagre clues as a means of tracking him down. He added to his remarks about the photographs:

Nobody should take the trouble to look for the bungalow. It has already been swallowed and heartily digested by the jungle, as I heard six months ago.

May it rot in peace.

4 No Ordinary Man

I was not tempted to search for the hut in the photographs or for any of the other jungle houses Traven used. The money I had for the project was not a princely sum and would only stretch, I estimated, to a film consisting largely of interviews with key witnesses. As I was sure that a straightforward account of the Traven mystery would make a strong programme, I was not too worried about this. I hoped that we would be able to get down to the Chiapas region for a couple of days, but I knew that the budget would not run to any lengthy investigation or filming down there. My chief concern was to find and choose the people who could contribute most to this complicated story so that we could tell it clearly and depict in some way the character of the author at the centre. In spite of my reading and research I was still struggling to form some kind of picture of the sort of person (or persons) it was who lurked behind the name of B. Traven. With this in mind, I turned again to the books and letters.

It was evident, as I had noticed before, that Traven's passion for secrecy did not spring from too modest a view of his own worth. It was true that there were one or two paragraphs in the letters of arch and embarrassing humility, but these were more in the nature of misjudged attempts at politeness than evidence of a humble disposition. Far more typical were the passages in which Traven outlined elaborate arrangements for others to follow, set out demands and, above all, boasted. As I had seen, he boasted that *The Death Ship* would be a commercial success and it was. When he addressed himself solely to the literary value of the work he was no less positive: 'In the

whole of German literature there is not another modern work
which describes the development of fear so minutely as this
novel,' he wrote to Preczang. Throughout the letters there is
the sense of a man who was pleased with himself. Perhaps
cockiness is the best description of this tone, which combined
an eagerness to put other people right with self-endorsement.
He swanked about his worldliness and he addressed his correspondents, as he addressed the readers of his novels, in the
manner of one who wished them to feel that here was an
authority. They could take it from him, he had been around
and seen a thing or two and his readers were receiving the
benefit, straight from the horse's mouth.

He let his publishers know, just for the record, that the events
leading up to the waiters' strike in *The Cotton-Pickers* had actually happened, he had been there. He wrote to Preczang saying
that some of the new material for *The Cotton-Pickers* might be
too strong for the Büchergilde to publish and that Preczang
had better cross out the passages about Mexican prostitutes if
the club had a lot of moralistic members. After all, said Traven,
he was writing about the *real* world – an emphasis which was
meant to remind Preczang of the uncompromising nature of
the work, and that the real world was something the author
knew all about. Lest there be any doubt on that score, Traven
explained that the tough milieu he inhabited called for different
relationships between the sexes from those Preczang, or his
members, might be used to. In the tropics, said Traven, you
had to be direct with women or be condemned to celibacy and
you paid for pleasures which you would get for free in Germany.

As he was at home with the ways of women, so he handled
the perils of a primitive existence. In the letters Traven
harnesses all the privations of his sojourn in the wilderness to
demonstrate his fortitude and his capacity for facing adversity.
His lengthy complaints about the hardships of life in the jungle,
which I had read before, seemed hand-crafted for the purpose
of arousing applause from the reader, who was quite clearly
expected to be awe-struck by so resolute and intrepid an author.
The mosquitoes, the snakes and 'the lizards as big and as black
and as strong as a man's arm' were called as witnesses to
Traven's grit. I did not doubt their evidence but I was intrigued, and on occasion amused, by Traven's need for them to

testify on his behalf. And there was something slightly sad
about all this showing-off by a lonely man. Whether from
vanity, shyness, or a sense of isolation, he was anxious to
impress and flaunted the experiences he was undergoing, possibly to distract attention from the great unspoken subject of
his past.

He wanted us to bow before the towering authenticity of his
writing. Everyone was to know and to mark that the world of
B. Traven was a true world, that the experiences were real. The
knowledge and the hardships of the books were the knowledge
and the hardships of his life.

If you want to know the bush and the jungle, its life and its
music, its loving and its killing, then you cannot live in the
Regis Hotel in Mexico City. You must live in the jungle
itself. You have to live with it, you have to love it, you must
be wedded to it. There is no other way. The jungle and the
bush only tell me their stories when I bury myself in them.

No ordinary man, he was suggesting, no ordinary writer
even, would undergo and survive the challenges which brought
forth the writings of the inimitable B. Traven.

Impenetrable jungle covered the broad flood plains of the
Panuco and Tamesi rivers ... Where there were settlements,
they huddled nervously together near the few railway stations.
Only a few Europeans lived here like lost people ... In these
depths where twilight reigns always, all the mysteries and
darkness of the world seems to lurk ...

There I live deep in the tropical jungle alone in a primitive
hut that I built myself like an Indian, without needing even
a nail.

It was quintessential Traven to let on that he had mastered
the Indian building skills. In his books he loved writing about
crafts, trades and the general doing of work, describing how
jobs were carried out, listing the tasks and difficulties of
apparently simple and menial occupations. He obviously
admired the talents and application of those who did these jobs
and was proud to show himself worthy of their number. As

Gales puts it in *The Cotton-Pickers*, 'There is absolutely nothing you can't learn if you go about it one step at a time.' There were few things, I guessed, that Traven would have admitted to not mastering. He was a voluble writer in his letters as well as his books, and in both there is the occasional sound of a know-all. His letters would spill over with opinions on how difficult it was to run democratic organisations like the Büchergilde, with comments on the corruption of justice, and the poor treatment of farmworkers in the United States, with descriptions of the tropical rains, and with information about prices in Mexico and the size of the apples that grew there. He even fell to lecturing Preczang on his own business, advising him that he should know that serialisation in newspapers or magazines never hurt a novel. Traven liked to hold forth, liked to expound, liked to inform and liked to have his own way.

There was an obstinate tone in his refusals to give any kind of biography to the Büchergilde, and even six months before the publication of his first novel he was fussing testily about how he might be categorised as a writer. In spite of his eulogies of the workers and the underdogs of the world, he did not want to find himself corralled in a school of literature by being labelled as a 'proletarian writer'. If this were to happen, he sulked, he would immediately write a novel glorifying capitalism in order to have the label removed. Carefully giving nothing away about his own background, as to whether or not he came from a worker's family, he went on in the same moody vein to protest that he did not think about workers as such. What he was interested in was people. The fact that the people he wrote about were, for the most part, workers was a coincidence, nothing more. The fact was he had spent most of his life with workers and he found them the most interesting and many-sided people, much more interesting than the likes of, say (and here he snatched an odd quartet out of the air), Coolidge, Rockefeller, Gloria Swanson and Tom Mix. That was not to say that he would only be writing about workers; in fact some of the things he wanted to write about would be of no interest to them.

There was little in this to help me guess at the man's origins, I could only note it as one more example of his determination to fudge the matter whenever possible. I speculated that perhaps it was the status of his birth which accounted for his secrecy, that he had come from a humble family and that this was something he felt troubled about, something which embarrassed him or made him feel ashamed. Hence he had always hidden it and contested all attempts to probe his ancestry. If this were so, perhaps he had written so vigorously and so movingly about the lives of workers as a repayment, a way of making up to his family and his class for his own abandonment of his birthright. This would be a kind of reversal of the theory of Traven as a guilty millionaire. Instead of a rich industrialist squaring his conscience for exploiting his workers, Traven was really a man of poor family compensating for a shameful rejection of his roots. But like everything else about this infuriating man, the fact that he obscured the status of his birth was open to an alternative construction. Was it not equally likely that he had not been born the son of a worker but that to reveal this would put in question his authority as a writer about workers? Perhaps it was the class of his parents and upbringing that he was concerned to hide. He had been born, say, so far from the lowest orders of society that B. Traven, the apostle of the oppressed, the chronicler of cruelty and exploitation had sprung, in fact, from the loins of the exploiters themselves. Might he not then have protected the authenticity of his work by concealing this? Such speculation was amusing but got me nowhere. Traven's ever-ambiguous response to the question of his origin could be explained by almost any theory. The fog of uncertainty would only be dispelled by the facts.

There was one matter, I noticed, on which he was not ambiguous. This was the question of his nationality. He told Preczang that he had first written several of his works in the English language before translating them himself into German and, in a letter to a Professor Strasser in Switzerland in 1929, he was clear and adamant about the country of his birth, albeit referring to himself in the third person.

B. Traven is an American; he was born in the United States; both of his parents were born in the States. His native language is English. Although he writes a good deal in German, he nevertheless writes about half, if not more, in English, because it is easier for him to put down first in

English difficult thoughts and connections and complicated dialogues, in order to clarify them for himself in words and sentences.

And he explained the apparent oddity of a native English speaker first publishing his work in a foreign language: 'The difficulty, not to say the impossibility, of finding a publisher in the United States for his books gave him the idea of rewriting his books in German and of offering them in Germany.'

Traven was irritated by the various European nationalities with which he was invested; they were all, he wrote, the inventions of critics who wanted to appear smart and well informed. Most commonly they made him, not surprisingly, a German but there was nothing in this, said Traven; why, he was not even of German race or blood. As if bored by the repetition he spelled it out for one correspondent: 'The publishers of the German edition of my books knew from the first day of our relations that I am an American born in the USA.'

If he were German he was risking drawing attention to the fact by being so loud and so specific in his denials. It was more like him to muddy the waters.

And here he was, at the same time, stating quite firmly that he was an American. Was this a straightforward diversion, or bluff to divert us from his real Fatherland? Or was it a double bluff, and he really was American? It was anyone's guess.

The accusation of being German seemed to aggravate him above all others; it was the charge levelled at him most often.

B. Traven is not a German; he was not born in Germany; he is not even of German descent. For the same reason he is not a German American, a German Mexican, a German Canadian; he is not a German emigrant, nor a German Argentinian, nor whatever else has been said about him in the reviews.

I was not sure what to make of Traven's apparent candour on this one point of his nationality. It was so out of character for him to provide any fact about his past, let alone to be so assertive about one, that it was as mysterious as his usual silence or obfuscation. I could hardly take what he said at face value, but his passion in this matter suggested that something was afoot.

The Traven of *The Death Ship* had pooh-poohed the whole business of nationality as being something of no importance, and I came across a declaration in one of his letters which echoed this. 'I am no German, since I have no right to number myself among them', it began (a slightly odd form of words, and less conclusive than his usual statements on this subject), and it went on:

> Personally I neither regard this as an honour nor as a shame, since I am – as most people are – as irresponsible for my nationality as for my date of birth or for the colour of my eyes. Whoever reads just one of my books will know that I never disguise my nationality.

Presumably Traven was referring to Gerard Gales, the American storyteller of the early books. It would be interesting to look more closely at Gales, to pick up what scraps of information are supplied about him. It might turn out that Gerard Gales was the author by another (even his real?) name.

Many students of the Traven mystery had identified the author with this American narrator of the first published works. The chief reason for this was Traven's insistence that he only wrote about what he had himself experienced or seen with his own eyes, a prosaic claim but one which provided a key to the books – they became autobiography.

Traven would not talk directly about himself but he was adamant that readers should discern his presence in the works.

> I am unable to chew things out of my pencil: others may be able to do so, not I. I have to know the people about whom I talk. They must have been my friends or my enemies or my neighbours or my fellow citizens for me to be able to render them well. I must have seen things and landscapes and persons before I can call them to life in my works.

And he was just as insistent about the specific experiences he attributed to Gerard Gales. He had told Preczang that the strike in *The Cotton-Pickers* had actually happened; likewise, *The Death Ship* was not a book that he had made up.

I think that the story is good and entertaining because I did not pick it out of the seams of my pants, because I did not invent it ... One simply tells how one saw things and how one experienced them.

The Gales character had knocked around Mexico and taken part in strikes; as a humble seaman he had sailed the high seas in a doomed crate, and, of course, he had penetrated the dark and inhospitable hinterland of Mexico. Perhaps Traven had, too, as he said:

There are people who make a trip through the Thüringer Forest and are able to write thereafter a jungle story. With respect I consider these men to be either poets or artists. I am neither a poet nor an artist, so I have to go right into the jungle if I want to write something about it.

In *The Bridge in the Jungle*, Gales introduces himself to a fellow American who has just sprung upon him. No names, of course, 'telling other people your name without being asked for it seems silly anyhow', but a brief explanation of Gales's presence is supplied.

I told him that I was a free-lance explorer and also the president, the treasurer, and the secretary of a one-man expedition on the look-out for rare plants with a commercial value for their medicinal or industrial properties, but that I would take any job offered me on my way and that I hoped to find maybe, gold deposits or precious stones.

In this, the last of the books featuring Gales, there are few hints about his past but the above description fits perfectly the wandering, turn-his-hand-to-anything Gales of *The Cotton-Pickers*. In that book, also, the facts about him are few but we learn that he is a hard-up American, familiar with, if not a member of, the Wobblies, the I.W.W. He implies that he comes from a working family and that he has travelled in the United States, England and Germany. The reader of *The Death Ship* knows that Gales travelled extensively in Europe, although it is interesting that there is no continuity of the character from book

to book. The name and the tone of voice are the same, but
there is no attempt to link the episodes in Gales's life. *The Death
Ship* is peppered with references to Gales's American background and he likes to imply a familiarity with Jackson Square,
New Orleans, or Lincoln Avenue, Chicago, a city he refers to
quaintly as 'Chic'. He appears to know Galveston, 'Philly',
Boston, New York, and Wisconsin, 'where people throw butter
on the fire to make the coffee boil quickly', but all these references are pretty shallow. There is little detail in them and
nothing that could not be picked up from reading and meeting
a few Americans. And they are often dragged awkwardly into
the narrative. Gales is also free with American slang, but he
uses it unhandily and seems to improvise much of it. 'Goldfish
in shit leave me alone!' is the sort of contrived locution he
comes out with.

There was not much more that could be garnered about
Gales's background and history from the novels, although there
is an early episode in *The Death Ship* which cunningly suggests
that the voice of Gales is, indeed, the voice of Traven. He
describes meeting an American couple in Rotterdam and telling them his tale of woe, about being left behind by his ship
and being unable to obtain any papers to prove who he is. They
listen and are fascinated, finding the story funny rather than
sad and the man, who owns magazines, fishes out a note and
gives it to Gales who then confides to the reader:

That was the first cash I ever received for telling a story.
Yes, sir.

Gales is thus established as a writer, too. But Traven cannot
resist spicing this little revelation with an irony which at the
same time throws its value into question. The man con-
gratulates Gales on his story-telling: 'You know, my boy, you
could make quite a lot of dough, the way you tell stories. You
are an artist.'

But what he is congratulating is the gift 'to tell a story the
way you did, a story that is not true but that sounds true'. So
is Traven also telling us a story that is not true but which
sounds true, or is he once more simply trying to confuse us and
throw us off the scent?

It was none the less possible to shape some sort of picture, however sketchy, of the Traven-as-Gales biography. I found an article from the *Texas Quarterly* of 1963 in which a certain Charles Miller had done this, adding some dashes of information, or guesswork, from sources other than those I had seen thus far.

According to Miller's speculative biography, Traven was an American, born in Chicago, Illinois, around the year 1900. His parents were Norwegian or Swedish and belonged to the working class. The boy Traven was put to work at the age of seven in the immigrant communities of Chicago, and thus received no formal schooling. But in between blacking boots, delivering papers and washing dishes he learned to read and spent long hours poring over borrowed books.

Miller's story went on to say that at the age of ten the young Traven was taken on to the crew of a tramp steamer as cabin boy. One of the first countries the boy visited as a merchant seaman was Mexico, calling at the port of Mazatlan on the west coast. Traven's love for the country dated from that time and as he made more visits to Mexican ports over the following years he formed the idea of making the country his home.

By the time Traven was about twenty he had travelled the world, was an experienced seaman and had picked up the rudiments of several languages. Some time in the early 1920s, claimed Miller, Traven gave up the sea and returned to Mexico, building his own palm-thatched hut in the jungle and living the hard and lonely life described in *The Night Visitor* or his letters to Preczang. Miller seemed to accept the Gales stories as fact, for he said that Traven's jobs in Mexico included work on the cotton plantations and oil fields, and that he turned his hand to cattle-driving, mining, trapping, working in a bakery, exploring and teaching English.

It was now, said Miller, that Traven started writing. By 1924 he had finished *The Death Ship*, *The Treasure of the Sierra Madre* and *The Bush* and despatched them to a publisher in New York. The manuscripts were returned to Traven and he was informed that they were not commercial and that, in any case, they would have to be turned into better English before they were publishable. Undeterred, the writer sent the same manuscripts to the Büchergilde Gutenberg in Berlin where they had a more satisfactory reception. Traven worked with the publishers on the German versions of these books, which had an immediate success.

Miller described Traven's insistence that the Büchergilde issue no publicity about him, his refusal to supply or have taken any photographs of himself and his unwillingness to meet either press or public. Miller quoted Traven's claim that he should be allowed to keep his personal privacy intact and that there would be no difficulty for good readers to discover him, for there was no avoiding the fact that, 'In every work of a writer the man behind it reveals his personality.' In spite of this, said Miller, the man who signed 'B. Traven' to the works had refused to claim personal glory, and had shunned public honours.

Charles Miller concluded his putative biographical sketch with a few words about the American publication of Traven's books before bringing the story as up to date as he could by describing the living Traven. Although Traven was a chronic traveller, said Miller, he had spent most of his mature life in the tropical regions of Mexico. He was a master of many tongues, not only English, German, French and Spanish, but also two of the unwritten Indian languages of southern Mexico. He chose not to answer most of the many letters written to him. The only way to get in touch with him was, like his publishers, to go through his agent, R. E. Lujan, of Mexico City.

R.E. Lujan of Mexico City was, I knew, more than an agent. This was Rosa Elena Lujan, the widow of the man Hal Croves, who had died in Mexico in 1969, and whose funeral picture I had seen in *Time* magazine. He was the man believed to be Traven. The name Lujan was not one further alias for me to grapple with, but her name before she married Croves and to which she had reverted according to Mexican custom. Señora Lujan was someone we would have to film. I had no means of knowing whether the birthplace and date of birth supplied by Miller were correct, but they, like everything in his summary, would fit with any picture of Traven based on his books. I had not heard before of his running away to sea as a boy, nor of the exact place of his first arrival in Mexico. I wondered, also, how Miller had discovered that Traven was such a linguist, particularly how he knew that he spoke the unwritten languages of the Indians.

There was one other paragraph in Miller's article which caught my eye. While running through some of the wild stories which had spread about Traven, Miller dismissed as myth the rumour 'being revived in Germany' that 'Traven was really Bruno Marhut (with various spellings)'. Miller was convinced that Marhut, as he referred to him, was certainly not the writer B. Traven. There had been such a man as Marhut – he was a brilliant young political writer who had flourished in Munich and narrowly avoided execution in the Bavarian revolution following the First World War. But, according to Miller, there was no evidence in Traven's books that they were one and the same man. It was, he said, merely an interesting myth. All the evidence suggested that Traven was in Mexico at the time Marhut was active in Germany. Far from escaping a death sentence in Munich, the writer was working at humble jobs in the New World.

This was interesting. Marhut, I presumed, was the same man as the mysterious Ret Marut (however his name should be spelled) whom I had read about in *Time*. Here was Miller saying that Marut was nothing to do with Traven; the *Time* article had suggested otherwise.

I felt that I had gone as far as I usefully could for the moment in extracting a picture, or a sense, of Traven from his books and letters. The next step was to make contact with those who had followed this hypnotising path before me to see what I could learn from them. My ambition remained merely to chronicle this mystery, to recount the investigations of others, but it would be untrue to say that the thought never crossed my mind that I might discover some new avenue of enquiry. I had no idea what this might be. But any detective taking over an unsolved case must feel that somewhere within all the evidence lies a clue, the significance of which others have missed. It is his hope that when he is face to face with the material he will sense some different meaning. Such thoughts at any rate filled my musings as I walked home from work on the spring evenings. I did not take them too seriously.

At the same time, and more usefully, I was trying to take stock of what I knew and what I was looking for. There were aspects of this extraordinary writer that I was confident I could now recognise: the defensiveness, the boasting, the concern for the dispossessed, the irony, the cockiness, the eagerness to lecture and instruct, his romantic attachment to the primitive, the secretiveness, the man-of-the-world air, the humour, the hatred of officialdom, the passion for anonymity. I must keep watch for these. They would all have their reflection in the man's life, whoever he was. Of that I was sure.

As to the physical person, or persons, there seemed to be three leading candidates. I decided that the best way to proceed would be to keep these three characters in mind as we accumulated reports and evidence, building up a picture of each and looking all the time for clues which would link any of them with what was known for certain about Traven, the writer. I could not be sure that any of the three would emerge as favourite, but at least this would be a good way of making sense of new material as I acquired it.

Firstly, there was the man who seemed to be described by the early books. He was an American, probably from the Midwest, a worker, possibly a member of the Wobblies, and he had spent some years doing a variety of jobs in Mexico before the books appeared. No one had put a name to this man other than the name the author had given him, Gerard Gales, though few appeared to believe that either Gales or Traven was the author's real name. This identity was, in essence, the person described by Miller in his article.

Secondly, there was the enigmatic person of Ret Marut. He was a journalist and writer, a dashing figure mixed up in a revolution in Germany in 1919, an anarchist, who might, or might not, have gone to Mexico. He was a mysterious character in his own right, let alone as part of the Traven riddle. He had sprung from nowhere and then disappeared.

Thirdly, and most promisingly, there was the old man who died in Mexico City. There were two names associated with him, Torsvan and Croves. I could not make out whether both names belonged to the one man or whether there might have been two separate people. But at least there was an authenticated death for Croves, as he was definitely calling himself in his later years. And he had apparently adopted some of the prerogatives of the author as time went on, for example the new editions of the books emanated from him. It was on the death of this man Croves that the world had mourned the passing of the author B. Traven. *The Times*'s obituary of Croves was headed: 'B. Traven. Writer of Powerful Tales Who Hid his Identity', and the *New York Times* declared: 'B. Traven. Secretive Author is Dead'.

But Croves's origins and history were obscure and there was one very odd factor about him. He had come on to the scene in the early 1940s at just the time that the books of B. Traven more or less dried up. After *General from the Jungle* in 1940, there were only a few short stories and one long novel, *Aslan Norval*, which came out in 1960 to a bemused reception from critics, who felt it had neither the calibre nor the subject matter of a Traven book. Yet the old man who produced this book was the man taken by the world to be the great writer. Croves himself had always denied that he was Traven, but there was nothing very strange about that – so would Traven have done.

5 'Der Ziegelbrenner ...
We Need You'

Hal Croves was going to be a central, if not the central, character in the film. His was the only physical presence connected closely with the Traven work and whether he was the author or not, whether he was the same person as Torsvan or not, no description of the Traven mystery could be sustained without accommodating his part; no solution would be possible without explaining who he was or was not. This did not seem too daunting a prospect; in fact, there was positive hope that we could get to grips with Mr Croves; after all, he had definitely existed – I had seen a photograph of him in his coffin. And there was his widow, Señora Lujan. She was still alive, living in Mexico City, and had evidently never doubted that the man she had married had been the author, B. Traven. She had translated some of the books into Spanish, she was the copyright holder of the B. Traven works – she must know as much as anyone living about the secrets.

The publisher Lawrence Hill, when sending us a list of the Traven books he had in print, had included Señora Lujan's address – Rio Mississippi, Mexico 5, D. F. – and we now wrote off to make our first contact with her. We knew that Señora Lujan's public statements positively identified her husband as Traven and our letter was phrased carefully to take account of that. We were anxious that she should take part in the programme and tell us as much as possible of what she knew. Reading the letter again now I see that we were nothing if not optimistic in our approach.

42

May 17th, 1977

Dear Señora Lujan,

I am at the moment doing some preliminary research into the life of the man I understand to have been your husband. Our aim is to make a short documentary film about him for BBC Television. I wonder if you would be willing to assist us by answering, in a letter, the questions which follow. We are hoping to bring a film crew to Mexico in July and would like to know 1) whether you would be prepared to talk on film about your husband's life and writing, or 2) if you would at least be prepared to talk informally to someone from the team to assist our research.

My questions are

1) Were you married to the man know as B. Traven? How and when did you meet? How long were you married to him? Did you have any children and if so how old are they, do they live in Mexico too?

2) What were the other names used by B. Traven during his life? i.e., was he also known as Ret Marut, Traven Torsvan, Hal Croves?

3) Do you know about his early life? Where was he born? What was his first language? When and how did he come to live in Germany then Mexico? Did he ever talk to you about his early life, or about his writing?

4) Could you describe his personality and his physical appearance?

5) Why do you think he was so shy of publicity? Did you have to enter into the game as well, that is if your husband was Hal Croves and B. Traven, did you too use the name Croves as well?

6) Who else who knew him is still alive and might be prepared to talk to us?

7) Who would you like to see given the task of writing his biography? Why? Is there anyone you would definitely not like to see doing this? Why?

8) Do you have any letters, personal possessions or photographs of B. Traven which we could use in our film? Do you know anyone else who has?

Please include in your reply, if you can, any other information which you think might be useful for us. I look

forward to hearing from you; thank you for your co-
operation,

    Yours sincerely,

JENNIFER MCKAY

Researcher,

'The Book Programme', BBC-2

The slight obscurity of question 7 should be explained – it was
a way of trying to gauge Señora Lujan's opinion of the various
theories put forward about Traven to see which she favoured
and which she might denounce as false. Had the Señora been
willing or able to write back with answers to this and all the
other questions the mystery would, I suppose, have been solved
then and there. But that was not how it happened.

The letter was despatched and we set about trying to line up
other interviews with people who had known the man Croves.
Lawrence Hill had met him and wrote to say that he would
be glad to help. He too, it seemed, believed Croves was Traven.
The film director John Huston had met Croves while preparing
his film of *The Treasure of the Sierra Madre*, indeed that was the
first occasion on which Croves surfaced in public. We would
need to tell the story of that first sighting and of subsequent
events and the best way to do that would be with Huston
himself. He is a greater storyteller, he would be a valuable
'name' in the billing of the film and he would perhaps stand
witness for us as to the quality of Traven's work. What was
more, I had read one cutting which suggested that Huston was
by no means convinced that Croves was the author, rather the
opposite. We obtained a telephone number for Huston in Mexico
and Jennifer McKay placed a call. She spoke to Huston's long-
time assistant, Gladys Hill, who could not have been more
friendly. Yes, she would ask Huston if he would be interviewed
about the first meeting with Croves, the filming and his
reported belief that Croves was not Traven. She knew that he
had spoken about this before and thought that he would do
it if he were free. We were to ring for an answer in a couple
of days.

In the meantime I rang Huston's agent, Paul Kohner, who
lived in Hollywood. Kohner had been involved in setting up
the filming of *The Treasure of the Sierra Madre* and had handled

the film rights for some of Traven's books. He was brisk and courteous on the phone. He had met Croves, he had corresponded with Traven and he would film an interview. I also rang Judy Stone, who had met Croves while writing the articles which she turned into her book, *The Mystery of B. Traven*. In July she would be at home in San Francisco, where she worked as film critic for the *San Francisco Chronicle*, and would, she said, look forward to our arrival. She appeared to be on very good terms with Señora Lujan, whom she referred to as Rosa Elena, and she gave me the Señora's telephone number in Mexico City. She urged me, also, to call Sanora Babb Howe, widow of the great Oscar-winning cinematographer James Wong Howe, who, she said, had been a friend of Croves. I did as she suggested and Mrs Howe, who now writes under the name of Sanora Babb, said she would be happy to talk to us about Croves, who was, she said, a mysterious person.

The arrangements were progressing smoothly. It was time now to ring Gladys Hill again to hear if Huston would take part, and here our luck changed. He had decided that he did not wish to be filmed, principally, said Gladys Hill, because he did not want to be drawn into any kind of argument about whether or not Croves had been Traven. If he were interviewed and expressed his doubts about Croves this would constitute a public snub to Señora Lujan – something he wished to avoid. That was his decision and his final word. It was a blow. We could paraphrase what Huston had been reported as saying in the past and I even knew of a brief snatch of film in which he described his first meeting with Croves, but these were no substitute for an interview expressly for us or for the opportunity to question him at length. I resolved to try again when we got to Mexico and to ask Kohner, when we saw him, if he would intercede for us in this matter.

Our next call was more fruitful. We now had a phone number for Señora Lujan and, spurred on by my impatience for a reply to our letter, Jennifer McKay made use of it. She spoke first to a maid who had no English and then to the Señora herself. The line was crackly and kept fading so the conversation had to be brief, but it was long enough to ascertain that Señora Lujan had received our letter and was willing, in principle, to be interviewed and to allow us to film in the house where she had

lived with Croves. She said that she travelled a good deal so
we would have to coincide with a time when she was at home;
July would probably be convenient for her but she wanted us
to give her some exact dates when we had them. There was no
time for further explanations or arrangements as the line was
disintegrating. The timing could still let us down and the
Señora's emphasis on her travelling could be a way of leaving
a door open for change of mind. It would not be the first time
someone had agreed to be filmed and then thought better of it.
With a Traven connection there was even more reason to
suspect that the cup might be dashed from our lips.

We sped ahead with other arrangements. A letter had arrived
from Michael Baumann, offering assistance. The Traven
grapevine had brought him news of our project and he was
keen to participate. Baumann had studied Traven as deeply
as anyone in the English-speaking world and, if we could meet,
he could guide us away from the culs-de-sac and along the
highways and byways of Traven scholarship. Unfortunately,
Baumann was not going to be in the United States when we
would be there, but he was coming to Europe for the summer
to visit Germany and Austria. His charter flight was going to
land in Paris, so I arranged for him and his wife to fly to
London for a day or so at the beginning of their trip in June.
This would be much cheaper than for me and a film crew
to fly to Paris. There was one great advantage in seeing
Baumann in June: it meant that at the very outset of the filming there would be the chance to bone up on Traven research and to clarify my thoughts in discussion with an
experienced toiler in the Traven vineyard.

In his second letter Baumann mentioned Robert Goss of
Oakland, California, 'the most important Traven researcher
in the U.S. to-day ... I am sure he will be most helpful to you.'
I rang Goss. He was as well disposed as Baumann had
promised and we arranged to meet in San Francisco. I was
unable to find Charles Miller, who had written the persuasive
account of Traven as an American worker. I traced addresses
for him in Mexico and the United States but there were no
replies to my letters and cables. On the other hand, I was able
to set up some further interviews in Los Angeles with Mina
and Herbert Arthur Klein, who had corresponded with Traven

in the 1930s and who had edited a collection of the short stories; and with Bernard Smith, who had been the editor of the first American editions of Traven's books.

We looked, as well, into the British publishing history of Traven's work. His agents in England, Curtis Brown, could tell us little or nothing and in a sweep of his various British publishers, Robert Hale, Chatto and Windus, and Jonathan Cape, we found no one who could remember handling the books or having any contact with Mexico. However, in Michael Howard's book *Jonathan Cape, Publisher*, I found a brief and tantalising passage, which persuaded me that Traven had reached across the Atlantic to leave his calling card in London:

> Also in the spring of 1940 Cape took over from Chatto the publishing rights in B. Traven's works ... The first title to be included was *The Death Ship* of which over a million and a half copies had been sold in Russia, and a quarter of a million in Germany until the book was banned and burned by the Nazis.
>
> Traven himself was an enigma. He dealt almost entirely through his agent, Juliet O'Hea of Curtis Brown, and his occasional letters to her from Mexico revealed an imperfect command of English. His exact whereabouts remained a mystery. One day, a few years after the war had ended, a nondescript ageing man arrived in Cape's front office, inquiring in a heavy accent about the sales of Traven's works. Jonathan was told, and at once asked his secretary to bring him up, believing that he might well be the author himself; but by the time she got downstairs again the man had gone.

If it had been Traven who had called at Cape's handsome premises in Bedford Square, he had been taking an uncharacteristic chance. But the sudden disappearance surely bore his thumbprint. I smiled to myself, too, over the epithet 'nondescript'. If it had been Traven and he had read this account, he would not have liked that.

Michael Baumann and his wife Friedl did not reach London until Monday June 20th, and it was after work on that evening that Jennifer McKay and I walked from BBC Television Centre

to the hotel where I had booked a room for them. What I
hoped for from Michael Baumann was a summary of the story
so far, a canter round the work that scholars and journalists
had done on the Traven case – as well, of course, as an exposition of his own views. Above all, I wanted to know more and
all there was to know, about Croves and Marut and the man
from the Midwest.

We met in the lounge of the hotel and made our introductions. Both Baumann and his wife were tired from their long
and protracted journey, but over a beer he told us how he had
first become interested in Traven when he was living in
Switzerland in 1963. Baumann was then casting about for a
subject on which to write his Ph.D. thesis. He read a series of
articles about Traven in a Swiss newspaper which led him to
read all the novels in German. He was struck by what seemed
to be the American origins of the works and decided to make
Traven his doctoral topic. He took his doctorate at the
University of Pennsylvania and was now teaching English at
California State University in Chico.

Baumann asked about our film and about 'The Book Programme'. Then I ordered some more drinks and began to
question him about Traven matters. He spoke slowly and
deliberately, choosing his words with care to make it quite clear
when he was reporting fact and when speculating; to distinguish
between probabilities and possibilities; to avoid journalistic
exaggeration, and to apportion credit to others where it was
due. I took him to be a close and conscientious scholar. He
was, I supposed, in his late thirties; his dark hair receded from
a high forehead, he wore spectacles and the quietness of his
voice added to a convincingly learned air. He began by paying homage to the work of the East German, Rolf Recknagel,
of whom he had written in a letter to me, 'without his initial
research . . . none of us would be anywhere, however much we
may disagree with him to-day'. Then we moved on to the substance of our meeting.

The first character we talked about was Hal Croves.
Baumann had never met Croves, but he had gathered together
such incontrovertible facts as there were. Croves, he said, first
turned up to meet John Huston in the winter of 1946–7. He
then disappeared but a Mexican journalist called Luis Spota

tracked down a man living under the name of Traven Torsvan
in Acapulco in 1948 and this man Torsvan was, it seemed,
identical with Hal Croves. In 1959 Hal Croves travelled to
Germany for the première of a film of *The Death Ship* and in
one hotel actually filled in the registration card as 'Torsvan
also called Croves'.

Michael Baumann added that the name Torsvan had turned
up for the first time in 1926, when a man described as 'an
engineer' and using the name T. Torsvan took part in an
archaeological expedition through the Chiapas region in the
south of Mexico. This man took photographs during the trip
and detached himself early to travel on alone. The leader of
this expedition, Enrique Juan Palacios, referred to the man
Torsvan as a Norwegian. All this was interesting. Traven had
written about the Chiapas region and he had taken photographs there for his book *Land of Spring*; there must surely be a
connection. But Baumann was unwilling to allow me to leap to
so simple a conclusion. It was not certain, he said, that the
Torsvan on the expedition was the same man who called himself
Torsvan later; there could well be two men with that name.
Baumann did accept that the later Torsvan and Croves were
probably one and the same, but, as he put it in his book, 'if
there is a seeming continuity in the persons of Torsvan and
Croves, we cannot yet attach the name of B. Traven to either,
or to the continuity itself. Both Torsvan and Croves explicitly
denied being B. Traven.'

So, what about the next candidate? Baumann is fluent in
German and had studied not only all Traven's work in that
language, but also the writings of Ret Marut and had compared the two. I could see as we sat round the table in the
Kensington Hilton that he was more than happy to put Croves
on one side and for us to turn our attention to the shadowy
figure of Marut.

Baumann explained that most of the research which had put
some flesh on to the name Ret Marut had been the work of
Rolf Recknagel. He had tracked down documents from which
he had been able to sketch a rough outline of Marut's career –
an outline, that was, of the fifteen-year period in which there
was any sign of the man, for Marut materialised as if from
nowhere and later vanished without trace. The name itself was

odd. Marut is the name of a kind of god in Hindu mythology.
The Maruts ride in shining chariots of gold and are depicted
as warriors wearing helmets and carrying spears. Their chariots
are carried on the winds, and they themselves are storm gods,
killing men with their lightning and splintering the trees of the
forest. It was a strange and romantic name for a man to give
himself. There was nothing to show that Marut had any
knowledge of Hindu religion and the Vedic myths, but he must
surely have known the meaning of the name. If he did, there
was a small, but telling, coincidence which seemed to
reverberate through all that I had learned so far. This man
Marut had chosen for himself the name of a storm god; the
writer Traven had chosen for his story-telling hero the name
Gales.

Marut may have been a pseudonym but, as Baumann told
me, he had possessed papers in that name. Recknagel had found
the first reference to Ret Marut in an almanac for the German
theatre season of 1907–8, where he was listed as an actor and
director. In 1908 in the town of Ohrdruf, Marut was issued
with a police registration card and in 1912 in Düsseldorf he
received another. They gave his birthplace as San Francisco

and the date as February 25th, 1882. Although born in San
Francisco, Marut's homeland was down as England. At least
it was originally so entered, but some time after the outbreak
of war between Germany and England in August 1914 the word
'England' was crossed out and replaced by 'America'. Within a
year Marut was supposed to have applied for German citizenship (in Düsseldorf in 1915), an application which was turned
down. Marut had tried two nationalities, English and
American, and attempted to sample a third. Since he was an
actor one might have expected there to be photographs but,
unlike other actors of that time, Marut seemed to have no
portrait photographs to distribute to agents and managers;
certainly none had survived. The only existing photograph
which showed his face was a bizarre one – a group picture
of the Red Indians from a production of *Peter Pan*, with all
the actors' faces covered in war-paint.

It was not, however, Marut's career as an actor which most
interested Traven-seekers. From November 1915, when Marut
arrived in Munich for the first time, his energies were chan-
nelled in a new direction and it was this period, said Baumann,
which held the key. Marut lived on the third floor of a block of
flats at Clemensstrasse 84, where the caretaker remembered him
all those years ago as a quiet and serious young man, friendly
and hard-working, hammering away at his typewriter far into
the night. The fruit of that labour was an anti-war novel of
limited circulation, *An das Fräulein von S ...*, and a radical
journal which Marut published himself – *Der Ziegelbrenner* (*The
Brickburner* or *The Brickmaker*). Baumann had a rare copy of one
of the issues of *Der Ziegelbrenner*, which he had brought with
him to London. He passed it to me now. On the outside it was
the size, shape and colour of a brick, and these bricks were
fired by Ret Marut to make comments on the imperfect world
he lived in and to help build a new society. The copy I was
holding was number three, dated March 16th, 1918. It cost 60
pfennig, was all in German and I could not read a word. I
flicked through the twenty-five or so pages within and looked
again at the red-brown cover. There was something strong and
business-like about the idea of a brick. It was an arresting image
and one which was to find a haunting echo much later in our
search.

Der
Ziegelbrenner

The first issue of *Der Ziegelbrenner* came out on September 1st, 1917, and from the beginning the magazine struck out vigorously against war, capitalism and authority. The first article of the first number had declared:

All of man's deeds, good ones and bad ones, start with thinking. Think good and you are good. Think bad and you are bad. Think war and there is war. And because everyone is thinking money, money and capitalism are to-day the only, the decisive, the most influential of all powers.

Der Ziegelbrenner appeared irregularly and was available to subscribers only. It continued until 1922 but the issues of the

---

Verlag: Der Ziegelbrenner.

Geschäftsstelle des Verlags:
München 23, Clemensstrasse.
Wir bitten, alle Zahlungen nur auf unser
Postscheck-Konto: 8350 Amt München,
zu überweisen!

last three years were published from cities other than Munich, for in 1919 Ret Marut had been forced to flee when the flame of the Bavarian revolution had been brutally snuffed out by troops sent by the Berlin government. Marut had been captured, but escaped and went on the run. He was thought to have left Germany in 1922 and was never heard from again.

How then was he ever connected with Traven? This in itself was a curious story. It had all begun with a poet called Erich Mühsam, who had been in Munich at the same time as Marut. Mühsam had been captured and imprisoned for five years following the Bavarian revolution, and when he was released he started a monthly journal, *Das Fanal*, in Berlin. In April 1927, in the seventh issue of this periodical, Mühsam printed an urgent call headed: 'Where is the Ziegelbrenner?'

Do any of the readers of *Fanal* know what happened to the Ziegelbrenner? – Ret Marut, comrade, friend, fellow fighter, human being, send a word, make a move, give a sign that you are alive, that you are still the same Ziegelbrenner, that your heart has not given way to party politics, that your brain has not calcified, your arm paralysed, your fingers stiffened. You eluded the Bavarians in 1919 though they already had you by the collar.

An amnesty had been declared and Mühsam wanted Marut to write an untainted and uncompromised history of the Republic of Councils in Munich. He had a high opinion of his former comrade.

You were the only one who was actively involved in events, yet who was able to see as if from a distance and from a height the terrible things that happened, the good that was being striven for, the deeds that were right, the deeds that should have been done that were even more right ...

We need you. Who knows the Ziegelbrenner? What reader of *Fanal* knows where we can find, reach Ret Marut? ...

Many are asking for him. Many are waiting for him. He is being called.

They continued to ask and they continued to wait because Mühsam received no answer to his stirring summons. He

assumed that the Brickburner was dead or beyond the reach of
his old circle. Then Mühsam came upon the early novels of
B. Traven. There was something about the tone of the author's
voice which struck Mühsam as familiar. The style of the writing, the attitudes, the opinions, sent him back to his old copies
of *Der Ziegelbrenner*. He called in an anarchist friend, Rudolph
Rocker, to help him, and together they compared the writings
of Ret Marut with the writings of B. Traven, and concluded
that the two authors were one and the same.

I liked this story. The idea of a long-lost voice from the
past speaking anonymously, yet clearly, across an ocean to his
old comrades was a romantic thought. There could hardly be a
more attractive way for Marut to let slip his secret. Yet it
seemed a pretty tenuous connection on which to base a theory
that Marut was Traven. There was no documentary evidence
of any kind to place either Marut in Mexico or Traven in
Germany. And then Mühsam so clearly wanted to find Marut.
In such circumstances it was more than possible that he had
convinced himself that the new mysterious writer with an
anarchist bent must surely be his fellow revolutionary. It was
not even as if Mühsam had any first-hand contact with the
Traven novels or their arrival from Mexico. He had simply, it
seemed, read them and shouted 'Eureka'.

Baumann continued to talk about Marut and made it clear
that he believed in the Marut–Traven connection. As he produced more and more links and similarities between the two
writers I became less and less sceptical, but I was unable to
forget that the whole edifice of an identification of Marut with
Traven rested on the chance recognition that Mühsam had
made. It was, at the least, a coincidence and doubt gnawed
at my mind for a long time to come.

Some other details were known about Marut. He could speak
English and kept prominently among his books volumes by
Shelley, Walt Whitman and, interestingly enough, Jack
London. Two young women played a notable part in the period
of his life that was documented. The first was an actress called
Elfriede Zielke; the second was another actress, Irene Mermet,
who became his partner in publishing *Der Ziegelbrenner*.

In the magazine Marut boasted that he had visited practically
every country in the world and had lived for many years in non-

German nations – a hint in that, I thought, of B.T., man of
the world. Of his origins Der Ziegelbrenner gave away little,
but there was one reference which chimed sweetly with Traven.
In answer to one anti-Semitic critic who attacked him, Marut
replied that there was no Jewish blood among his ancestors,
not that he was especially proud to be of undiluted Aryan
blood, for a man could not help his nationality. And, lo and
behold, *Der Ziegelbrenner* was also fond of surrounding himself
with a cloak of secrecy and drama. The magazine had to print
its address of publication – Clemensstrasse – but all correspondence was through a post-office box number and the shutters
were firmly up against any enquirers. Many issues carried the
line: 'No visiting allowed. There is never anybody at home. We
have no telephone.'

In a letter to a female reader, Marut explained his retiring
stance:

> I am but a product of an era with the heart-felt wish to dis-
> appear again back into the continuum, with the same
> anonymity with which I must to-day shout out my words
> before you ... I have not the slightest literary ambition. I
> am not a writer, I shout. I want to be nothing but – the
> word.

Now this did sound like Traven. Slightly more high-flown
perhaps, but the same wish to dissolve the person into the work.
Mind you, Traven did tend to be schoolmasterly in his instructions about anonymity while Marut could become positively
angry, as here in the issue of November 9th, 1918:

> I shall always and at all times prefer to be pissed on by dogs,
> and it will appear to me to be a greater honour than to be
> pissed on by readers of *Der Ziegelbrenner* with letters that
> attempt to sniff out holes in my garment in order to pin me
> down, for no-one else has the opportunity of boring himself
> into my flesh.

He sounded as if his dislike of being identified was a physical
disgust, almost a fear of contamination. And this curious and
vivid imagining was matched on occasion by bizarre behaviour.

Marut, it was said, used to address public meetings on revolutionary causes – but he did so with the lights out, in darkened rooms, so he could not be seen. And he, too, had a way with names. He wrote as *Der Ziegelbrenner* in his periodical; he published a novel (advertised in the magazine) as Richard Maurhut; he called himself Ret Marut. No one knew what his real name was, nor where he had come from. The same person or no, Traven and Marut were alike in many regards.

Michael Baumann had discovered many other telling similarities of style and ideas in his exhaustive textual study of Traven's books and Marut's journalism, similarities which carried more weight with him than the few biographical similarities. We talked about them briefly that evening in the hotel, but we were going to cover this in the interview on the following day and by now Baumann and his wife were looking weary. They had had a delayed and extended journey compounded by jet lag, so we decided to break up for the evening and continue when we met for the filming.

6 A Man with No Name

The next day I met Baumann and his wife as arranged at the BBC's Lime Grove Studios. The sylvan name of this building belies its appearance, for it is an ugly and irregular block whose large blank side walls loom unkindly over the surrounding private houses. The studios were once used as movie studios during the high summer of the British film industry. On June 21st, 1977, though, my needs were modest and we were filming not in one of the big television studios but in a conference room on the ground floor.

I began by asking Baumann why he was sure that Ret Marut was somehow involved in the Traven work. For a start, he said, the timing fitted. Ret Marut disappeared from Germany and from Europe in 1922 or 1923 and in 1925 a man who wrote novels in the style of Ret Marut began writing letters to German publishers from Mexico. The styles of the two men were similar, they exhibited some of the same ideas, they used similar expressions, they seemed to be influenced by the same thinkers, particularly by one man, Max Stirner, a German anarchist philosopher of the first half of the nineteenth century. His ideas were strongly individualistic and anti-authoritarian, he attacked governments, religions, and all ideas or organisations which might divert a person's attention away from his loyalty to himself. (Interestingly enough, Stirner was not his real name, but in his case the true name was known, Johann Kaspar Schmidt.)

Baumann continued with a catalogue of similarities between the writings of Marut and Traven. Both writers insisted time and again on the importance of personal indignation as a means of changing the world; they inveighed against authorities of

57

every kind; they hated bureaucracy, planning and identity papers. They were both romantic Christians, and compulsive Bible students; they were against wars, nationalism, the lies of the press, capitalism, and communism.

Baumann then reminded me of what was for him the final piece of positive evidence – that Señora Lujan had said soon after her husband's death that he had been both Traven and Marut. Baumann was forced to admit that he knew of no documentary evidence which linked Ret Marut with Mexico, and for me the case was not yet proved beyond a reasonable doubt. Señora Lujan's testimony I would be able to evaluate better if and when we met. Meanwhile, as I could not read German, and had been unable to examine *Der Ziegelbrenner* closely for stylistic echoes, it was impossible for me to feel the full force of the internal evidence which Baumann found so telling. With no personal disrespect to him, I was sceptical of research where so much of the weight of the evidence depended on interpretation, especially as I was in no position to check the strength of the case or gauge what might have been omitted. I adopted this rather solipsistic approach because I had already discovered that much of what was written about Traven was make-believe or wishful guesswork and I wanted to stumble towards my own opinion, even if that meant withholding judgement on strong probabilities.

Another doubt which lodged in my mind concerned the nature of the evidence. Granted there was a quantity of it and its accumulated weight was considerable. But it was circumstantial or it was internal; what it was not in any degree was direct and incontrovertible. Not one scrap of paper, not one eye-witness from Germany could be found to say for certain, yes, Marut did go to Mexico and, yes, he was Traven. Amidst so many other clues this lack of direct proof appeared all the more glaring by its absence. Was such evidence not there because it had simply not survived or been lost? Was it not there because it had been meticulously destroyed? Or was it because it had never existed? Until some piece of unarguable proof turned up there would always be a small doubt about Marut going to Mexico, however many pointers suggested that he had. It was a doubt which might never be dispelled.

We continued with the interview. Baumann was sure that

Marut had gone to Mexico, but he recognised that this raised large problems which many other scholars had skipped over. First he gave me an outline of these difficulties, and then provided a haunting and plausible solution.

The first problem, said Baumann, was that while he was sure that Ret Marut's hand was discernible in the Traven works, Marut could not possibly have been in Mexico when the adventures described in the early Traven books took place. Since most people who read these early books (the Gerard Gales stories) felt that what was described in them *did* actually take place, Marut could not have been writing down his own adventures – there must have been someone else. There was, said Baumann, evidence that the storyteller of these books had lived in Mexico for as many as twenty years before Ret Marut could have got there.

The second problem was that the speed at which the Traven books came out in the five years after his first appearance made it extremely doubtful that Marut could have written them all himself. He had not been long enough acquainted with Mexico to write them from his own experience and, even if he had, there was not time for him to write so many books so quickly starting from scratch – certainly not under the difficult conditions which Traven described in his letters to Preczang.

Baumann repeated that most readers had taken these novels and stories to be true adventures which had actually happened, and he reminded me that Traven had let the world know from the beginning that whatever he wrote he had to have personally experienced.

I asked Baumann how he could explain away this conundrum. If Marut had gone to Mexico and sent back the books and yet there was not time for him to have lived Gales's adventures, meditated on his experiences and turned them into novels and stories, what had happened?

The answer, said Baumann, was that the early works of B. Traven were not the work of one man. A telephone rang at that moment in the room where we were filming and we had to stop to answer it. It was a wrong number, but the pause gave Baumann a chance to step out from under the warm lights for a minute or so. When we began again, he developed his explanation.

The idea had first been put forward by a Swiss journalist called Max Schmid, who suggested that an American had been what he called the 'Erlebnisträger', which means the 'carrier of experience', for the Traven books. It was this American who had written the original manuscripts of the early novels and stories, and Ret Marut had somehow met this man, recognised the literary value of these works, and begun to translate them into German.

Who, I asked, was this other man? 'We don't know,' said Baumann, but he was probably an American Wobbly, some kind of vagabonding worker. The first German version of *The Cotton-Pickers* had been called *Der Wobbly*, and there were many such men knocking around Mexico between 1910 and 1925, most of them without work, individualistic, anarchistic, hoboes, who were often well read. Baumann's guess was that this American partner had actually written the manuscripts and had probably tried to get his stories published in the United States and failed. Then somehow Marut came on the scene. Some readers had even suggested that this mysterious American co-writer had been done away with, to leave Marut as the sole originator of the books.

When I questioned Baumann about this tantalising hypothesis it became clear that it was *only* an hypothesis. No one had ever been able to discover who the other man was nor find any trace that he had existed, let alone explain how, where and when he and Marut had met. The evidence was all from inside the works. No one knew what had happened, said Baumann, but evidence might turn up one day. He even felt that it was possible to isolate some of the characteristics of the two men as revealed in the books. Marut, who he thought was the senior partner, was more of a teacher, a little pedantic and lecturing; a man eager to explain exactly what the world was about. The American 'Erlebnisträger' had no such systematic philosophy and was much less concerned with putting the world to rights. Baumann also thought he recognised that the earliest stories were cruder in style and had a different, and slightly more patronising, attitude to the Indians than the later ones in which Marut was more prominent or the initiating partner.

The 'Erlebnisträger' theory did have the virtue of keeping all three of my leading characters alive. Croves was there in

Mexico, so was Marut – and they were possibly the same person; and the American Wobbly, who walked so forcefully out of the books, had now donned the mantle of the 'carrier of experience'. There was still no firm clue to where any of these three had been born and brought up, but here was one way in which all of them could have a hand in the making of B. Traven.

An additional complexity had been added, however, by Baumann's assertion that the books were originally written in English. In spite of claims that Traven was an American I had seen no hint previously that the German manuscripts sent from Mexico were not the originals. Now, no sooner had I managed to sketch a rough map of the terrain I had to explore than I was being asked to consider the possibility that the latitudes and longitudes should be reversed. There was no alternative but to stick to my chart and be ready to turn it on its side if Baumann turned out to be right.

I wanted to conclude the interview with a question that I planned to put to everyone we talked to. It was my intention that the finished film would end with a round of our interviewees emphasising the unfathomable nature of the case of Traven.

QUESTION. Do we know who B. Traven was?
BAUMANN. In my opinion we do not know who B. Traven was. It may take a good deal of searching before we find out.
QUESTION. Do we know nothing?
BAUMANN. We know that the works exist. We know that Ret Marut was one of the mysterious entities that formed the B. Traven complex and I personally believe that an American adventurer, an American worker, was the other entity that was involved. But who either one of these people was – at the moment we do not know.

I stopped the camera and we finished filming for the day. The Baumanns were to fly back to Paris that afternoon, but there was time for a drink and further talk. Michael was worried about his performance in front of the camera. He had been nervous but I had reshot one or two of the questions so that he could correct stumbles or omissions. He was relieved to have the

ordeal over with. I raised the subject of the *B.T. Mitteilungen*,
or *B.T. News Reports*, which Baumann had mentioned to me
on the previous day. These were, he said, a series of typed and
roneoed publications, written in German, which were sent to
publishers during the 1950s. He showed me one that he had
brought with him. It was a cheaply produced sheaf of typed
sheets, stapled together like the newsletter of any small club or
society. The first issue had come out in 1951, published jointly
in Mexico City and Zürich by Traven's then Mexican agent
and translator, Esperanza Lopez Mateos, and his European
agent, Josef Wieder. The newsletter ran consecutively with the
page numbers continuing from issue to issue up to page 290,
and ended with Wieder's death in 1960. They contained news
items about the publication of Traven books, stories about his
life, about Mexico and about the question of his identity; they
appeared to be no more than advertising leaflets designed to
stimulate sales by drumming up interest in the elusive and
secretive author. This was a startling reversal of attitude by
Traven, who had in earlier years forbidden publicity and
advertising. The purity of idealism had dissolved into a hokey
commercialism.

There was, though, nothing very different from the old
Traven in some of the heroics the author was credited with in
the *Mitteilungen*.

> He had to drink out of dirty puddles when there was no
> other water available. He was immersed with his horse in the
> mud up to its saddle and, as happens to everybody, fell with
> his horse down some gorges thus tearing his face and hands
> in the undergrowth, ripping his clothes and injuring his
> knees and shins.

Nothing very new, either, about the immodest claims for the
work itself: 'How is it that B. Traven's books possess such an
incredible power? . . . There is a truthfulness in the books which
thrills the reader.' It certainly sounded from the extracts which
Baumann translated for me as though B.T. himself had a hand
in the newsletters.

A 1952 issue contained what was described as 'the authentic
B.T. biography'. I recognised it as the basis of Charles Miller's

version of Traven's life. Baumann paraphrased it in his book, as follows:

Among its claims were that Traven was born 'at the turn of the century in the Midwestern region of the USA'; that his 'native language' was English and that he wrote his books in English; that his parents, though of Scandinavian descent, had been born in the United States and that, 'through both parents, Traven came from a long line of seamen'; that Traven had earned his own living since the age of seven; that he had never gone to school; that his school had been life, 'hard and inexorable life'; that he had arrived in Mexico for the first time at the age of ten (that is, c. 1910), when he was working on a Dutch tramp steamer that plied the Pacific Coast; that he had been living in Mexico for forty years (that is, since c. 1912) with the exception of short and longer periods during which he had travelled 'to other countries and other continents'.

This, then, was a Traven biography deemed suitable for advertising purposes by the author's agents. It agreed with the one biographical fact Traven had been willing to vouchsafe, namely that he was an American, and in all respects it slipped very neatly over the shoulders of the 'carrier of experience'. There was an interesting discrepancy between this account and other likely guesses in the matter of age. If this was Traven and he was born around the year 1900, then he was eighteen years younger than Marut; if this was the 'Erlebnisträger', then we were looking for a younger man than I had hitherto suspected.

The most bizarre contents of the newsletters were still to come. Baumann showed me issue number six which, he said, displayed a peculiar and vindictive streak in the author (Baumann was sure that Traven had written much, if not all, of the newsletters). On pages 38 and 39 was an article which recorded instances of a curse which befell those who spread false rumours about Traven or who tried to track him down or otherwise broke his rules. Through some dark power, apparently, Traven brought retribution on those who crossed him. The article was headed: 'The mills of the Lord grind slowly but ...'. The mills of Traven, we were meant to infer, ground somewhat more swiftly.

The piece referred firstly to a cutting from a leading Mexican newspaper, which read as follows:

> It seems that many people actually knew B. Traven. On the thirteenth of August *El Sol de Pueblo* published a notice, according to which the famous novelist had died in Angelopolis, where he had lived with the adopted name of Jacob Torice. *El Sol* declares furthermore to have obtained this information from the author Guillermo Jimenez.

The *B.T. News Report* added only a laconic postscript: 'Guillermo Jimenez, a promising author of histories and biographies, was drowned ten months ago, aged only 28, in Acapulco.' Thus perished those who bore false witness against B.T. The article continued with further instructive stories.

> A certain Dr Dampf, who spread a lot of nonsense about Traven and maintained that he had known Traven personally, thus trying to draw attention to himself, died three years ago after a long and painful disease, without humanity taking any notice whatsoever of his pretended scientific researches.
>
> Heinrich Guttmann claimed to have once been the editor of the Berlin *Vorwärts* and also to have assisted at a public burning of Traven's books by the Nazis. Who could believe that Jews were admitted as spectators during such an event? Guttmann was also the first who circulated the Traum*– [Traven]–Marut story and published this nonsense very soon after his arrival in Mexico ... He was found fourteen months ago one morning on a road in the centre of Mexico City with his head crushed and his body mutilated. The police recorded that he had had an epileptic attack (in fact he was an epileptic and hereditary syphilitic and therefore incurable) and that, as he lay helpless in the street, he was run over by several lorries.

* *Traum*, the German word for 'dream', was an anagram of 'Marut' and also similar to Traven. This word play was said to establish a connection between Marut and Traven.

The reporter Erwin Egon Kisch who brought the Fred Maruth [sic] legend back to Europe in 1945 after it had already been rejected by several serious journalists, died four years ago in Prague.

There was a wild, fairy-story quality to all this. An avenging angel, strange deaths, men struck down in their prime: it had a childish ring, but there was little doubt that the writer was in earnest.

Baumann told us that the advent and commercial nature of the *B.T. News Reports* had led to speculation that there was some kind of conspiracy around the Traven works. The theory was that Traven had died in 1931 or 1932 and that the manuscripts of his unpublished novels and stories had fallen into the hands of a small group of people who had produced them as new works at intervals over the ensuing years. This group, it was said, had taken the proceeds from both these new books and the already published titles, and had naturally done all it could to preserve the secrecy of the author's origins and to disguise the fact that he was already dead. This would explain why someone suddenly decided to start peddling the Traven works in the 1950s, unthinkable behaviour for the Traven of earlier years. It would also explain why the Traven *œuvre* more or less came to an end around 1940. It was reasonable to suppose that the author had died with a number of finished, but unpublished, manuscripts and that these could have been eked out over the next eight years. After that there could be no more Traven works and it was significant, so this argument ran, that the one novel, *Aslan Norval*, which did appear after this time was an uncharacteristic work, rejected by several publishers and hooted out of court by some critics.

Baumann did not espouse this conspiracy theory, but the fullness of his explanation of it told me that it carried some weight with him. He did not put any names to the exploiting group, but if such a conspiracy had existed it must have been in Mexico. Perhaps he was looking back to the time when Esperanza Lopez Mateos and Josef Wieder had been in charge of the Traven canon. I wondered about Esperanza Lopez Mateos. A conspiracy theory is greatly enhanced by a sudden and unexplained death – she had committed suicide in 1951.

A beautiful, talented and well-connected woman, mixed up
with a faceless author, dies by her own hand at just the moment
that there seems to be a change of ownership of the works.
Who could ask for a better plot?

Before they left us for a brief tour of London, Michael and
Friedl Baumann passed on some of the latest titbits of Traven
discoveries. Evidently Rolf Recknagel had found a hitherto
unremarked birth certificate among the papers kept by Señora
Lujan in Mexico. It was in the name Johann Christof Friedrich
Gale or Galey (exactly which Baumann was not sure) born in
Lübeck, Germany, in February 1884, the illegitimate son of a
working-class woman. The question had flown through the
world of Traven scholars – was this the true birth name of
B. Traven? There were two clues which supported this hypothesis. Firstly, the name Gales was, of course, the name of the
apparently autobiographical hero of the early novels and,
secondly, here was a haunting geographical resonance: the
river on which the town of Lübeck was sited was the river
Trave. Alas, it was too good to be true. Baumann himself had
been able to show that the child to which this birth certificate
referred had died five months after his birth in the summer of
1884. This was not the author's real name, though there was
no explanation as to how this document had found its way to
the house and effects of Hal Croves.

An interesting development which had not yet crumbled into
dust was a claim that Ret Marut had been in London in 1924.
Baumann said that the evidence for this had been winkled out
of the American State Department by an application under
the Freedom of Information Act. I made a note to apply myself.
It would be a happy convenience if we could end our account
of the Traven mystery in London on our return from Mexico
and the United States.

At last Jennifer McKay and I said goodbye to the Baumanns.
They had been patient with our ignorance, helpful with our
misconceptions, ever willing to elaborate and to explain. I had
been fully briefed for the Traven mission and I was ready to test
out the theories on the people we would meet and against any
evidence we might come across. There was still no way of
knowing, if there ever would be, how many men I would be
dealing with: Traven, Croves, Torsvan, Marut and the man

from the Midwest could turn out to be five men or one. We had
to know more about them all.

When the Baumanns had left for Paris on their way to
Austria I went back to the office to make the final arrangements
for a domestic journey. On the following day I was going to the
Isle of Man for a few days to make a film about the author of
Watership Down, Richard Adams, who now lived on the island.
We flew with the same camera crew to Liverpool, and on to
Douglas. I bought a paperback at Heathrow Airport to read
on the way, a novel called *Ripley Under Ground* by the crime
writer, Patricia Highsmith. I suppose that I finished my newspaper and turned to the book somewhere over Worcestershire,
and before we had left the airspace of that county I was
hypnotised by what I was reading. It told of a conspiracy to
make money by faking the paintings of an artist who had died.
For a time after the artist's disappearance his friends exhibited
and sold the work he had left behind him, but when this ran
out, well before the market was saturated, they began forging
new work. The conspirators had to make up a story to explain
the continuing supply of pictures and the continued absence
of the artist.

> Tom had reflected a moment then said, 'What's the matter
> with Derwatt being still alive somewhere, sending his paint-
> ings to London? This is if Bernard could keep going.'
> 'Um-m. Well – yes. Greece, maybe. What a super idea,
> Tom! It can go on for ever!'
> 'How about Mexico? I think it's safer than Greece. Let's
> say Derwatt is living in some little village!'

The dead painter's pictures soon began arriving from
Mexico. The mysterious artist allowed no interviews or photo-
graphers; no one knew the name of the village where he lived.
It was just as it could have happened with Traven, even to the
choice of Mexico. So Miss Highsmith must have heard stories of
a Traven conspiracy too. My suspicion was borne out somewhere over the Irish Sea, when one of her characters raised
the subject of the absent genius. 'He's living in Mexico, isn't
he?' asks one man. 'Yes,' came the reply, 'and he won't say
where. Like B. Traven, you know.'

7 To the United States

I planned that we should leave for the United States on July 3rd but the curse of Traven, as threatened in those *B.T. News Reports*, decided otherwise. No one was found crushed to death by lorries, thank goodness, but both Robinson and I were struck down by our reactions to the jabs we received from the BBC doctor. I went to bed in a pool of sweat for three days; Robinson was poleaxed on our return from interviewing Richard Adams on the Isle of Man. There was no alternative but to postpone our departure for a week, and I informed everyone I had been in touch with of the delay. The most important of these was Señora Lujan in Mexico City. I sent her a telegram with the new dates. My fear was that Señora Lujan would make some excuse and avoid me, perhaps leave Mexico for the time I was there. There were examples of Traven himself doing just this when he knew enquirers were on their way. With Señora Lujan I need not have worried. Four days after I had sent my telegram and two days before we set off I received her reply:

REYURTEL DATES YOU MENTION AGREEABLE STOP
EXPECTING YOU ANYTIME DURING JULY STOP KIND
REGARDS ROSA ELENA LUJAN

There were no more delays, and on the morning of July 10th, Robert Robinson and I met at Heathrow and caught the morning TWA flight to New York. Robinson has lived by his wits as a freelance journalist and broadcaster for some twenty years. At the time of our journey he was nearly fifty, a man of medium height, bald with long strands of sandy hair arranged to cover

68

most of the bare acreage of his head. A stranger, though, would be most likely to notice first his sharp and intelligent features, a reflection of the precise, agile and humorous cast of his mind.

I had been on several filming trips with him before and far from recoiling from the prospect of living cheek by jowl with him for a month, I looked forward to it. He is not, I would say, a good traveller, choosing, as he does, to compare everywhere with England or preferably London, or better still Chelsea (where he lives) or the south London suburbs (where he was brought up). But his complaints, though regular, are in large part ritualistic and take the form of protracted and amusing descants on long popular themes: the absence of *The Times*, airports, early-morning noises in hotels and American food, which, he claims, has had all the flavour syphoned off and released into the elaborate descriptions on the menu. For all this he is a cheering companion and a perceptive observer, who likes to look behind the obvious differences between peoples and places to find the human similarities which link them. On the Traven odyssey he was my partner almost throughout. We discussed and argued at every turn and though we were not always in agreement, I was fortunate to have such a steel on which to sharpen my theories, and thankful for a colleague who would often glimpse a promising spark where I saw only smoke. If I fail to do justice to his part in my narrative, the lapse is all mine. It was he, let it be remembered, who first intoned for my hearing those three strange syllables 'B. Traven'.

Now that we had eventually set off we were in high spirits, anticipating the fun of visiting new places and excited at the work before us. We toasted our mission with plastic beakers of wine and talked over our schedule. Intent on draining every penny of value from our air fares, I had optimistically arranged to shoot some other stories for 'The Book Programme' while we were in the United States. I had made dates with Erskine Caldwell in Arizona, with the thriller-writer John D. McDonald in Florida, and with a writer then on the crest of a wave in America, John Cheever, who lived in the suburbs of New York. But even at this stage I could see that the Traven trail was going to dominate our waking hours.

I dozed off on the plane re-reading *The Death Ship* and found myself drifting in and out of sleep, wondering about the name

'Traven'. If it was a pseudonym it still must have come from somewhere, have some meaning or contain some reference. I had heard, I forgot where, that it was an obscure piece of German sailors' slang meaning to load objects into the hold of a ship. Assuming that the author of *The Death Ship* wrote from personal experience, this sounded plausible, but it was impossible to trace the provenance of this derivation. I had with me an article from *The Times Literary Supplement*, in which George Woodcock doodled with the name. He, too, found 'traum' (dream) as an anagram of Marut and with a simple change made this into 'trauen' and then into 'traven'. 'Traven', he said, was the German verb 'to dare', 'to adventure' – it fitted; 'betrauen' (B. Traven) meant 'to entrust' or 'to authorise', and as B. Traven was the name to which the anonymous author entrusted his work, that fitted, too. For good measure, Woodcock took the name Torsvan, gave it a German rather than Scandinavian spelling and came up with 'Torswahn', meaning 'fool's delusion' – another fit, especially with *The Treasure of the Sierra Madre*. Finally, he turned to Hal Croves and with a quick flick of the wrist transformed it into 'Hal Covers'. Another bull's eye. Woodcock saw all this wordplay as evidence of Traven's ingenuity in the manufacture of his camouflage. Possibly. It certainly reflected the ingenuity of detectives driven to desperate solutions.

In New York I called at the offices of Alfred Knopf, the first American publisher of Traven's books. There I met the chairman, William Koshland, explained to him my interest in Traven and asked if I could see their file of letters from the author or his representatives. Koshland was interested to hear of the film and promised to help. The file, he thought, would be with Alfred Knopf's own papers, but he could get hold of it and suggested I return on the following day. I did so and Koshland handed me the folder containing such letters as he had. I did not have time to study them fully then and there, but Koshland was kind enough to give me the run of a photocopier and I was able to take copies of most of the letters.

We filmed John Cheever on July 13th and arranged to rendezvous with the film crew the next morning at the BBC's offices on Fifth Avenue, where we were to begin the Traven filming by interviewing Lawrence Hill. Robinson and I had

already worked out our questions for Hill so we took the evening
off, he going out to see a film, I to dinner at a friend's apartment
on West 79th Street. There were four of us to dine and I held
the company spellbound, as it seemed to me, with an exposition
of the unfathomable mystery of B. Traven. As we neared the
end of the meal the lights in the apartment suddenly went out.
There was a squeal of joy from my three companions, all New
Yorkers, when they realised that the lights in all the surrounding buildings had gone out as well. There were shouts and
laughter from the apartments all around and we went to the
window, where we could see that the whole of the northern half
of Manhattan was in darkness. The lights of the city from below
the park burned on but, as we watched, they too were abruptly
extinguished.

My companions told me it was essential that we go out on
to the streets, and my protests that we would all have our throats
cut were howled down. Sure enough, there was a great deal
of happy promenading going on. We watched amateur traffic
cops directing traffic, saw a few looted shops, had some more
drinks, talked to total strangers who agreed that this was ter-
rific, quite like the old days of the 1960s and so much nicer
than the last blackout. All was still dark when I took a taxi
back to the Algonquin Hotel at about two a.m. and the thought
crept up on me that the Traven filming might not get off the
mark. It seemed a little extreme for the curse of B.T. to take
out the whole city of New York simply to prevent me from starting my film, but he nearly achieved his purpose.

The following morning there was still no electricity, no hot
water and the city was eerily quiet. The film crew, I learned,
had been up half the night shooting news material of the blackout, so we arranged to meet at the hotel at lunchtime. I called
Lawrence Hill and explained that we could not film where we
had planned because we could not plug in the lights there, and
suggested that, as it was a fine day, we could still go ahead and
film the interview in Central Park. He agreed and drove up
to the Algonquin just after lunch, an eyecatching and slightly
eccentric figure wearing a floppy sun hat, short-sleeved sports
shirt and driving an open Volkswagen. So, at about three
o'clock on the Sheep Meadow in Central Park, we outstared
the evil eye and began our filming.

Hill explained that his interest in Traven went back to his
first job in publishing, when he worked as a salesman for Alfred
Knopf's in the early 1940s. One of the books on the firm's list,
which Hill had read and enjoyed, was *The Death Ship* by a mysterious author with no first name. There were other books by
Traven on the list, which Hill also read, but in spite of Hill's
best efforts as a salesman, they only sold moderately, attracting
a coterie rather than a popular following. Many years later Hill
started his own business, and one day a young man came into
his office with the manuscript of a collection of Traven short
stories which he had been authorised to place with an American
publisher by the author and his agent-wife. Hill published the
stories and went on to publish a whole chain of Traven books,
many of which had not been issued in the United States before.

The contracts for these books were signed by Rosa Elena
Lujan and all correspondence was with her; not once did Hill
receive a letter from Traven himself. Señora Lujan assured
Hill that the corrections on the material she sent from Mexico
had been made by the author himself, but even so these books
which were being published for the first time in the United
States all needed extensive editing. In the summer of 1967 Hill
went down to Mexico to discuss the publication plans with
Señora Lujan.

The address he was directed to was in the middle of Mexico
City, and there he met Rosa Elena Lujan and a man he took
to be Traven but who, when he introduced himself, held out
his hand and said, 'Croves'. When Hill said that he had always
admired the books and that it was an honour to be publishing
them, he took it as significant that Croves did not demur. He
described Croves as a man of below-average height, with strong
features, a large prominent nose and an air of profound seriousness. Hill believed that Croves was Traven, and that he had
been Ret Marut in Germany, yet he said that Croves looked
much younger than the 77-year-old he had been led to expect.
(Marut would have been about 85 at this time.) Croves,
said Hill, had a noticeable accent. At the time it sounded either
German or Scandinavian, though, in the light of his belief that
Croves was Marut, Hill was now sure that it was German.

On the day after this first encounter, Hill was invited to
lunch. It was, he said, what you would expect a lunch party

in a rather cultured upper-class Mexican home to be like. There were several other guests, among them an artist who was to illustrate one of the books. At the table, Señora Lujan sat close to her husband so that she could repeat for him any remarks he missed through his deafness. Robinson and I were interested to know how the assembled company had addressed the man they assumed to be B. Traven. Hill could not remember what he himself had called him, but Señora Lujan had referred to 'my husband' or 'the Skipper', which was a pet name, and also, Hill thought, to 'B.T.' I was doubtful that Hill had remembered aright about this last name, for I had heard that Croves always resisted any overt indication that he was Traven. More telling was Hill's description of how he had sat down with the artist and Croves after lunch to discuss the illustrations for the children's story, *The Creation of the Sun and the Moon*. Croves had spoken and behaved like the author of the book, offering perceptive and intelligent ideas. When Robinson pressed Hill about this, he replied that he had assumed that he was talking to Traven and there was no reason to believe that he was not.

We asked Hill why he thought Traven had so wanted to remain anonymous. In a way, this was a deeper mystery than the man's identity. We hoped that, if and when anyone discovered who Traven was, it would throw some light on the man's reasons for hiding. In the meantime, Hill had several possible explanations. There was Traven's own claim that he wanted to be judged by his writing alone and did not want the evaluation of his work mixed up with what his personality was like, whom he slept with and all the other details that go with the public relations of authors. But, said Hill, there was obviously something more than just that involved. Taking Traven to have been Marut, he pointed to the man's background in Germany, where he had narrowly escaped death after the Munich revolution. Many of his friends had been killed then and it was understandable that he should wish to strike out the memories of that period of his life. Señora Lujan, herself, had told Hill that this was the reason why her husband had denied all these years that there was any connection between Traven and Ret Marut. And the Munich episode had left another legacy: a persistent and undying fear that there would be reprisals, at first, perhaps, from the right-wing forces which had destroyed the Bavarian revolution; later from the Nazis, who had sprung forth from that counter-revolution and who had banned the works of B. Traven. If Traven was Marut, he might not feel safe even in Mexico. The long arm of revenge could reach across the Atlantic Ocean, as the fate of Leon Trotsky, another fugitive in Mexico, would have reminded him.

Hill's speculations were interesting, but he offered no clues as to who Marut really was or where he had come from and, again, no definite proof that he was the same man as Croves. Hill admitted that there was much still unknown about Traven and probably always would be. Of course, there was Señora Lujan. But Hill raised a powerful caveat about the value of her contributions and about the depth of her knowledge of her husband's life. She had been married to him only for his last fifteen years and she knew about the rest of his life only by hearsay, or by the letters, diaries and so on that she had found in his files. It was hard, he said, to reconstruct a whole life from files.

We thanked and said goodbye to Lawrence Hill, who wished us luck in our search, and drove cheerily away in the July sunshine. Eugene Carr, the cameraman, and his team packed the camera gear into their van and also wished us well for the rest of the film. They were to remain in New York for other assignments. Robinson and I returned to the Algonquin, which was about the last place to get its electricity back, and made ready for the next stage of the journey – to San Francisco. There we were to meet Judy Stone, someone else who had met Croves and believed him to be Traven. We were not sorry to be leaving New York. The city had surprised itself with its vulnerability. The scale of looting induced a state of shock and self-recrimination. For the outsider it was like eavesdropping on the postmortem to a family suicide.

8 The Hohenzollern

I do not wish to tell you more about the novel right now save that you may rest assured that in the whole literature of any country you won't find another novel like this one; it is absolutely unique and it can never be imitated.

I hardly needed to glance down to the typed signature to discover the author of the letter I was holding. The same confidential tone in the boasting, the same belligerent endorsement of his own work proclaimed it to be by the hand of the man who had written those letters to the Büchergilde Gutenberg in the 1920s. The pay-off confirmed it:

> Very truly yours
>
> B.Traven.

We were on the flight to San Francisco and I was reading through the letters I had photocopied at the offices of Alfred Knopf. There were fifteen of them. The letters were typed, they were all from post-office box numbers in Mexico City or Acapulco and they were from three different parties: B. Traven, M.L. Martinez and R.E. Lujan – although all three appeared authorised to deal formally, and to Knopf's satisfaction, with the Traven works. Only one letter, from Lujan, was signed by hand.

The boasting letter above was the first in the collection, dated September 23rd, 1937, and sent to Alfred Knopf himself. I had

never heard of *Indian Weekend*, the novel it referred to so glow-
ingly, and presumed that it was an alternative title for an earlier
work. Traven, his English still inexpert, asked for an advance
of five hundred dollars and then made great play of stipulating
a condition. 'I am afraid you will have to accept it no way
round.' He was, in fact, about to make a generous gesture.
Traven insisted that Knopf deduct from his advance the sum
of $309.01, the balance of the advanced royalties paid on *The
Death Ship*, which were still unearned by the book's sales:

> When I offered you *The Death Ship*, you paid me without any
> hesitation so generously the asked-for thousand dollars – in
> spite that the book so far has not met with the financial suc-
> cess both of us had expected you kept all the time religiously
> to our unwritten agreement. For this reason I can no longer
> keep your money, much as I might be in need of.

It was a gentlemanly act, for authors are not best known for
their willingness to pay back advances, and Traven concluded
it elegantly, 'I am sure that you too will feel better on seeing
The Death Ship from now on sailing without that heavy ballast
in her bowels.'

I flicked through the five other letters from Traven. They
were largely about arranging payments or about other
publishers' editions, but a flash or two of his character shone
through. I noted him casually establishing his American
nationality in a letter of March 24th, 1945, when he wrote:
'I asked [them] ... to present all accounts at the American consulate so that *our* consul may okay the money as honestly earned
...' There was some further self-advertisement – 'The book
[*Treasure*] is by far better than a picture can ever be made from
it' – and also something of that eagerness to please with which
it often went hand in hand. An editor had obviously suggested
that a small cut should be made in a new edition and Traven
was almost ingratiating in his response: 'Please, tell Mr de Graff
that I agree with him one hundred per cent on that the four
lines he mentioned are disturbing. I almost think that if I were
to write the book to-day I would mostly not use these lines
myself.'

And then only seventeen days later came the last letter in

the file that was from Traven himself. Thereafter, they were all from M.L. Martinez, until July 21st, 1955:

Dear Mr.Koshland:

We wish to inform you to send after July 30,1955 no longer any mail referring to B.Traven or checks to the undersigned address but instead

       to
          R.E.Lujan
          Apdo.2701
          Mexico,1,D.F.
          Mexico.

The check for $41.63 (Jun.30,1955) also arrived. Thank you.

                  Faithfully

                        Casa M.L.Martinez.

And Martinez was no more.

There was an interesting letter, too, in 1954, asking a Mr Joseph Lesser, who was a public notary, but who had clearly never met Traven, to certify that an enclosed document bore a true signature of B. Traven. A previous similar document, said the letter, had lost its usefulness now that Esperanza Lopez Mateos, who was referred to in it, had 'passed away'. 'So we again need a Mexican citizen to hold the rights referred to as only this way we can protect the interests of Traven successfully in Mexico ...' It was probably just a way of arranging payments legally in Mexico while maintaining the anonymity of the author, but such arrangements might be used to conceal many things – a conspiracy even. I might have allowed my mind to run wildly and dangerously along these lines had it not been for the recognisable hand of B.T. in the letters, and the clear understanding of all concerned that Martinez was acting with his approval.

The end of the correspondence was none too happy. Traven and his agents felt that his books were not being pushed enough and they negotiated to buy back the unsold copies and the printing plates. They implied that the anti-communist feeling in the United States (this was the McCarthy period) was the reason why a publisher 'will, for convenience sake, not push a book if said book by certain power groups is considered too hot'. The funny thing was, said the Traven camp, that behind the Iron Curtain there was pressure to cut out some passages from the books because they attacked dictatorships in general and the communist rulers in particular. In fact, the East German publishers claimed that if they put out the books uncut they and their printers might end up in a Russian labour camp.

> So it turns out [concluded one of the letters to Knopf's] that certain influential people in the States claim that the books by T. show a definite communist leaning, whereas the pressure groups behind the iron curtain maintain the firm notion that these books are harming the communist system if published as T. wrote them. Your opinion sir.

The correspondence was concluded sadly in April 1956 with a letter from one Sergio Lujan, a forwarding agent of Laredo, Texas, asking Knopf's why he had not received the promised shipment of four hundred repurchased books. It was an odd coincidence that this intermediary should have the same name as Traven's agent. They could hardly be related, as this man referred to Rosa Elena as *Mr* R.E. Lujan of Mexico City. A simple error, no doubt, but every typing mistake in the Traven story was beginning to seem charged with sinister meaning. I put the Knopf folder away in my battered briefcase. Robinson was dozing happily in anticipation of a first sight of San Francisco; I decided to do the same.

The city was no disappointment. Its position is spectacular, on a steeply hilly site opposite the entrance to a huge bay, and the builders have served it well with streets of interesting and attractive houses. The place has an organic and authentic feel. We were told by a native that the city's genius lay in its having been built by whores and pirates. It owed nothing to the puritanical and matronly hands which had squeezed the life out of so many other American cities. San Francisco was, of course, the place that Ret Marut claimed to have been born in, though I held no hope of finding any clue to that. All the city records were consumed in the fire and earthquake of 1906 – as Marut must surely have known – so San Francisco was a highly convenient place to say you came from if you had something to hide: so convenient that it was even something of a joke to claim a pre-1906 birth there. I knew, also, that Judy Stone had combed the newspaper birth columns for 1882 on the off-chance that his parents were sufficiently well to do to advertise his arrival. She had had no success.

Robinson and I had a happy bonus at the airport. The hire-car company with whom we had made a booking had no 'intermediate' cars available, and asked if a white Thunderbird would be acceptable for no extra charge. We graciously consented. Thus, on the afternoon of our arrival, we were able to visit Judy Stone at her house high up on Connecticut Avenue in a car which was larger, flashier – more to our taste in every way – than we might have expected. We filmed her on her patio a couple of days later. She was a most eager and helpful witness, understandably keen to draw attention to her book but full of ideas and contacts for us. She is a tiny, energetic and fast-talking woman, obviously infatuated with the Traven mystery. At the time we met her she was film critic of the *San Francisco Chronicle*, and she brought to her work on Traven the skill and push of a long career in American journalism. Her brother is the great I.F. Stone of *Stone's Weekly* and, as she made us welcome, she reminded me that 'Izzy' had done something for a programme of mine some years before. We did not waste much time on such niceties, for we were keen to hear, and she to tell us, of her Traven knowledge and experiences.

She had first become entangled in the story at the end of 1964, when she was planning a Christmas holiday in Mexico. At that time she had read several Traven books and thought she would like to interview the author. An acquaintance, who had worked on a Mexican film made of Traven's novel *La Rosa Blanca*, said that she would never obtain an interview and in any case no one knew Traven, only his agent Hal Croves. She wrote to Croves asking for an interview with the author, and received a reply, couched in a somewhat stilted English, which read in part as follows:

But in one point I'm afraid I will disappoint you. I will not be able to arrange a meeting with B. Traven because at the

moment he is travelling in the tropical regions of southern
Mexico and surely will not be back within many months.
I am very sorry that I cannot be of any help to you in this
matter, at least not at present.

However, Croves himself invited Judy Stone to visit him, and
eventually in 1966 she did so.

She was met at her hotel by Señora Lujan, who introduced
herself as Mrs Croves, and took her to the house in Rio Mississippi, where she was introduced to Croves himself. He was
a rather frail old man, in his late seventies or early eighties,
not more than five foot seven inches tall. He had blue eyes, thick
glasses and he was very deaf – something which affected all Judy
Stone's talks with him, for she found it almost impossible to
ask him questions. He either could not, or would not, hear them
so she waited for him to bring up the topics of conversation.
He spoke English to her and she was struck by his accent, which
sounded Germanic but not quite German.

Judy Stone referred to Croves as Traven, and we asked her
if he had ever acknowledged this or implied it in what he had
said. Most of the time he had been careful not to, but once,
and only once, he slipped and used the word 'I' when he should
have been referring to Traven. Then he caught himself and
went back into the role of Croves. All his friends addressed him
as Hal and his wife and stepdaughters called him Skipper, the
pet name that Lawrence Hill had mentioned.

When Judy Stone returned for a second visit to Mexico in
November 1966, she was astonished to read that *Siempre* magazine had just published an interview with B. Traven, the first
ever. It did not contain any new information and the biographical content was the usual 'authorised' story (like the version
in the *B.T. News Reports*) that he was an American born in
Chicago in 1890, now a Mexican citizen; but it carried photographs of the inside of the house in Rio Mississippi and
mentioned that the author was often called Hal. Judy Stone
learned later that this interview had taken place on the promise
that the name Croves was nowhere to be mentioned and, to
be sure, when she met him again there was no hint that anything had happened. She hoped, even expected, that after the
Siempre article he would be willing to talk about himself openly

as Traven and she was baffled and irritated when he remained
simply Hal Croves.

Croves's behaviour did change in one way: his friendliness
was now mixed with a more obvious resentment towards the
press. Judy Stone remembered accompanying Croves and
Señora Lujan on a drive to San José Purua, where *The Treasure
of the Sierra Madre* was filmed. At first the old man was silent
and withdrawn, then he began to talk about the filming,
describing how Lauren Bacall, Humphrey Bogart's wife,
had driven to Mexico City to buy some different food from
the chicken they were always eating. Judy Stone asked if
Croves had liked Humphrey Bogart, and he started to tell
her how warmly he felt about the actor when he suddenly
stopped and said, 'Oh, I forgot, there's a newspaper woman
here.'

Of all the things that Croves said to Judy Stone during her
several talks with him, the strangest was his very first utterance
on the day they met – 'Forget the man. What does it matter
if he is the son of a Hohenzollern prince?' She was stunned by
this extraordinary remark, though her own initial caution and
the difficulties caused by Croves's deafness prevented her from
pursuing its implications just then. Soon afterwards she had
lunch alone with Señora Lujan, who admitted that her husband
had lived in Germany calling himself Ret Marut and that during that time, while he was engaged in fighting the political
system there, his mother had told him that he was the illegitimate son of a member of the Hohenzollern family. This had
upset him and he had never forgiven her.

Judy Stone found an opportunity to return to this sensational
disclosure, and this time the Señora vouchsafed that her husband had been the son of Kaiser Wilhelm II and that his mother
had been an entertainer, a singer of some kind, probably of
Scots or Irish descent. She had discovered this when she had
travelled with her husband to Germany for the première of the
film of *The Death Ship*. They had visited Berlin and he had taken
her to a square which had a connection with the Hohenzollerns.
He had become very agitated and excited by the surroundings
and had told her then that he belonged to that royal family,
forbidding her ever to let on about it.

I was interested to learn that the Kaiser story had such

support from central characters in the drama, even seemed to
have originated from them. And Judy Stone had found one or two
surprising lines in *Der Ziegelbrenner*, which gave some circumstantial support to this romantic solution. In one copy there
was a kindly reference to the German emperor and the penulti-
mate issue contained a lyric fantasy about the death of a king,
which, oddly for a revolutionary magazine, expressed great
sympathy with the monarch. It was strange, too, that this
anarchist publication had been able to challenge the authorities
in time of war with apparent impunity.

There was a postscript to Judy Stone's account of the Kaiser
connection. When Croves died on March 26th, 1969, she went
back again to Mexico City and Señora Lujan showed her for
the first time Croves's study on the third floor of the house.
Three items in that room caught her attention: a picture of
a bridge over the river Trave in Lübeck; a copy of the *Almanach
de Gotha*, the dictionary of European royal families: and a
photograph of Kaiser Wilhelm II – not the usual trappings of
the anarchist's study. It could all have been elaborate set dressing, one more sweep of brushwood over the trail, or it could
have been a final tacit confirmation by the old man that the
Kaiser had been his father.

On that same visit in 1969 Judy Stone attended the last rites
of Croves, and it was clear that all present believed they were
at the funeral of B. Traven. The ceremony took place at Ococingo in the Chiapas, a tiny town on the edge of the jungle. Judy
Stone remembered with amusement that the school-children
had been let out from school, but had no idea who it was that
had died; an irony she felt Traven would have enjoyed because
he had hated nonsense about funerals. He had once written that
you should go off into the jungle and die where rejected dogs
could pick your bones and get something to eat, and Judy Stone
had been pleased to spot a couple of mangy dogs waiting at
the small airport in Ococingo when she arrived.

In the evening, she recalled, there had been a parade by
candlelight, accompanied by simple music, to the poorest part
of town, where the ashes had been put on a table and the
Indians had come to pay their respects. The evening had ended
back at the bug-infected hotel where some Mexicans had come
to serenade the visitors with a marimba band and a bottle of

liquor was passed back and forth through the high window – much more like a real Traven funeral.

The following day she flew in the tiny three-seater plane as the ashes were dropped over the jungle. She remembered being surprised by the click of the bones against the window as the ashes fell. There had been a blue haze over the mountains because the Indians were burning in preparation for planting. 'It was very moving because Traven really shared the feeling of the Indians that land was the most vital part of life and, finally, he was part of their land.'

Judy Stone showed me that the printed programme for those last ceremonies was headed, unambiguously, 'The Chiapas Homage to B. Traven'. But before we concluded the interview Robinson pressed her again about the man Croves. Was she absolutely sure that Hal Croves was B. Traven?

She replied: 'I don't think there are any absolutes in this case. When I interviewed him I felt very certain that Hal Croves was B. Traven and that Ret Marut was B. Traven ... I thought that when he died the mystery would finally be cleared up but instead there was additional obfuscation and today I'm not sure – I think the man I met was B. Traven. I don't think that conspiracies can be carried out so completely by people.'

In spite of the obfuscation she remained unconvinced by the idea of 'the carrier of experience'. Other writers had had a burst of creativity and then slowed down, she said, and the rush of early books from Mexico could easily be explained in this way. *Aslan Norval* may have been considered a forgery and was certainly not up to the previous quality of Traven books, but he was an old man when it came out. He would not have been the first writer to suffer from failing powers.

But if there was only one man involved, Judy Stone believed that we would probably never know who that one man really was. The only thing she was sure of was that he was illegitimate, for a preoccupation with illegitimacy runs through the writings of *Der Ziegelbrenner*, the novel of Richard Maurhut and the books of B. Traven. On one occasion Marut heaped praise upon Strindberg's play *Crown Bride*, a folk-like story about an unmarried mother who kills her own child. He described it as a 'mighty drama', and claimed that it was in some respects a better work than Goethe's *Faust*. The subject matter seemed to affect him powerfully.

This thought was in accord with my own reading of Traven's books and it stayed with me to the very end of the search. His obsession with the question of identity, his passionate denial of the importance of one's birth or nationality did not prove illegitimacy, but they were symptoms of some painful stone lodged in his bowels, a nagging hurt which could never be removed and never forgotten. Perhaps his birth, his parentage, his blood did not coincide with his own estimate of himself, or he would not allow them to. Born too high perhaps? Or too low? Born with too little dignity and too little love? In Traven's story 'The Night Visitor', the ghost of an ancient Aztec speaks of the purpose of life – 'For love, and for nothing but love is man born into this world. It is only for love that man lives.'

We finished the interview, packed up and said our goodbyes. We had to move on to take some shots by the docks and we had to squeeze in some lunch. The cameraman, Dave Myers, took us to a shack down by the harbour where we ate a shrimp salad and drank a glass of wine. Robinson and I were encouraged by the camera crew's enthusiasm for the story and even more pleased to hear that both Dave Myers and his sound recordist knew some of the Traven books. We were worried throughout that we were becoming obsessed ourselves with a story no one else had ever heard of. This did not make the tale any less gripping, but Traven was not well known in Britain and that was a nettle we had to grasp. Myers, as I said, did know a bit about Traven. Somehow, looking at him, I might have expected it. He is a short man, with a relaxed, laconic manner and an aura of having knocked around the world. He is a joy to work with because nothing surprises him and nothing is impossible. It soon became obvious that his laid-back 1960s' style could quickly be jettisoned when some fast work was needed and his sparse and vague verbal communication could be sharpened up when stale food was served in a restaurant.

The next day we filmed Robert Goss, the man Michael Baumann had said was the leading Traven scholar in the United States. Robinson and I had already visited him at his modest apartment in Oakland across San Francisco Bay. He had a mass of cuttings and bibliographical material and an encyclopaedic knowledge of the Traven canon. He had been a teacher of German but had been made redundant and now, at the age of about forty, was a student again at Berkeley University. It was there that we filmed him, on the grass under a tree in the garden of the Berkeley art museum.

Goss had met neither Croves nor Señora Lujan and he showed none of the sureness in his conclusions that Judy Stone had exhibited. I took this caution to be as much a reflection of his careful and scholarly nature as any lack of strength in the arguments. He had made a close study of everything Traven had written and most of what was written about him, and he brought a hypercritical eye to each piece of evidence. He was far from sure that Croves provided all the answers. He, like Baumann, pointed to Croves's late appearance on the scene, to the small amount of work which was produced after that time and to the problems surrounding the last novel, *Aslan Norval*. It had been turned down by several publishers because it was unlike anything previously written by Traven; it had a different set of characters, well-off people, with no sight of the underside of society, where Traven's heart had formerly lain. It was not good enough to put this down to the waning powers said Goss: 'If Croves was B. Traven why didn't he write like B. Traven?'

Goss was suspicious, because there was a lot of money tied up in the Traven books. Señora Lujan evidently claimed to have over five hundred different editions and there had been at least seven films made. Goss had even attempted to estimate how much the copyrights could have yielded since 1948, possibly as much as a million dollars.

Goss had spent many hours discussing the problems with Baumann and he, too, now believed that there was definitely more than one person involved in the authorship. Ret Marut could not have written the books alone. Almost the whole of *The Cotton-Pickers*, said Goss, showed that the man who had written it was an insider, someone who knew about the way the radical labour unions were organised in Mexico. The Wobblies and other groups were on their guard against infiltration by informers and it took time to gain their trust, much more time than Marut would have had if he had arrived in Mexico in 1923 and was sending off his stories early in 1925. There were some ex-Wobblies who said that Traven's accounts were utterly authentic and that he must have worked alongside the organisation or been in it. Goss had even heard a claim that Traven lectured in America well before his books were published in English.

One interesting, if outlandish, suggestion from Goss was that the other man who had helped Marut was on the run from fellow Wobblies as well as from government agents. This would explain why the central character in the early Traven books always takes the humblest jobs at the lowest pay – unlike most Wobblies who would have secured better-paid jobs and looked after each other's interests. Goss said that the Germans spread around millions of dollars during the early part of the First World War in an attempt to initiate sabotage or subversion which would keep the United States out of the hostilities. The main leadership of the Wobblies had nothing to do with this but there were men who did accept German money and who then became fugitives from their fellow workers. One theory had it that 'the carrier of experience' was just such a man, taking the lowest of jobs, avoiding other Americans, frightened of revealing who he was.

I thought that this was an over-elaborate life history to dream up for a man we did not even know existed. In any case, I did not feel it was necessary to explain how the author had acquired every job mentioned in his novels, as if the books were a kind of diary. They were *novels*, not autobiographies. The experiences related in the books provided a rough diagram of the author's past, not a detailed portrait. A Traven biography could never exclude them, but nor could it be composed by slavishly assembling each and every incident.

Robert Goss was sure that there was an American hand in the novels somewhere, whether or not that of a renegade Wobbly. Like us he recognised the show-off quality in Traven's writing. He said there was a pedantic, schoolmasterly tone on occasion and Traven's whole manner of address was of a man telling his readers astounding exotic things that no one would ever have told them before. And then, in the middle of amazing them with this straight-from-the-shoulder truth, he would sometimes slip in 'a big windy story', what Americans call a tall tale. Goss said there may be other countries where this was typical but it was certainly a very American thing to do. I knew about tall tales. The previous year Robinson and I had been filming in Nebraska, where a local folklorist had explained that the tall story was the archetypal Midwest joke. It sprang from the determination of the early pioneers not to be downcast by their abysmal surroundings. Thus, in a desperate and defiant humour, they would exaggerate both the bounties and the horrors of their lives. Special pictures were made up purporting to show how the prairies supported huge jack rabbits or wheat that grew twice as high as men. Settlers would send messages home like: 'Huge difficulties. No ordinary man could survive here. I'm doing fine.' I remembered Gales in a restaurant in *The Cotton-Pickers*.

Antonio scattered a large soupspoonful of green chili sauce into his soup, and I took two heaping ones. I've already said that half a teaspoon of this fiery sauce seasons the soup so highly that it's impossible for a normal person to eat. But then, I'm not normal.

Goss was right; it was an American trait but hardly one that proved an American helped write the books.

Goss had further arguments against the books being solely the work of Ret Marut. To begin with, he said, Marut was an aesthete and a stylist, had some money of his own and was, by his own admittance, not a member of the proletariat; the Traven books, on the other hand, were surely written by a man who had known what it was to be a worker. Then there was Traven's German, said Goss; it was peculiar. When the books had first been published in Germany several critics had commented on the language. One of them thought they might have been a bad translation from another language but eventually concluded that the author was just using Americanisms. Goss himself had analysed a passage of forty pages from *Land of Spring* and found over two hundred 'barbariisms of style' and twenty or so 'glaring errors in simple German grammar'. How could Marut have forgotten his correct German so quickly?

Finally Goss argued the philosophical and political differences between the Traven books and the writings of Marut. Like Baumann, he described Marut's anarchism as being essentially individualist, while Traven's was co-operative. In *Land of Spring*, he said, Traven proclaimed that European-style individualism had had its day; that the Indian was racially superior to the white man because he was innately co-operative, and would thus dominate the world for the next thousand years.

These arguments had to lie on the table for the moment. Like Michael Baumann's, they depended on the interpretation of internal evidence and, also like Baumann's, they were the result of long and careful study of the works. We had been blown both ways in windy San Francisco: first, by Judy Stone, towards the view that Croves was definitely Marut and Traven; then the mist had rolled in through the Golden Gate, obscuring that single apparition, and Robert Goss swayed us back to an open and complete scepticism. Fortunately, we had no need yet to make up our minds.

9 The Game Is Still Going On

We had only two days in Los Angeles in which to prepare and film five interviews. I was beginning to feel that I had over-reached myself in setting up further film stories with Caldwell and McDonald. Even if we had time to go to Scottsville, Arizona and Tampa, Florida, which I doubted, I wondered if we would be able properly to research and do the extra reading for two new subjects. Our minds were overflowing with Traven. Robinson and I were spending meal times, drink times and journey times, debating and arguing the significance and provenance of what we had read and heard. He, with a more romantic disposition, was strongly inclined to the notion of 'a carrier of experience', a faceless and nameless American haunting the mystery, always out of sight; I, with a more pedantic turn of mind, thought that our author would turn out to be one man alone, but which man? Marut, Croves, Torsvan and the Wobbly shared our table for every doubleburger, sat down with us in every bar and jostled for space on the back seat of our hired Plymouth. With the four of them still on board we would have no room for Caldwell and McDonald to join our party. I cancelled the extra stories.

After arriving in Los Angeles we drove straight out to Malibu, where we were to visit Mr and Mrs Herbert Arthur Klein. We motored at the gentle, consistent speed registered by all traffic in Los Angeles. The whole city suggests indulgence. It appears to be permanently in a trance-like state, induced by its size, its sunshine and the dreamy motion of its auto-mobiles.

Malibu is on the ocean and Herbert and Mina Klein have

89

a brown-painted house in a private road right on the beach,
surrounded by rock stars and film directors. It is one of the great
surfing beaches and the Kleins, although no longer young, still
practise the sport and write books about it. They are professional writers and have written also about scientific subjects,
Germany and painting, and they have translated and edited
a book of stories by Traven, in whom they first became interested when Herbert was a newspaper correspondent in
Germany in the 1930s. They welcomed Robinson and me,
gave us tea and chatted with us about the people we had
seen.

The Kleins' first-hand knowledge of Traven came from a
two-part correspondence with him, the first instalment of which
had begun when Traven spotted a favourable review Herbert
Klein had written of the American edition of *The Death Ship*.
In 1935 Klein wrote in all innocence, asking for some facts
about the author so that he could write some articles about him
and his books. In reply he received a long letter from Traven,
who grudgingly agreed to take up Klein's offer but only on his
own terms. The letter was an attempt to manipulate the young
journalist by alternately buttering him up and lecturing him.
Here again was the know-all, this time the old literary hand
advising a novice on how to get a break. Klein had offered himself as a translator but Traven would not hear of it:

> Why the devil does a guy who can write such an intelligent
> review like that offer his services as a translator? ... Know
> what you are? You are an essayist, a critic par excellence.
> You can not only make a name for yourself as a writer of
> articles on hundreds of subjects but you can make money,
> good money ...

When we filmed the Kleins the following day, Herbert Klein
read out extracts from Traven's letters in a slow, deliberate
voice. I could see that the letters were closely typed but little
else and when I asked if we could take copies of them, Klein
refused, saying that he felt himself betrayed by a previous
researcher who had been shown the letters in confidence and
then wrote an article based on them. He and his wife were
generous in what they read to us, however, and I thought I

detected that their enthusiasm for the Traven game was over-
coming their planned caution.

Klein continued reading. After the flattering opening,
Traven had then proffered advice in the manner of a horny-
handed old pro. It was tough, he said, finding publishers who
would take your work.

Before I had sold a book to Germany I had peddled my
stories around to all magazines and editors that exist, or then
existed, in this country (by which he meant the United
States, said Klein) and all I sold in five years of constantly
firing at them was five bucks, believe it or not.

He was offering a clue to test Klein's good intent. 'But if you
tell this to anybody before I tell you: "Now you may tell it,"
we are through with this for ever. You will get your chance
if you are all set to get it.' He was toying with Klein. There
was more in this lofty tone when he turned to the request for
some facts about himself.

I'm not so very hot on the proposition. I don't want American publicity. It flares up and dies at sunset. Nothing behind.
My work carries all the publicity I want, if my books are
not considered good, no publicity can make them any better.
The books have to be good and they will be read, if not today,
then so much surer tomorrow.

This messianic flavour was familiar. Traven was playing hard
to get, but, with a great show of magnanimity, he said he might
see his way clear to sending a few facts, if it would help young
Klein make his mark in life. 'These facts, of course, will not
be the sort of facts about movie stars. You would not expect
such facts from me.' They would provide the kind of information useful to the intelligent essayist he took Klein to be: 'And
don't forget, half a hundred magazines and papers of the British
Empire are ready to buy any intelligent articles you write about
B.T.'

This last was the kind of tall story television producers tell
about their viewing figures. There was no mistaking the belligerent tone of the self-praise. It was the same I had seen in the

letters to Knopf and Preczang, the authentic sound of B.T. shouting and waving his fist at a world he could not hear and could not see, in case it was not taking enough notice of him. He would send Klein enough material for a hundred articles – on one condition.

Of course, you will understand that whatever I send you printed or written must be returned inside of three days. Also, all letters I am writing you, this one included. That's my condition. Take it or leave it.

B.T.

That was not quite all. There was a postscript answering Klein's ingenuous thought that, as he was living in Los Angeles, which was not far from the Mexican border, he might one day wander down south and meet Traven. The author warned him off in characteristic fashion.

If you cross the border at San Diego you are still some two thousand miles away from the hut that I am living in. But I am frequently in Los Angeles and in the public library there, where I was once told when I asked one of the attending ladies if she could tell me something about who B.T. was. 'Oh, that guy,' she said, 'oh, he's just a bum. We have a few of his books here because they were gifts and we could not refuse them. He is a sort of drunken sailor or something. We have got real books here too. May I help you?' Whereupon I said, 'Thank you, Miss, I wanted only to know whether this building is fireproof or not.' And she said with dignity, 'Of course, sir. We can assure you of that.' So I said, 'What a pity.' So ended our conversation and the lady may still be wondering what I meant with 'pity'.

For all his obtuseness, Traven sent a little book of 'facts' within a month, and, true to form, accompanied it with elaborate suggestions – instructions would be a truer description – of how the material should be used. He even wrote out passages as if he were Klein, using the first person. Klein was supposed to hark back to when he was a newspaperman in Germany and then slip in his stuff about the mighty author. Like this, he suggested:

I, being used to hear our workers in general talk about their motor cars or radios or a new better-paying job they were after, was surprised to hear the workers I was with talk about books by Gorky, Sinclair Lewis, Upton Sinclair and many others I did not know – among them, B. Traven, whose name was mentioned most frequently.

This casual reminiscence might then continue: 'It seemed there was not one man or woman at the table, or anywhere around us, that did not know all the books written by that strange man, B.T.'

Traven went on in this vein, which was either shameless or desperate, at great length and had the cheek to add that he was, naturally, not saying that Klein should write his article exactly on these lines – though if he wanted to copy it out word for word he was, of course, free to do so. He indicated which American publications Klein should send his articles to, suggested some titles, to begin with: 'What Mystery about B.T.?' 'You may explain with quotations that there is no mystery about B.T. other than that he wishes to be left alone.'

Some more titles were suggested: 'Adventure Yarns or Philosophy?'; 'Unknown B.T. and Why?' and 'Fiction or Propaganda?', in which Klein was supposed to say that Traven had no desire to reform anything, only to open the eyes of his fellow men to look at the world in a different way and to leave it up to them to change things if they felt it necessary.

The advertising purpose of all this effort on Traven's part was shown by his firm instruction that Klein was not to mention any book which had not yet been published in the United States, except two which were announced as in preparation. I was interested to note that the commercial attitude of the *B. T. News Reports* of the 1950s had marked no change of heart, for here in the 1930s Traven was hustling away to push his books. What the *News Reports* tried to do later by stirring up controversy, Traven was trying to do here by browbeating a young journalist. Such tortuous methods were necessary for an author unwilling to come out and face the world in person. Herbert Klein smiled as he recalled for us how he had driven himself for three days non-stop in an effort to copy out all the material

Traven had sent before the magic curfew was rung and he had to send back the letters.

The interesting sequel to this correspondence with Klein took place nearly eight years later in 1943, and helps establish a continuity between the different eras of Traven dealings. Mina Klein now took up the story and described to us how she had seen in *New Republic*, next to an advertisement for a 'dinner-forum on India's place in the democratic world', a single advertisement under the heading, 'Books'. 'The Story of an American Sailor Aboard a Death Ship. The most exciting and sensational sea story of this time.'

Mrs Klein wrote away to the address given, Casa M.L. Martinez, Post-Office Box 2520, Mexico City, saying that she only wanted the book if it was *The Death Ship* by B. Traven. There was a familiar ring about the reply.

> Your guess is perfect; the book is by B.T. How can there ever be any doubt – there is no other book like it in the whole world and you know it ... Read it and then pack it up neatly and send it to a friend of yours who serves in the Navy or in the Merchant Marine or in the Army or with the Marines or send it to anyone you appreciate – you cannot make a better gift. Very truly yours,
>
> M.L. MARTINEZ.

A second letter confirmed Mina Klein's instinct that the Martinez letters were written by the same person who wrote the Traven letters. This time it was not just the style of the communication which was familiar; there was a clear echo of earlier contacts in the conditions laid down. Martinez would send some articles about Traven: 'but we must insist that you return within five days every magazine sent you, postage paid by you. Whenever one copy is returned you will receive the next.'

Martinez set out the same conditions to Mrs Klein as Traven had to Mr Klein. The same tone of voice was audible in the correspondence to Knopf from Traven, Martinez and R.E. Lujan, and my conclusion was that throughout the years from 1935 to 1955 there was one ventriloquist manipulating the mouths which spoke to the world on behalf of B. Traven.

Herbert Klein relished every by-way and cul-de-sac of the

Traven mystery, and had coined his own word, 'Travening', for what he described as 'the frustrating and totally endless search, and running around ... the search for identity'. The justification for it all was the great quality of the books written by this anonymous author. When we finished the interviews with the Kleins the mist had still not lifted from the ocean, but, in any case, we had no time to take even a short walk along the beach. Robinson, the film crew and I had to whisk ourselves back to Hollywood, where we had an appointment with Bernard Smith.

In the 1930s Smith was a young editor at Alfred Knopf in New York and it was he who handled the first three Traven novels published in the United States: *The Death Ship*, *The Treasure of the Sierra Madre* and *The Bridge in the Jungle*. I had seen his name in the Knopf letters and from those references it was evident that the work he had done had been much to Traven's liking. He lived in Santa Monica now, but drove in to a house in Hollywood where we had arranged to film. He was a short man of an athletic, almost military bearing. His hair was nearly white, neatly parted down the centre and lying close to his head, and his voice, like his entire manner of address, was firm and clear. He was a most agreeable witness, sure and precise in what he had to say and exuding an air of competence and energy.

Some time in 1933 an English manuscript of *The Death Ship* arrived on Bernard Smith's desk in the Knopf offices. He felt as he read it that here was authentic proletarian literature (something for which there was a great vogue at the time), written by a man who had been a worker all his life and who was expressing a true working-class point of view. What was more, he was doing so with boldness and vigour and without dreary propaganda or a party line. Much supposedly prole-tarian literature was synthetic and middle-class in its origins, but here, thought Smith, was the real thing. There was, though, an enormous problem, for the book was not, in Smith's view, written in English but was a direct word-for-word translation from the German, complete with German sentence structure. Smith told Alfred Knopf that there was no hope of publishing the book as it stood but that he was willing to try to rewrite it – if the author would give his permission. Knopf wrote to

Traven suggesting this ploy and the author, in his reply, asked
for a sample of the editor's work. Smith provided such.

He told us: 'I rewrote the first, I would say, twenty or twenty-
five pages of *The Death Ship*, sent it to him and back came a
letter, from him to me, saying he was enormously enthusiastic
and that I had a free hand to do anything I wanted. Whereupon
I rewrote the whole book.'

Smith was scrupulous about not claiming more for himself
than he deserved. 'I don't want anyone to misunderstand what
the nature of the rewrite was. It was not any literary contribution from me, that is to say I didn't add anything to his narrative
or to his characterisation. I merely put his translation from the
German into acceptable English.'

The final version, said Smith, kept some of the roughness of
the original. It was a working-class novel by a working man
and a certain awkwardness was part of its quality. The next
two novels were suitably restyled, again with the full approval
of the author.

This seemed a powerful argument against theories that the
books were based on English manuscripts written by an American. Surely, if that were the case, enough of the English would
have survived to make the versions sent to Smith more convincing? And no American would so forget his native tongue as to
embarrass himself in this way. The Kleins had mentioned that
in one letter from Traven he had spelled the word 'here' as
'hier', as in German; now the man who first saw the English
manuscripts sent from Mexico testified to their Germanic style.
Robinson pressed Smith again on this point, for it was important to get it absolutely clear. There was no question about it,
said Smith, Traven wrote originally in German. The colloquialisms he put into the mouth of Gales in *The Death Ship* were
not real American colloquialisms, and Smith had to find substi-
tutes for these attempts at slang which were all part of Traven's
effort to pass himself off as an American.

Smith received even more stringent instructions about avoiding publicity than the Büchergilde had. There was to be no
publicity about the author of any kind, and if any journalists
enquired about him they were to be told that nothing was
known. Smith was ordered not even to say that the books came
from Mexico, it was to be as if the manuscripts had fallen into

his hands from the skies. Such was the depth of Traven's mania for secrecy that he wanted to know who opened the letters in Smith's office: did he open his own mail or did others sometimes see letters addressed to him? Smith replied that he was the only person to see his mail – a fib, but he wanted to encourage Traven to write freely.

In spite of this, Bernard Smith did attempt to meet the man who sent him the books and letters signed B. Traven. He was left clutching at the air but the lengths to which Traven went to avoid discovery were proof to Smith, if proof were still needed, that the obsession with anonymity was no mere whim. In 1936 Smith planned to take a month's holiday in Mexico in September and what more natural than that he should write to the author, whose work he had been instrumental in publishing, to suggest a meeting. The reply, which came swiftly, was evasive.

Last week in August I shall leave for California, Dakota and Wisconsin where I have to see some people, how they are doing. I may be back in Mexico about the first week in September but I am not sure of that and you had better not rely on my being there ...

So there was to be no meeting, but Traven promised that he would see to it that the holiday was a success. Smith and his wife made their trip as arranged and, on their arrival in Mexico, they were met by a car and an attractive young Mexican woman who handed them a letter from Traven. The letter said that the young woman, Miss Mary, was to be their guide and translator and that the car was theirs to make use of for the duration of their holiday. Each morning during that month-long trip a letter from Traven was delivered, outlining a schedule of visits and activities for the day. They covered every hour from early morning till late at night, a complete guide to everything the Smiths should see in Mexico and information on how to live safely and economically. Traven had taken an immense amount of trouble in preparing this home-made Baedeker-by-instalments and Smith was grateful for what he interpreted as a gift of thanks.

The daily letters were all supposedly written before Traven

had taken off for Dakota and Wisconsin, but Smith was not
convinced by this cover. He was sure that Traven was at hand
watching their progress through Mexico. Both he and his wife
felt that there was a small man following them wherever they
went; they saw him, or thought they saw him, a shadow-like
figure in the gloomy corners of cathedrals or watching from afar
as they sat over a drink. They were convinced that Traven was
shyly escorting them, monitoring their tour to check that all
was going well. But, of course, he never made himself known.
The Smiths might have questioned Mary, their guide, about
the unseen benefactor, but here, as always, Traven had antici-
pated the danger of discovery. In the second letter of the series
Traven requested just one favour of Smith: 'Please do not mention my name to Miss Mary. Nor about our connections. She
doesn't know me. And any asking about me would only upset
and confuse her.'

This was obviously absurd, said Smith, she must have known
him or had some contact with him, but the American couple
acceded to the request. They never mentioned Traven's name
to their guide nor did they ask her any questions about how
the trip had been arranged.

Smith's contact with Traven ended with the publication of
The Bridge in the Jungle in 1938. He had no solution to unanswered questions which still loomed over the author's life.
He took Croves to have been Traven and to have been Marut,
but all this was on his reading of the same research that I had
seen. The mania for privacy he had recognised in Traven
was due, he thought, to his political background in Germany,
but there was another aspect to it. Smith believed that once
Traven realised that his need for anonymity and secrecy stirred
up good publicity, he played the game of hide and seek for all
it was worth. And it had paid, had it not, asked Bernard Smith,
otherwise why would Robinson and I be in California asking
him questions?

When I stopped the camera, Smith shook hands with us all,
wished us luck and hurried away. We had kept him longer than
intended, and he was late for a lunch appointment. He left us
thinking over what he had said. We were finding more and
more supporters for the Marut–Croves–Traven identification
but the character of B. Traven the letter-writer, B. Traven the

invisible guide, and B. Traven, the American who had forgotten his English, became ever stranger and more complex.

Our next location was near by at Paul Kohner's offices on Sunset Boulevard, a striking dark brown and cream painted building of the size, and with something of the welcoming aspect of a private house. Kohner, in his early seventies, had spent all his working life in the film business and was a leading Hollywood agent handling the affairs of, among others, Charles Bronson, Liv Ullman, Ingmar Bergman and John Huston. He had recently been the subject of a fulsome biography by his brother, which was entitled *The Magician of Sunset Boulevard*. When Robinson and I had called on him the previous afternoon, we had shared his hallway with an anxious actorish-looking couple, who had turned the suntan into a work of art: a thinly dressed girl of bland good looks and a white-suited young man whose muscles seemed permanently flexed to support a tonnage of gold bangles. Eventually, we had been ushered into the office and met Kohner, a jolly-looking man, with a voice rich and liquidy, as if he had just eaten an ice-cream. At that first meeting he had not been forthcoming. He had made us do the work, explaining about the film and what we wanted to ask him, while he listened and made the occasional comment. He had seemed preoccupied and I wondered if the interview would be a success.

When we returned for the filming there was no sign of this unbending manner. Kohner sat at his large desk, on which were piled several heaps of letters, papers and scripts, and carried on his business breezily while we set up lights and camera. He was most friendly and accommodating and talked at length when the interview began.

He first came into contact with Traven in the early 1930s, when he was in charge of production for Universal Pictures in Germany. He read *The Death Ship*, liked it and managed to get in touch with the author through a lawyer in Switzerland. From this first contact a lengthy correspondence had flowered, intermittent and slight to begin with, but later regular and full. It continued after Kohner's return to the United States and established a strong relationship between them. We asked if we could see the letters but Kohner refused. The previous day he had shown us the expensive-looking volume in which they were

carefully bound but we had not been allowed to look inside.
Today he did not have the letters with him, and, in any case,
the rules would have been the same. Kohner had acted as
Traven's agent for film adaptations of his books and no doubt
the letters contained business discussions of a confidential
nature. I knew also that the two men's friendship had suffered
a rift and that the correspondence had been broken off
abruptly. Kohner may well not have wished to make the cause
of this public – the letters reflected, after all, a private as well
as business friendship.

Robinson asked how the author had signed his letters. At first
it had been just 'T.', said Kohner, later 'B.T.', but these initials,
like every word of the letters, had always been typed. Not one
had been signed by hand. There was an occasion when Kohner
had needed Traven's signature in order to complete the contract for the film sale of *The Treasure of the Sierra Madre*, and
he had arranged for the signing to take place in Mexico. He
received a tiny, barely decipherable signature with a 'T.' as
the only visible letter. I asked Warner Brothers in Los Angeles
for a copy of the film contract but the only one they produced
had the signature 'B. Traven, by Paul Kohner', witnessed in
Los Angeles on September 4th, 1942:

right or its renewals, so far as it arises from any violation
assigned to and shall be paid to said Warner Bros. Pictures,

Kohner, like Bernard Smith, tried to meet Traven. He travelled regularly to Mexico to visit his wife's family and suggested meetings which, on two or three occasions, the author
actually agreed to. Time and places were fixed for the rendezvous and Kohner followed the arrangements but Traven never
turned up, on one occasion acting out a ludicrous and melo-
dramatic charade to excuse his absence. As Kohner waited in
his hotel room in Mexico City, a messenger arrived at exactly the
time appointed for Traven's appearance, and brought a note
from the author. The note said that he had suddenly been taken

ill in the taxi on his way to the hotel, that he was now in hospital and would write again the next day. Kohner remembered how the next letter had read: 'They have locked me up here. They've taken a lot of blood from me and pumped me full of God knows what. I'm afraid that they are going to ...'

The note broke off like the end of an episode of *The Perils of Pauline*. Kohner, play-acting in return, replied that he was worried that something might have happened to Traven and that he would call the police to effect a rescue. He knew full well that the author was playing a game and felt that by joining in he might entice him out of his corner. He did not succeed.

Soon afterwards there was another near miss. Kohner and his wife were invited to tea by Esperanza Lopez Mateos, Traven's translator and representative, and they were certain that this time the author would put in an appearance. Tea was served in a large room, which was divided in two by a curtain. The afternoon went by and no Traven appeared, but Kohner's wife noticed the dividing curtain moving suspiciously, and she was sure that there was someone, Traven, hovering there out of sight. Kohner did not give in to his impulse to go over and pull the curtain aside and he and his wife left the house still without a sight of B.T.

Many of Traven's letters to Kohner were actually aimed through him to his wife, Lupita Tovar, a famous Mexican film star. Traven was infatuated by her. He considered himself her patron in some way, sent her newspaper cuttings about herself and programmes from cinemas where her films were playing – there was not a word printed about her in Mexico that the author did not obsessively cut out and post on. He wrote at length to Kohner extolling Lupita's virtues as an actress and asking why her career was not better managed. (Here was another reason why Kohner might wish the correspondence to remain in the family.) In the bossy, know-all manner he often assumed, Traven advised Lupita on what films she should make and of the failings of those she had made – he had seen them all several times. He offered advice on how she should improve the quality of her voice, suggesting himself as the elocution teacher she needed. He sent her a specially-written film script called *Mercedes Ortega Lozano*, with the bizarre sub-title, *The Story of a Flipped Woman*.

This absurd fan worship almost enticed Traven to reveal himself. He wrote asking Lupita to meet him in Acapulco. She travelled down with some friends,and when they arrived in the resort a little Mexican boy brought a note from Traven, which specified a meeting place – a remote spot on the coast – and a time, six o'clock. Her friends drove Lupita to the appointed place, where she got out of the car and walked down to the beach alone. She waited for half an hour but Traven did not materialise. She thought she saw a figure lurking further down the beach but it came no closer and, in the end, she returned to the car and drove back to where she was staying. The next day a messenger delivered an angry letter from Traven, haranguing her for bringing bodyguards to the rendezvous. He had asked her to come alone, what was the matter with her, didn't she trust him? It was clear that he must have been there on the beach watching her, once again unable to bring himself to remove his mask.

Some time after this Kohner's friendship with Traven collapsed and the happy coda to this relationship occurred only years later. One evening in Mexico City in the late 1960s, Paul Kohner found himself sitting next to an attractive woman at a large formal dinner party. Her place card named her as Rosa Elena Lujan, but she introduced herself as Mrs Croves.

Kohner realised who she was and said that she must know about his relationship with Traven. He asked if the time had not come to patch up the old quarrel and to try to get some more films made of Traven's books. Señora Lujan was sympathetic, and soon afterwards Kohner and his wife were invited to tea. It was a tearful meeting at which the old man Croves said how sorry he was that this *rapprochement* was taking place so late in his life.

This was an important moment for us. Here was a man who had established a friendship by letter with B. Traven telling us how he later met Hal Croves and took it for granted that the two men were the same. Hill and Judy Stone were never allowed past the mask of Hal Croves, so Robinson pressed Kohner about this.

QUESTION. Did he either introduce himself to you or speak of

himself or imply that he was Croves? Or did he specifically
say or imply or behave as if he was Traven?

KOHNER. He didn't have to say anything to me because we
recalled the many years that we corresponded and the many
incidents that happened. And he thanked me profusely for
the many times that I sent him packages down to Mexico
... He knew very well, as far as I was concerned, the game
was up. He knew that I had accused him, in that unfortu-
nate last letter that I sent him, that he had invented this
figure of Croves and he must not play that game with me,
because he didn't have to. Anyhow, I assure you it was
Traven, and Traven was Croves. There's no doubt about
that.

QUESTION. No doubt in your mind?

KOHNER. No doubt in my mind. No doubt in my wife's mind.
No doubt in my son's mind.

Kohner took down from the wall a framed colour photograph, which showed himself and his wife with a very old-
looking Croves. As he held it up for us, Robinson asked him
once more.

QUESTION. Are you convinced that the man Croves is also the
man who produced the works signed B. Traven?

KOHNER. Yes, indeed. One and the same man.

The three- or four-hour meeting, at which that photograph
was taken, was the first and the last between Hal Croves and
Paul Kohner. Croves died the following year. I was impressed
by Kohner's certainty that the old man he met was the same
man he had corresponded with thirty years before. According
to Kohner he had had not a moment of doubt, for they had
picked up naturally from the shared references and memories
of the earlier contact. Kohner's evidence did not tell us if this
one man had written all the books and written them alone, or
where he had come from or what his real name and identity
were, but it did tie the letter-writer of the 1930s to the Croves
of the post-war years. If Hal Croves was the man who had
written the letter signed B. Traven to Paul Kohner and who
had behaved in such a characteristically elusive and irritating

manner, then it did look as if it was he who had written the bossy
Traven letters to Klein and Knopf in the same era, and thus
to the Büchergilde in the 1920s. Croves and Traven were both
disguises of the man who had complained to a far-away editor
of the privations of the jungle; who had badgered Herbert
Klein to return all his letters within three days; who had stalked
Bernard Smith through cathedrals and Lupita Kohner along
a beach; who had hidden behind curtains and sent cryptic
notes; who had advised publishers how to publish, journalists
how to write, actresses how to act and agents how to handle
their wives' careers.

It did look like this, but Robinson and I still refused to con-
cede that it was definitely so. After all, it was not impossible
that Croves had been an impostor, that he had read Kohner's
letters to Traven and bluffed it out when they came face to
face. It would have been a prodigious piece of trickery for such
an old man, but it was a possibility we were stubbornly clinging
to. What we had to do was to find out more about Hal Croves.
If by some chance he was not the author, we had to discover
the clues by which we could eliminate and expose him, and
if he was the author we had to uncover his history and origins.

10 'Into a Far Country'

One person who could tell us about Croves was Sanora Babb Howe, the writer and widow of the great Hollywood cinematographer, James Wong Howe. She and her husband had been good friends of Croves, whom they had first met when he came up and introduced himself on a film location in Mexico in 1951. We now turned off Sunset Strip in Hollywood and a short distance up the hill came to Sanora Babb's rough plastered, Spanish-style house. She opened the door to us and bustled about in a homely manner to make us welcome in her comfortable and unostentatious home. We set up the camera in a large living-room, which was cluttered with papers, books and mementoes, and where, in a crowded corner, I noticed a clutch of movie awards, including two rather tarnished Oscars. Sanora Babb brought us all a beer and then settled down to answer our questions.

It was obvious from the beginning of our talk that she had always believed that Hal Croves was B. Traven. In our questioning, we asked her only about Croves, and her account of the old man's character fitted harmoniously with the notion that he was Traven. She and her husband had been very fond of him. He was a vigorous and energetic man, who could sometimes be blunt and down to earth, but was generally mild of manner. He was a gentle, kind and thoughtful friend to Sanora Babb, who spoke of him with warmth and affection.

The friendship was not uncomplicated. However amusing and charming a companion Croves could be, he established around himself a no-man's-land into which not even good friends were allowed. Friendship with him was conducted according to certain rules which were no less forceful for being unspoken; he would tolerate no questioning of his past, no speculation about his origins and no hinting that he was anyone but Mr Hal Croves. He was, in short, as obsessive about secrecy as Traven himself.

The rules that Sanora Babb and others went along with emerged from a series of jolts and rebuffs, by which Croves made his feelings known. For Sanora Babb the first indication that she had to tread warily with Croves came when she and her husband were dining with him soon after they had met. She blurted out that she thought that Croves's accent sounded Scandinavian, and that his appearance was rather Scandinavian too. The effect of this simple speculation was immediate: Croves became silent and huffy and, by a combination of icy stares and sulks, made it clear that there was to be no more of this sort of talk if their friendship was to continue.

One occasion, which remained etched in her memory, was when she transgressed the most dangerous of all barriers. She was entertaining Croves to tea in her house and in the course of talking about the books of B. Traven, she made the ultimate gaffe of referring to Croves as if he were the author. He let the comment pass unremarked and left soon afterwards only to return later that evening, when he pushed a note through her door instructing her never under any circumstances to address him as if he were Traven. He compounded this secrecy with some odd behaviour the following day. He called again on Sanora Babb and asked in a perfectly friendly way if she still had his note and, if she did, could he please have it back. She fetched it and handed it to him, whereupon he dramatically tore it up before her eyes and left.

She had ample opportunity to get used to these antics, for Croves seemed unable to prevent himself from brandishing a constant suspicion about the world, even when he believed himself to be alone or unobserved. Sanora Babb remembered an occasion when she was meeting Croves for lunch in Mexico City and she caught sight of him arriving ahead of her in the distance. He had not spotted her and stood in the doorway of the restaurant glancing suspiciously to the left and right before slipping quickly inside. It was for all the world as if he were making sure that he was not being followed by a secret agent or a detective. Strange behaviour, punishing stares, furtive notes and sulky silences were all part of the Hal Croves that Sanora Babb knew.

She had some letters from Croves relating mainly to negotiations over various uses of the Traven stories. They were signed 'Hal', 'H.', 'H.C.' and 'H. Croves', and were all firmly labelled as being from the author's agent.

Hal, H. H. C, Most Sincerely *H. Croves,*
H. Croves.

In 1953 Croves wrote a letter about a contract: 'As to the signing itself I have no authorisation to sign B.T. all I can do and what I have done for years is to sign on behalf and for B.T. to which you may add your signature as a witness.'

In another letter of the same year: 'By your letter you refer to the story as 'your' story. It isn't mine, it is T.'s story and remains his although I had to make a few changes.'

On another occasion he excused himself for quickly accepting an offer from Canadian radio by saying that it would take weeks to get an answer from T., so he thought he had better take the responsibility himself. There was a five-page letter to Sanora Babb's husband about the script for a film of the story 'Macario', in which Croves negotiated about what dialogue might or might not be cut, what sort of actor should be cast, how scenes should be shot – all this with only a couple of references to what T.'s opinions were. In the light of the domineering views Traven was in the habit of expressing about his work, I thought that Croves was taking a bit of a chance with his freewheeling attitude. It was unlike the Traven whose letters I had read to allow an intermediary to barter with the content of his work. An agent could bargain over the money, certainly, but Traven would have had his own views about how his stories were to be altered for filming. In his letter Croves was making no secret that it was his own opinions, not the author's, that he was offering, and there was every indication that these were to be binding. What had happened?

At first reading of this correspondence the thought flashed through my mind that the hints thrown out by Baumann and others were on target. Traven was dead. There was no need for Croves to worry about riding roughshod over the precious works because Traven was in no position to cuff him for speaking out of turn. Croves was signing for Traven, failing to get in touch with him, making terms on his behalf because now there was no Traven, only an agent. All these letters were written in 1950, or later, and I remembered that Alfred Knopf had received no letters from Traven himself after 1947. From then on they had all come from Martinez and Lujan. Did they, with Croves, make up a triumvirate of conspirators? It was a tempting conclusion.

There was another explanation, less likely to make the heart race, but far more probable in the light of all I was learning about Croves. If Croves's opinions were derived directly from the man who wrote the books, if he had truly inside knowledge, if, in other words, he was Traven, then he could write as he did with impunity. If, as Sanora Babb, Kohner and others suspected, Croves could declaim with confidence about the stories because they were his own, one problem, at least, was solved. There was an interesting line I spotted in one of the letters, which reinforced my thoughts on this. Sanora Babb had written to Croves mentioning that she had a heart ailment and Croves replied, just as B.T. would have done, telling her exactly where she could have it cured, an institute in Mexico City, that he knew all about.

> I know more than half a dozen cases which had been given up by every doctor in the City, being told they would not live more than two years more. They went to that Institute and without being hospitalised they were cured fully within six months ...

I detected the same ring of schoolboyish exaggeration in this claim by Croves as in the early letters of Traven.

Sanora Babb had a particular reason for believing that Croves was Traven. One evening when she and her husband were at dinner with Croves and Esperanza Lopez Mateos, Esperanza overstepped the mark by referring to an Indian wife

Croves had taken in the south of Mexico. There was an angry exchange and Esperanza stood up from the table, asking Sanora Babb to leave with her. When the two women were outside, Esperanza told her friend that it was true that Croves was Traven and added that she was not revealing this just because she was angry; she thought Croves would want her to know, even if he would never tell her himself. Croves was then based at Esperanza Lopez Mateos's house, and soon afterwards, when he was away on a long trip to the jungle, Sanora Babb was shown drawers full of manuscripts – some in German, some in rough English – which Esperanza said were his.

But if Sanora Babb were sure about Croves writing the books she freely admitted that she was sure of little else.

> Well, after knowing him many years, I still feel that no one really knows his secret. I doubt if his present wife knows, she met him late in life. And the things I have read seem to be another elaboration of his mystery. I just think that Traven died with his secrets and that nobody really knows.

The shadow of Traven was falling across the grave marked Croves from most stations of the sun, but the darkness it cast was leading to further obscurity. I noted Sanora Babb's scepticism about Señora Lujan's knowledge of the truth. It was a little irritating that our chief Mexican witness was already under suspicion. We would soon have the opportunity of judging for ourselves.

Before we left Los Angeles, I telephoned Harlan Ellison, who had edited a late collection of Traven stories called *Stories by the Man Nobody Knows*. I wondered how he obtained manuscripts and what dealings he had had with the author or his agents. Ellison said that he had first spotted some of the stories in American magazines like *Manhunt* and *Fantastic* and had tried to get hold of Traven. He had been referred to a literary agency, who, in turn, had referred him to Hal Croves.

Croves authorised the collection and provided three original stories, which Ellison had rewritten considerably. At the time he had wondered if the stories were truly by B. Traven or whether Croves was some kind of impostor, who was passing off his own inferior work. Ellison no longer doubted their

authenticity. There was one story about a basket-maker that was
'pure Traven', and he was inclined to discount any discrepan-
cies in style among the others on account of their Traven-like
plots and structures. It was possible, he thought, that the author
had been ill or quite old while he was writing this material
because, for example, there were a great many typing mistakes.

Ellison had managed to keep a faint question mark flickering
over the head of Hal Croves, and I recounted what he had told
me to Robinson as we drove from Beverly Hills to Los Angeles
airport in the soothing stream of the morning traffic. He
remained more sceptical than I about Croves being Traven and
here was more evidence, to go with the odd accent and the lack
of new works, that it might not be as certain as our witnesses
assumed. To Kohner, Hill and others, our scepticism about
Croves must have seemed perverse, but we were trying to establish the truth to our, rather than other people's satisfaction. The
only way to tell hard fact from guesswork masquerading as fact
was by striking everything with our own sounding hammer. We
hoped that, with practice, our ears would become attuned to
telling the true from the fractured notes.

Our plan for Mexico was to pick up the story of Hal Croves
from his first appearance in the early 1940s to his death in 1969.
If we shook it hard enough some answers would surely fall out.
I had asked Paul Kohner if he would ring John Huston on our
behalf to see if he would change his mind about giving us an
interview. Now that Kohner had met us and suffered our worst
he would, I hoped, tell his old friend that we wished him no
harm. Croves's first entry from the wings had been to meet Huston and we wanted to hear the story from the man himself. The
next step was to see Luis Spota, the journalist who had tracked
down the man called Torsvan in Acapulco. It was generally
accepted that this man Torsvan was none other than Croves,
but we wanted to question Spota about this and to film him
telling his story. Then there was Gabriel Figueroa, who was
one of Hal Croves's best friends. He must know something. And,
of course, there was Señora Lujan, widow of Hal Croves and
owner of the B. Traven copyright.

As we flew down over Baja California my thoughts went
back to Ret Marut. The last that any of his friends ever heard
of him was a postcard sent from Rotterdam to fellow revolu-

tionary Erich Mühsam, said to be at the end of 1922: 'In a
few hours' time I shall board a ship to take me across the Atlantic. With that I shall have ceased to exist.'

Had that ship taken him to Mexico where he had translated
himself into B. Traven and later Hal Croves? There had been
mention of Mexico in *Der Ziegelbrenner* and the long poem
Khundar, which appeared in the issue of April 30th, 1920, had
ended with the words:

> Salvation will come through questions of searching and
> wandering. Therefore let us go wandering only where there
> is truth, wisdom, salvation and light.
> And when he had so spoken he left from there into a far
> country that same evening.

What better far country than Mexico for a man to re-create
himself in? It was always a land of secrets and shadows, where
ancient stones guarded the prerogatives of old gods. There were
the pyramids, which had witnessed the bloody rituals of the
Aztecs; the temples, which had housed the ceremonies of the
Mayans. It was a place where the obscurities of the past enveloped the present, where a man could hide or disappear. One
of the great gods of Mexico is Quetzalcoatl, the feathered
serpent, adopted by the Aztecs from the Toltec people, who
had inhabited the valley of Mexico a thousand years before
them. Quetzalcoatl, bringer of agriculture, the arts and the
sciences, was also the creator of man. He journeyed to the
underworld, collected the bones of the dead of previous worlds
and gave them life by sprinkling them with his own blood.
Marut had ceased to exist in his previous world, and he might
well have made his way from Europe to Mexico for his own
resurrection. Mexico was also a new country, born out of revolution and still with the potential for radical change. As such,
it would have made a proper refuge for Der Ziegelbrenner.

My own image of Mexico was culled largely from old movies:
a land of jolly peasants, laughing revolutionaries, wicked
generals, lusty women, rattlesnakes, heat and dust. It was, in
fact, a moist and cloudy afternoon when we arrived at Mexico
City airport and the first impression was of being surrounded
by uniforms – customs men, soldiers, policemen, porters, drivers,

despatchers and airport officials. Succumbing to the attentions of a persistent tout, we clambered into a mini-bus taxi along with several parties of Americans taking their Mexican vacations at the wrong time of year, the rainy season. We drove into the city, gazing out of the windows at the streets damp from the afternoon rain and crowded with overloaded bicycles and kamikaze Volkswagens. The road in from the airport was seething with an animated pavement life, much of it centred on the open-spit-roasting of scrawny chickens.

We were the last to leave the taxi and I had to brandish the address of the Hotel Bristol several times before the driver was able to set a course. His ignorance of our quarters was not to be blamed entirely on his youthful inexperience, as it transpired that few taxi-drivers in Mexico City were aware of its existence, in spite of its standing with the staff of Her Majesty's Ambassador. It is a modern, clean and serviceable hotel on a corner overlooking a wide and open road junction, which is empty by day and crossed by screeching vehicles at night. This is a pleasant part of the city, where there are still many older houses, of no more than two or three storeys, and near the grand boulevard of the Avenue de Reforma. The British Embassy, a stylish old mansion, is just round the corner. Everyone agrees on how beautiful Mexico City *used* to be and disagrees on how big it is – twelve or thirteen million were the most popular guesses at its population. To those like Robinson and me, fresh from Los Angeles, the city carried itself with a distinctly European air.

I rang our cameraman Emilio Cesar and he came over to meet us for a drink and to hear the filming plan. He is a tall man, quite heavily built, with the face of a Mexican from central casting: gleaming white teeth, dark eyes and a black curly moustache. He was a little nervous at the first meeting, but his English was good and then, as throughout the week, he was eager to please. As I ran through our schedule he listened and offered the occasional 'No problem', or 'It will be O.K.' – comments he was to use later with a defiant optimism in the face of manifest impossibilities. My heart fell when Emilio told me that he had just come back from New York with a brand new camera. I like old, well-tried cameras which have passed thousands of well-exposed, well-focused film through their innards. Emilio assured me that the new one had been well tested, and he himself had shot ten rolls of film in New York without a hitch. Unseen in the background I thought I heard the Curse of Traven slipping the lead into the boxing glove. He had left us alone since his clumsy assault on New York, but I sensed that he had been travelling with us, biding his time for another strike. I was not mistaken. On the first shot of the first day's filming in Mexico City, the new camera revealed its interesting new faults, in particular a tendency to change speed or switch itself off in the middle of a shot. The radio microphone also refused to work. We foiled the Curse over this by using other mikes; the camera, however, was a different matter.

A reserve camera was fetched, which worked for a time, but it was not as flexible a piece of equipment and so we were limited in what we could do. Emilio exhibited a confidence about curing the camera problems which was at first reassuring, and later, as I realised he was trying to raise his own spirits as well as mine, acutely depressing. He worked like mad trying to mend the equipment in the evenings, he chased all over the city to borrow other cameras, he raced round trying to keep to our schedule. There were other breakdowns. As Emilio moved from embarrassment to fury over them, I swung from frantic, albeit internal, irritation to a resignation that, I liked to fancy, was attractively Latin.

Daily, and sometimes hourly, we were cheered or cast down by bulletins on the health of the camera. Even when all was working smoothly, we suffered the agony of wondering whether the wretched thing would go on the blink at any moment. I cancelled our trip to the Chiapas in order to make up lost time and to lead a fight back against the Curse, who had caught us with another kidney punch. He had seen to it that Kodak in Mexico had completely run out of the film stock we were using. Emilio had been confident in advance that we could buy all the film we needed in Mexico, but he had reckoned without the Curse – and without the fact that Kodak were just beginning to manufacture stock locally rather than import it. So, even when we laid our hands on a camera that worked, we had nothing to put in it. Once more we fought off the hand of fate. Emilio borrowed a roll or so of film from every other cameraman in Mexico; and I had some cans flown down from New York.

None of this, of course, was visible at that first drink in the
Hotel Bristol; neither was Emilio's chief lieutenant, Pablo. We
never learned Pablo's second name although he accompanied
us daily, usually in the role of sound recordist. He was a thin,
bespectacled man in his middle years, who had the stooping
gait of one who might be used to regular beatings. He was ever
willing and, as far as our lack of a common language allowed,
friendly towards us, but he seemed ill at ease in his rôle as sound
recordist, indeed he often looked at his recording machine as
if he were seeing it for the first time. It is not unusual for sound
men to appear distant or to be in a world of their own. They
spend their days in earphones, listening not to what those
nearest to them are saying but to what the microphone is picking up. Pablo with his nervous and halting manner was more
distant than most, absent-minded even, and Emilio may have
noticed this, for he would often shout at Pablo for, say, neg-
lecting to switch on his machine when the camera started.
For all this, Emilio was a likeable and energetic cameraman,
whose pictures, when we later viewed them, were perfectly
satisfactory.

11 John Huston Meets Mr Croves

The air in Puerto Vallarta was like soup; the temperature in the nineties. Robinson asked me why John Huston, who could live anywhere he wished, should choose to live in such a damnable climate. I could only assume that, as the town was a holiday resort, this sultry drenching was not a punishment administered all the year round. Huston, in any case, was known as a friend of Mexico, he had first visited the country when he was eighteen and had been a regular visitor or resident ever since. We were there because Paul Kohner had interceded on our behalf and Huston had now agreed to see us.

Gladys Hill, Huston's long-time assistant, sent a lorry down to the airport to pick up us and our equipment, and I opted to sit in the open back to feel some movement in the otherwise still air. We were driven along a flat road past the new hotels which were colonising the beaches round the town. The jungle was yet to be completely tamed and the new developments had an unfinished and impermanent look. The town itself was a tight cluster of houses on the steep sides of a valley, which burst out of the blue jungle to the sea. Huston, I had been told, was the godfather of Puerto Vallarta's new standing as a fashionable resort. He had shot his film of Tennessee Williams's *The Night of the Iguana* in what was then a tiny isolated village, and when the filming was finished Richard Burton had bought a house here for himself and Elizabeth Taylor. The lorry fought its way painfully up the narrow cobbled streets, and the Burton house, evidently a landmark in the town, was pointed out to us. Huston's house was hard by and we were greeted at the door by Gladys Hill, who promptly provided drinks for us all. Emilio

was a little nervous at filming such a god of the movie industry
as Huston and, before the great man made his appearance, we
discussed carefully where to place the camera in the huge cool
and shady room into which we had been shown. The room
flowed uninterrupted on to a long open balcony and we set up
there.

John Huston had been the first human being to report a
meeting with Hal Croves, at the beginning of 1947. At that
time, following the success of *The Maltese Falcon*, Huston was
one of the new champions of the movies, and he was setting
up a film that he had wanted to make for some time, an adapta-
tion of *The Treasure of the Sierra Madre* by B. Traven. Previous
plans to film it had been interrupted by the war, in which Huston had served in the U.S. Army as a documentary film-maker.
While he was away, Warner Brothers, who owned the rights
to the book, twice almost put the film into production. The story
was eventually kept for Huston and towards the end of his time
in the army he started work on the screenplay.

John Huston was more than usually faithful to the books he
adapted for the screen, and, when he had begun work on *The
Treasure of the Sierra Madre*, he had written to the author through
a post-office box number in Acapulco. A correspondence developed, in which Traven wrote long expansive letters offering
suggestions about how the film should go, and Huston asked
him to come to Hollywood to collaborate on the script. This
brought a strange reply. Traven would consider the request,
but, if he came, he would have to make the journey northward
by stages in order to acclimatise himself slowly to the different
latitudes. This would have taken months so Huston pressed on
and finished the screenplay himself. He was still anxious to have
Traven work on the film, and it was arranged that Huston
would go down to Mexico City, where the novelist would somehow make contact with him. We wanted Huston to tell us what
happened then.

Huston soon padded barefoot into the room and shook hands
all round. He was dressed in a khaki pyjama-like shirt and
trousers and exuded an air of briskness, which I guessed might
be his practised manner for meeting strangers. The Traven
mystery, he said, was becoming rather like Shakespeare, the
more information we had about it the deeper it became so that

it was superseding the works, if not in importance, then in attention. Robinson asked Huston if he would give us his own estimation of Traven's quality as a writer. Traven, he said, was above all a passionate defender of the victims of society, a man who hated injustice and had found a great battlefield in Mexico on which to join combat with it. His books were 'marvellous affirmations of his faith in the beaten man', and while he was no stylist, his stories were permeated by a great and single-minded vision. This is what had first attracted him to the work.

And so to the time when he was waiting for contact with Traven in an hotel in Mexico City. Huston said to us it was the Baumer Hotel, and stuck to this when I wrote to him about it later, but earlier accounts had it as the Reforma. Huston told us the story with some relish, pausing for effect to draw on his cigar and lowering his soft, beguiling voice. He is a good actor as well as a writer and director, and this was a tale he enjoyed telling.

Huston always slept with his door unlocked, and, shortly before dawn on the morning of the day on which he was to meet Traven, he awoke to find the shadowy figure of a man standing by the foot of his bed. The man took out a card and handed it to Huston, who switched on the light and read it. It said: 'Hal Croves. Translator. Acapulco and San Antonio.' Huston could now get a good look at his mysterious visitor. He was a little man, thin and rather frail-looking, and his clothes hung loosely on him. His faded khaki shirt was fastened with a cheap gold pin and he seemed slightly awkward in his manner. He had a long nose, white hair and grey-blue eyes. Huston spoke first. 'How do you do, Mr Croves?' The man replied, 'I have a letter for you from Mr Traven,' and he handed it over. In it Traven said that he was ill and unable to come and that in his place he was sending his old and intimate friend Hal Croves, who knew as much about his books as he did himself and who was as well qualified to advise about the country and locations. Croves could represent him in every way and furnish Huston with all necessary information. The men shook hands and Croves left the room while Huston dressed.

The two men breakfasted together and over the next few days their conversations about the film were carried on through several meetings. Croves liked the script, which Huston showed

him, and said that he was sure that Traven would like it too,
indeed Croves's thoughts about the screenplay were distinctly
similar to those Traven had expressed in his letters. Clearly this
was someone who knew the author's mind well. He suggested
several places where the story could be filmed and was, in Huston's words, 'obviously an old Mexico hand'.

The idea occurred to Huston that this slight, elderly man
might be Traven and that the letter was a kind of coded admittance of such, with its 'he will represent me' and 'he knows as
much about my work as I do'. Yet Huston found it difficult
to match this hesitant man with what he knew of Traven from
his books and letters. Croves was uncomfortable in conversation, saying little and speaking in short sentences, whereas
Traven, in his letters, was expansive, enlarging on his points
and expressing himself freely and easily. A film script Traven
wrote of his book *The Bridge in the Jungle* was extraordinary for
its rambling digressions and elaborate expositions on the philosophy of the camera. As Huston saw it, Croves reduced matter
to the bare essentials, the bone structure, while Traven was
always putting on flesh. In this their personalities were strik-
ingly different. Huston could not make up his mind about
Croves, but hired him to work as a technical adviser on the
film.

The filming of *The Treasure of the Sierra Madre* began in April
1947. The production itself was something of an adventure as
it was rare then to shoot almost a whole film on location, let
alone to do so far away from the studios. Extras were hired
in Mexico, but the leading players and the sizeable film crew
flew down from California to begin work in Tampico on the
Gulf coast, before moving to the main location near the village
of San José de Purua, about 140 miles west of Mexico City.

True to his usual practice, Huston stayed fairly close to
Traven's novel, rearranging some of the book but retaining all
the main elements. It is a powerful morality tale about greed
and riches, which traces the adventures of three down-and-outs
who band together to search for gold in the wilds of Mexico.
Humphrey Bogart was cast as the unscrupulous Fred C. Dobbs
and Tim Holt as the young Curtin, two no-hopers who come
together at the beginning of the film when they are cheated
out of the wages they have earned at a construction camp. In

the flophouse, they meet Howard, a voluble old prospector (played by Walter Huston, the director's father), whose stories fire their imaginations, and the three of them set out for the mountains of the Sierra Madre, where, thanks to the toughness and know-how of the old man, they find gold and build a mine.

As Howard predicted, the gold dust brings with it fear and distrust. When the old man goes off to help some Mexican Indians who have taken him for a medicine man, Dobbs, by now inflamed with his suspicions, shoots Curtin, leaves him for dead and travels on alone with all the treasure. But Dobbs is killed by bandits, who take his mules but ignore the bags of gold dust. The other two treasure-seekers come upon the site of his murder and discover that their struggle, the privations, the greed and the killing have all been for nothing: the wind has risen and scattered the gold dust back over the mountain. The land which gave up the gold has reclaimed it. Old Howard, who has by now decided anyway that he will live quietly and simply with the Indians, roars with laughter at nature's joke. This ironic fable about the corruption brought by wealth was an unconventional subject for the Hollywood of the 1940s, and Huston needed the support and protection of his producer, Henry Blanke, in the face of pressure to reduce the sting.

When the filming began the technical consultant, Hal Croves, turned up at the set as arranged and soon created considerable interest; after all he was present and the author was not – a strangeness in itself, as it was known that Traven lived in Mexico. And then Croves disliked any questions about Traven. Occasionally, some brash spirit would go up to him and ask point blank, 'Are you B. Traven?', and Croves would either turn away or smile and go on to some other subject. Huston flinched when he witnessed these direct confrontations and he never challenged Croves in this way.

The rumour that the 'technical consultant' was really the author soon spread around the company, and Croves's shy and reticent behaviour did nothing to discourage it. He avoided the stills photographer, and when cornered refused to have his picture taken, though he was once snapped unawares, sitting on the ground in singlet and wide-brimmed hat watching the filming. He would get angry when he heard Traven referred to casually in the first-name convention of show business

as 'Bruno' – a popular guess as to what the enigmatic 'B.'
stood for. Not that Croves ever offered an alternative Christian
name.

The filming went well but the physical conditions – the heat,
the insects, the accommodation – were tough on actors and
crew, who were used to the comforts of Hollywood, and Warner
Brothers were worried by the rising production costs and the
seediness of the story and characters. The studio suggested that
the Bogart character, Dobbs, should not be killed at the end
of the film, but Huston, with support from his producer, resisted
this ham-handed interference. The 'technical consultant', said
to be earning a hundred and fifty dollars per week, was not
proving all that useful. He was reticent and offered few ideas,
and thus Huston consulted him less and less. One suggestion
Croves did make was that the director had miscast his father
in the rôle of the old prospector Howard. In the book, argued
Croves, Howard was so ancient that he could hardly stand on
his own feet any more and he was only kept going by the dream
of gold. Walter Huston was a good enough actor but Croves
was sure that Traven had someone much frailer in mind. In
his view, and he was certain that Traven would agree with him,
Lewis Stone would have been much more suitable for the part.
This was not the kind of advice John Huston needed, and he
stood by his father, who won an Oscar for his colourful por-
trayal of the old gold miner.

One embarrassing incident took place during the filming,
which led to Croves's becoming even more of an outsider to
the rest of the company. At a celebration one evening, the
centre of attention was a young doctor, who was attached to
the film unit to look after any injuries and illnesses contracted
by cast or crew while working in the wilds. In the evenings the
doctor treated Mexicans from the local villages and even
carried out operations. Such was this young man's popularity
that at the climax of a party his trousers were taken down and
his private parts painted with mercurochrome – evidently a
great honour. There was much laughter all round and John
Huston then received the same compliment. The horseplay
continued until it came to Croves's turn and, this time, the
clumsy joke was not received in the spirit in which it was offered.
He became angry and fought off those who laid hands on him,

and they in turn stood back and left him alone. Such liberties were not to be taken with Hal Croves. When the filming was finished, Huston flew back to Hollywood and he never saw or corresponded with Hal Croves again.

Our interview with Huston ended with one obvious question unasked. He had said beforehand that he did not wish to be asked outright whether or not he thought that Hal Croves was B. Traven. His reason for this was that he was by no means convinced that the two men were one and the same, and if he voiced his doubts publicly they would stand as an accusation against Señora Lujan, something he wished to avoid. This was why he had refused our first request for an interview. As we talked over a drink and Huston pointed out the site of the new house he was building a few miles up the coast, we asked him why he had doubts about Croves. It was, he said, because of the difference between this quiet little man's character and the largeness of spirit and generosity with words which were evident in the writings of Traven. We kept our bargain with Huston in the film and I break the confidence now only because I have since discovered that Huston has pronounced in public about Croves on other occasions. In a recent book he was quoted as saying,

'I liked Croves, but he wasn't my idea of the Traven who wrote with that sort of devil-may-care grandeur, let-the-chips-fall style that we know from his books.'*

With a friendly, 'Goodbye lads,' Huston hurried away to a lunch appointment. Gladys Hill put the lorry again at our disposal and we went down to a restaurant on the beach to have lunch and ponder over what John Huston had told us. Robinson, mindful that our film was about a mystery, was happy that we had one more reason for doubting the credentials of Hal Croves. The more uncertainties we found, the more we could stir up a flavoursome brew. But Huston had not been close to the Traven story for some time. His conclusions dated back to his experiences thirty years before, when, according to reports, he thought differently.

* *The Cinema of John Huston* by Gerald Pratley, Tantivy Press, 1977.

The film of *The Treasure of the Sierra Madre* opened in January 1948 and was a success both at the box office and with the critics. James Agee wrote: 'This is one of the most visually alive and beautiful movies I have ever seen', and *Time* magazine called it 'one of the best things Hollywood has done since it learned to talk; the movie can take a place, without blushing, among the best ever made'.

John Huston won that year's Oscars for best director and best screenplay, and his father took the Oscar for best supporting actor.

In that same issue of *Time* which reviewed the film (February 2nd, 1948) there was a story headed 'Technical Adviser', which described the part that Hal Croves had played in the filming and concluded that by the end of shooting, Huston was pretty sure that 'uneasy little Mr Croves was Traven himself'. *Time*'s sister publication, *Life*, printed the photograph of Croves that had been taken surreptitiously on the set. It reported that Huston's view of Traven was that he was a proud man who no longer took an active part in human affairs, that in public he disintegrated and became ridiculous, so, in order to keep the name of Traven free from scorn, he disguised himself as somebody else.

Six weeks later both magazines received testy replies. *Life* received a letter, signed H. Croves, from San Antonio in Texas. It began, 'I am writing to comment on your review of John Huston's film *The Treasure of the Sierra Madre* in which you claim that I am B. Traven, the author of the book on which the picture is based.' Croves insisted that he was not Traven and was apparently writing on the author's behalf as well as his own: 'In Traven's opinion it is of no use to comment on anything printed or said concerning a person. But I have not yet reached that Olympian state of wisdom.' He then launched into Huston:

> Mr John Huston being convinced, as he himself said, that I was Traven, and then paying me a lousy hundred dollars a week, only shows publicly in how low an estimate he is holding Traven, the man or the woman, as the case might be, whose story gave Mr John Huston the chance of his life time.

He continued in this cantankerous vein,

> Never again will Mr John Huston have an opportunity
> to direct a picture based on any other of Traven's books.
> Traven does not need Mr John Huston or Traven would,
> only eight weeks ago, have signed a contract which would
> have netted Traven thirty thousand dollars, possibly
> royalties also, for the picture rights to another Traven book,
> and which picture Mr John Huston was to direct.

'Yah, boo, sucks,' he might have added.

This certainly sounded like the Hal Croves who had refused
to submit to the horseplay on the film set and it echoed the
B. Traven letters to Preczang, the Kleins and others. It was
a voluntary, written by Croves, for his client B. Traven, but it
was in the style of the master composer himself.

> A writer of books like the ones Traven created and which
> have been published in twenty different countries, loved and
> admired, or, yet, perhaps severely criticised still when
> nobody any longer can remember a movie director who,
> once upon a time, long long ago, did a picture based on
> a story by said writer ...

Not prettily expressed, but the message was clear.

The letter to *Time* magazine came not from Antonio but from
Mexico City, and was signed with the full name Hal Croves.
It was chattier and lighter in tone, almost as if Croves were
demonstrating that he had more than one identity – that on
film locations he might seem one sort of person, in San Antonio
he was another, and in Mexico City yet another. 'I was never
"hired" by Mr John Huston,' he began,

> when I was introduced to a certain gentleman – one of the
> very few genuine gentlemen in the caravan that Warners
> shipped to Mexico for their boo-ba-booing here – he looked
> at me hard and sharp for two seconds and asked: 'Suppose
> you had something to do with that picture in general, or,
> let's assume, with the music or sound effects, what would
> you suggest?' After I had talked for about four minutes, he
> interrupted me short and said: 'You're on!'

Huston's account of their first meeting had touched a nerve of vanity and Croves was huffy:

> Mr John Huston will never be a great writer, because he is a bad observer. On location I wore any odd or old clothing as the going was mostly rough; but when I presented myself at the hotel I did not wear 'Faded khaki' as Mr John Huston claims, but was dressed immaculately in a new and expensively tailored suit as would be proper if one is to meet somebody whom he believes important at so swanky a place as the Reforma hotel.

Rattling on, Croves repeated his argument that if he were the author it would mean that Huston had 'hired' Traven for a hundred dollars (not a hundred and fifty as he says) a week, 'that same Traven who a few months earlier had been offered between seven hundred and fifty and a thousand dollars a week'. Either Huston was a cheapskate, he implied, or he didn't believe that he was Traven at all.

'Who is who now and what is what ... ?' asked Croves with immense cheek. It was a question that he had done his best to make unanswerable. He signed off jauntily: 'That's all now folks, thank you.' The first appearance of Hal Croves had begun with a business card in a darkened hotel room and had ended with the catch-phrase from a Hollywood cartoon.

The next chapter in the Mexican story took place later in 1948, and to hear about that at first hand I had arranged an interview with Luis Spota.

12 El Gringo

The filming of *The Treasure of the Sierra Madre* created a small Traven industry. The mystery of the unseen author was widely rehearsed and a story went around that *Life* magazine was offering a reward of three thousand dollars to anyone who could discover the identity and whereabouts of Traven. The hunt was on. Journalists searched places connected with Traven – Mexico City, Acapulco, Tampico, San Cristobal de las Casas – and fanned the wild rumours about who he really was. This gust of activity died down when the *Life* reward turned out to be nothing more than a publicity stunt dreamed up by the Mexican publisher of Traven's books.

The journalists lost interest – except for one, who had been determined to track down Traven before there was any talk of the reward and whose determination remained undimmed by discovery of this hoax. He had become fascinated by Traven's books, intrigued by his secrecy and for six years already had been brooding on the mystery. He was young, he was ambitious, he was single-minded, and he was willing to discard scruples to succeed.

Luis Spota is now a prominent figure in Mexico, a best-selling novelist and a leading television presenter with his own weekly current-affairs programme. The British Embassy had found his address for me and when I telephoned him he invited us to film at his house, in the Coyoacan district in the south of the city. He turned out to be a good-looking man of about fifty, dark-haired and with glasses, and he spoke English well with a strong, rhythmic accent. He introduced Robinson and me to his attractive wife, and provided us with a stiff drink each. Emilio was on a search for some more film stock and arrived late, but Spota, used to the delays and broken appointments of filming, waited with good grace. He dug out a copy of the *Mañana* magazine containing the article which had made his name and which was the subject of our questions, and every now and then would leap up to consult it in order to remind himself of some detail. His memory did not need much jogging and by the time the camera turned, Spota, a natural performer, had warmed to his task. He spoke freely and engagingly, even though parts of his story did not show him in a very favourable light.

In the early 1940s he was a young office boy working on a magazine called *Asi* in Mexico City. He aspired to be a reporter, and lived in awe of his boss, a journalist called Gregorio Ortega, who was teaching Spota his trade and who, one evening, gave his young protégé a copy of *The Bridge in the Jungle* to read. As they walked home from the office together, Spota asked about the author of the novel and Ortega outlined the little that was known, adding that the few facts were surrounded by a tissue of fiction and legend. The person who discovered Traven, said Ortega, would be a great reporter. These words stuck in Spota's mind and fired his ambition: 'I was a young man then. I was impressed by the possibility of become a great, really great, newspaperman in my country and, if possible, all over the world. So I started an obsession.'

Spota began by reading his way through Traven's novels, and over the next few years made enquiries of everyone who might give him a lead. He learned that Esperanza Lopez Mateos was the author's representative; he heard the tale that Traven had been an anarchist in Munich; he heard stories of the evasive Hal Croves meeting Huston. Through a third party and via a post-office box number Spota even managed to write to Traven. In the brief typed letter he received in reply, the author slipped him with an amusing sidestep. Never listen to other people's advice, wrote Traven, not even his own, because people always gave advice according to the state of their liver. That was all. In six years Spota had not got very far.

His break through came by way of a friend who worked in one of Mexico City's leading banks, the London and Mexico. This man knew that Spota, by now working for *Mañana* magazine, was seeking Traven and mentioned to him that there was

a security box at his bank in the name of Berick Traven Torsvan
– was this any help?

Spota's instinct told him that he was on to something. 'I used
to have a very good feel as a reporter, every reporter must have
a good feel. This time I feel something. I went to the bank,
made some moves, not always legal – but we are reporters anyway – and I get a small short cut to this box.' Inside the security
box he found evidence that it had been rented in Torsvan's
name since 1934 and a letter for a Maria de la Luz Martinez
at Post-Office Box 49, Acapulco.

Spota went to Acapulco, where, in his words, he 'made some
friends at the post office', and kept watch. A dark Mexican lady
of about forty came to collect letters from P.O. Box 49 and Spota
followed her to 901, Costa Grande Avenue, about a mile from
the town centre. A sign outside proclaimed that this was Cashew Park, a sort of beer garden specialising in a drink made
from the fruit of what the advertising leaflet called 'the most
aristocratic tree of the tropics – The Divine Cashew Tree'.

PARQUE CACHU

CASHEW PARK

901 Avenida Costa Grande
‹Camino de Pié de la Cuesta›

Tome los camiones "Aviación" o los
Pasito-Parque Cachú-Mozimba
Cerramos todos los días a las 21 Hs.
Permiso de Operación No. 2575

VISITORS WELCOME

Surely, you have enjoyed cashew nuts and you have
liked them; but you have never seen a cashew tree,
never seen or tasted a cashew fruit, never seen
a cashew nut in the raw. Come and rest in the
shade of the most aristocratic tree of the tropics:
The Divine Cashew Tree
One mile and one eighth from the center of Acapulco
on the highway to Pie de la Cuesta
Welcome:
We close at 9:00 P. M.

CASHEW PARK
Parque Cachú

Through the gate Spota could see that the gardens were full of cashew trees, under which there were tables and chairs. In size, the holding was about 30,000 square metres, and besides the fruit trees there was a house and a large vegetable patch. The whole place was surrounded by a high wire fence. Maria de la Luz Martinez lived here with the owner of Cashew Park, who was apparently an American, known locally as 'El Gringo'.

Spota was well pleased with his reconnaissance, but before attempting an assault he had one other check to make. All foreigners had to register with the authorities in Mexico and Spota had previously searched the government records in vain for any trace of B. Traven. He now searched again, looking for the name Torsvan, and this time he was lucky. No. 30666 of the Immigration Services' Form 14 – the application for an identity card – was in the name of Traven Torsvan, filled in on July 12th, 1930. It carried two photographs, full face and three-quarter profile, of the younger Torsvan, who cut a dapper figure in a dark jacket, light shirt and bow-tie. He stared firmly out from rather hooded eyes. His nose was prominent, his mouth tilted down at the sides and his left ear stood out, large and shapely.

According to the details on the card Torsvan was an American Protestant, born in Chicago on March 5th, 1890. He was 1·68 metres tall; his hair was fair; his nose, straight; skin, white; eyes, blue, and he was clean-shaven. In 1930 he had been single and an engineer: he had entered Mexico in June 1914 through Juarez on the border with Texas. His permanent address was given as 17 Isabel la Catolica in Mexico City, but the diligent Spota dug out from another file the more up-to-date address in Acapulco. So, the owner of Cashew Park was an American *and* he was the owner of the bank security box *and* his Christian name was registered as Traven. Spota went back to Acapulco to stalk 'El Gringo'.

Spota and a colleague, Fernando Lopez, posing as post-office workers on holiday, visited Cashew Park on the hot afternoon of July 17th, 1948. They were startled to be met by a mass of dogs, about twenty-five of them of all sizes and colours, barking menacingly. Señora Martinez came out and quietened them. Spota recognised her as the woman he had followed. The two reporters ordered some food and began chatting to the Mexican woman, who told them that she had married the master of the place around the time they had bought this land, about eighteen years earlier. Her husband was a strange man, she said, he didn't have many friends and didn't talk to people much. He worked a lot in his garden or in his office and he had a large library with books on all kinds of subjects, in both English and Spanish.

As they were talking, the heavy afternoon rain began to fall and drove them indoors to the café. The reporters could hardly believe their luck, for they were not the only ones driven in by the rain: in from the garden came 'El Gringo'. He was a short slight man with fair, greying hair. His face and neck were very tanned, his eyes bright blue, and his lips thin; it was the man from the immigration card, but much older. He looked fragile but healthy, Spota thought. He seemed worried by the visitors and wanted to know who they were, but after a while he relaxed and came to drink with them. When he heard that Spota and his friend were on holiday, Torsvan immediately lectured them about what they were doing wrong. They shouldn't go to resorts like Acapulco. What they ought to do was visit the romantic and beautiful places of Mexico, which he was only too pleased to talk about and list for them, places like Tabasco, Chiapas, Durango, Oaxaca–the wilder and more out of the way places.

He told them stories; he talked about the Mexican Indians and their superstitions; he spoke proudly about his garden. The talking went on for over four hours and the old man seemed to enjoy himself drinking with the two pretenders, so much so that when they left he shook hands with them and urged them to return. The reporters had enjoyed themselves, too, and were confident that, with a little effort, 'El Gringo' could be deceived into giving himself away.

Two days later they did return; Torsvan was working on his land but eventually joined them for a drink. The afternoon got off to an uncomfortable start, for El Gringo was annoyed by a suggestion that the song birds, which abounded in the trees, might be caught and kept in cages and he was made nervous by the camera the journalists had at their table. When he had relaxed he gave the reporters two bossy little homilies. The first was to Lopez, who knowing that Torsvan was registered as a Protestant, said what a good and tolerant religion this was. Their host immediately proposed that Lopez should convert to Protestantism, that when he returned to Mexico City he should buy a good Bible (Torsvan told him where) and that he should begin studying it. Both reporters were taken aback by this evangelical fervour.

Next, on that July afternoon, Torsvan expounded on a subject of greater interest to his fellow drinkers, the matter of a person's identity. Of what value was a birth certificate, asked Torsvan? Someone might present a birth certificate as evidence of identity but could anyone prove that the presenter and the individual named on the certificate were the same? Spota recalled how the hero of *The Death Ship* was a man tormented by the desire of others for proof of his identity. ' "You ought to have some papers to show who you are," the police officer advised me. "I do not need any papers; I know who I am," I said.' How interesting that the old man in Acapulco shared this preoccupation.

Torsvan and Señora Martinez left to go to the cinema, and Spota and Lopez left also. They considered doubling back to search the house but then thought better of it. Not that scruples had made a sudden and uncharacteristic appearance; they were simply afraid of the twenty-five unfriendly-looking dogs and of Señora Martinez's brother, who lived next door and carried a gun. In any case, things were going well for them. 'El Gringo', though cautious, had lowered his guard and Spota, fighting to his own rather than the Marquess of Queensberry's rules, was about to land a distinct foul blow.

He intercepted Torsvan's mail. To Robinson and me, Spota was a little shame-faced about this: 'You know all the ways can lead you to God. A good reporter has many ways to get the things he wants. Well, now it's history – I made a friend in the post office and I am a little indiscreet and we have a great curiosity.' Whether or not money changed hands was not quite clear, but certainly Spota was able to see all the letters arriving at P.O. Box 49.

The first fruits of this arrangement, a couple of family letters to Señora Martinez, were of no use to the news hounds. They waited. On July 20th they visited Cashew Park again and their

host lent them some books to read while he worked. Spota was
handed *Man, the Unknown* by Alexis Carrel and as he flicked
through it a small piece of paper fluttered out. It was a post
office receipt for a parcel sent on September 13th, 1938,
despatched from Acapulco to an address in Zürich, Switzerland
– the address of Joseph Wieder, the European agent of B.
Traven.

On the same day, the skulduggery with the post paid off. Spota
intercepted a letter to Martinez which came in a personalised
envelope from Gabriel Figueroa. Spota was acquainted with
Figueroa and knew that his sister-in-law was Esperanza Lopez
Mateos, Traven's translator. It was an envelope to open. Inside,
there were three letters. One was from Figueroa to Señora Martinez, in which he explained that Esperanza was very ill and
asked Señora Martinez to 'inform Mr Traven that his film *The
Treasure of the Sierra Madre* has been a great success, and that
I will send him newspaper cuttings etc.' The second enclosure
confirmed a close link between Martinez and Traven: it was
a note from a Swiss bank for the account of M.L. Martinez,
which Figueroa described as 'a slip from the bank for Mr
Traven'. Then there was a short letter to Esperanza from
Wieder in Switzerland referring to this money advance, and
at the bottom of this letter was another, written with obvious
difficulty by an unsteady hand. In content it was only a further
message about the money but its significance for the reporters
was that it appeared to have been written to the author by
Esperanza on her sick bed. For Spota this was enough; he was
convinced that the man in Acapulco must be Traven and that
triumph was at hand.

He returned once more to the garden at Cashew Park and
engaged 'El Gringo' in another lengthy conversation. For five
hours Spota tried to lead him on. They talked about American
politics, Mexican politics, and the virtues of the cashew nut
before Spota again brought up the subject of Traven. Torsvan
carefully dodged the hints and questions and referred always
to 'the author of the books' as a quite separate being. Spota
was offered a meal with Torsvan and, while breaking bread
at the man's table, he maintained his pursuit. Torsvan, aware
or not of what Spota was up to, began sowing the seeds of what
were to become further mysteries. He said he knew that the

author Traven had not written a line since 1934 or 1935, and
that it was clear that something strange had happened or that
illness had struck, for in the book *The Rebellion of the Hanged*
there was a startling change in style early in the work. He didn't
know what, but something, surely, had affected the author. He
dropped further clues, suggesting to Spota that the man he
sought was in Davos in Switzerland; did Spota know about
Davos? He did, the TB sanatorium in which Thomas Mann
had set his novel *The Magic Mountain* was there. Quite right,
said Torsvan, that's where he should look for Traven. It was
not only TB patients who went to Davos, he said cryptically,
mental patients could also be treated there. Spota tried to make
sense of what he was hearing. First, this man Torsvan seemed
to string him along with the notion that he could be the author;
then he pointed him in quite other directions. These were
complications Spota could do without, and he resolved to bring
this game to a conclusion.

On Tuesday July 26th, 1948, Spota mustered his troops for
a frontal assault, taking Lopez with him and deploying a photographer Enrique 'Fatty' Diaz. The ground he chose for the
encounter was not Torsvan's home soil at Cashew Park but the
village square of Mozimba on the outskirts of Acapulco, where
'El Gringo' went every afternoon to collect mail and buy a
newspaper and food. Spota hid in a parked car and watched.
At ten minutes to six he spotted Torsvan, in dark glasses, walk-
ing slowly up the street. He looked a vulnerable, almost pathetic
figure, this little man in baggy trousers, who, in the evening
sun, cast a long shadow. He carried a large shoulder bag and
a gasoline tin, and he was intent on his newspaper.

'Fatty' Diaz was signalled into action, and he stepped out
of the shadows and began taking photographs. Torsvan took
fright when he saw him, he covered his face with his hands and
hurried away, while Spota and Lopez left their car and gave
chase. Torsvan turned, shaking with rage, and shouted at them:
'This is an abominable thing to do ... you and your photo-
graphers', but the hard-nosed Diaz continued to snap away and
again the old man turned and fled. Spota smelled blood and
he and Lopez soon caught up with Torsvan, who stopped and,
still trembling, asked: 'Why do you follow me? Why are you
taking photographs? Why don't you leave me in peace? I am

a good man. I don't do harm to anybody. Why are you doing this to me?' Diaz took another photograph.

The pictures were in the *Mañana* magazine that Spota handed to us. They showed a scrawny old man hurrying across a dusty street with the two young journalists, one on each side. There was a picture of the three of them on a street corner, under a palm tree, and one of the old man desperately turning away to avoid the camera. Indeed, for all Diaz's bulldozing style none of the photographs caught Torsvan full face. But the pursuit worked. Eventually Torsvan relented and having cadged a piece of chewing gum from his pursuers agreed to talk with them in a cheap and broken-down bar. He was still angry and when accused directly of being Traven he snapped back: 'You are a son of a bitch. I am not B. Traven.'

The stories tumbled from him. The man who had written the books had left the country some years earlier during the rule of President Cardenas, when foreigners had had to register; Traven was in fact his cousin, and in any case he was dead. Spota pressed him: why had Traven left Mexico? Because he did not want any difficulties, said Torsvan. And his real name was a secret which no one would ever discover because the author had taken every possible precaution to hide it. Beers were ordered. The questions continued and Torsvan changed his tune. B. Traven was not a nom de plume, after all, but the real name of the author. Torsvan said his own Christian name was Berick but the author's Christian name was Barbick. An ancestor, a Norwegian seaman, had visited the coast of Maine in the United States and had been particularly well treated by the residents of a town called Barbick there, so the name of the town had been passed on as a family name. Then Torsvan switched again, pretending now not to understand or not to hear the questions.

Spota became impatient and irritated. He came clean, confessed his name and occupation and said that he had papers that could prove Torsvan was Traven. There was still no surrender. 'Why do you keep asking me if I am the writer? I have told you that I am not the person you are looking for. Why are you trying so hard to hurt me?' In reply to Spota's insistence, Torsvan offered an interesting story which was perhaps the origin of the 'other man' theories I had heard from Baumann

and Goss. The fact was, said Torsvan, that the man Traven
had not written the books alone, there had been more than
one person involved. He, Torsvan, had had a hand in one of
the books and received a share of the royalties for that particular work, hence the money he had been sent from Switzerland. If Spota were to read the books again, more closely, he
would notice that in some of them there were things that only
a clever woman could have written, perhaps that woman was
Esperanza Lopez Mateos. And what is more, said Torsvan, the
man Traven had only witnessed for himself a very little of what
he had written about; most of the stories consisted of things
he had been told at second hand. Traven had worked in the
oil fields of Tampico but he'd never worked on the land with
the peasants, which was why, said Torsvan, there were so many
mistakes in his books. Traven just didn't know Mexico that
well.

This last was a plausible tale but Spota was unshaken in his
belief that he had made his catch. For now, though, the talk
was getting him nowhere and he and his colleagues allowed
Torsvan to leave. A meeting was arranged for the following
Friday at Cashew Park.

When the journalists arrived for this final encounter they
were met by Señora Martinez, who said straight away that the
photographer, 'Fatty' Diaz, was not to come in and would have
to go away before the others could enter. Torsvan was working
in his yard, treating some wood against woodworm but after
a couple of hours he changed, joined the visitors and invited
them to eat at the house. It was a fairly humble dwelling, Spota
noticed, and he guessed that Torsvan had built it himself. They
sat in a small room which sported a picture of Franklin D.
Roosevelt and one of General Marshall. Spota commented on
an old typewriter which was on a desk near the window. 'Yes,'
said Torsvan, 'I write a bit for American magazines using the
name Kraus. But many of my articles have been rejected
because they are no good.' This would hardly be the case, he
suggested, if he were Traven.

For lunch they had roast duck. Torsvan, aiming to even the
account a little, began by teasing his guests and when they had
finished eating he told them that the bird had been Señora Martinez's pet, which she had nursed when it had a broken leg as

a baby. Having wrong-footed his guests with this unlikely tale, he insisted they listen to an old legend he wanted to tell them. About a hundred years ago, he said, there were three hunters: one wanted to kill a deer, one a tiger and one a wild goose. There was just one special place where they could bag these animals, they were told, and they would have to go out very early in the morning. So, at first light the hunter who was after the wild goose left the camp to stalk his prey. The day dragged on and he saw no sign of the goose. Eventually it became dark and he had to return to the camp in a foul mood only to be greeted by his colleagues who were laughing at him. They had caught their animals but he had gone in search of a wild goose and found only a phantom – because you can never catch a wild goose, it doesn't exist.

Torsvan meant the story to have great significance to his guests, and there was no need for them to ask who the wild goose was meant to represent. He sipped his drink and continued on the offensive. He was definitely not B. Traven, he did not believe they had proof and if they published anything about him he would simply leave Mexico and go to his country, the United States. He went further and told Spota that he would kill himself if he published his story, and that Spota would have to live with a death on his conscience. Spota was unmoved. 'I said to him: "Well, that's your choice. That's your problem, not mine." I was very cynical then. And I published the story and fortunately for literature and for humanity, he did not kill himself.'

The story was carried in the issue of *Mañana* for August 7th, 1948, and, with it, Spota achieved his ambition to be recognised as an ace reporter, even winning a prize as Mexican Journalist of the Year. There was an interesting postscript. A month after publication, the editor of *Mañana* received a letter, which was sent from England and postmarked London. It was a typed letter from B. Traven, himself, saying that Spota was a liar and that he, Traven, was living happily in London. The man in Acapulco was certainly not him.

Spota reacted swiftly to this threat to his new-found fame. 'With the smartness of a reporter I took the letter to the Technological Institute of Mexico and we discovered this: the paper it was written on was Mexican; the ink of the typewriter was

Mexican; the glue of the envelope was Mexican. So it was easy to see that he had sent the letter to a friend in London and the friend sent the letter back to Mexico.'

Spota was a little embarrassed about the whole episode now. He had broken confidence, he had broken the law, he had hounded an elderly man and when Robinson asked him if, looking back, he would do the same again, he said that he would not. 'Now, because I am older and because I understand the man and his reasons better, if I got the chance to get him again I would keep my mouth shut and not do a single thing to uncover his secrets. I think that the man has a right to be himself.'

Spota's sleuthing had made it look certain that Torsvan was the author, Traven. If he were not, why on earth should Traven go to the length of writing to deny it and arrange for the letter to be posted in England? It would be most convenient for the anonymous Traven to have the wrong man identified. The only reason for him to take action to challenge Spota's claim was if the journalist was right. And there was the great bank of circumstantial evidence which Spota had accumulated. Torsvan received moneys from B. Traven's agent in Switzerland, moneys which were payable in the name B. Traven; he was in close touch with Esperanza Lopez Mateos, the author's agent and translator; he lived with Maria de la Luz Martinez, the chief contact for Traven at that time; Torsvan knew about the Mexico Traven wrote about, in particular the Indians of the south; he had a detailed knowledge of the Traven canon, and he was wont to boast about the qualities of the author.

It was still just possible to cast Torsvan as a member of a conspiracy. His conflicting stories and explanations would be the perfect way to hide a plot and if, say, Torsvan had got hold of the works but not written them, if that were an explanation of his extreme secrecy, it was more than likely that, when cornered, he would spin a web of confusion around himself. He was tied to the issuing of the books and the receipt of money for them, but that didn't prove that he had written them, nor that he was the rightful recipient of the money. And perhaps the claim that there was more than one writer involved was true. It would explain the absence of a single Traven figure and why no one was permitted to come close to the author.

I felt I was struggling as I played with this hypothesis. Every-

thing Torsvan said and did fitted with an explanation which
made him Traven. To be sure, he denied it but that was only
to be expected; there was never much chance that, after twenty
years of hiding and deliberate confusion, the author would turn
round and own up when finally tapped on the shoulder. And
there was an enticing ambivalence about Torsvan's attitude towards Spota. At some moments he had seemed on the point
of going along with him and admitting that he was the author;
at others he had drawn back, faked a lack of interest, pretended
not to hear or understand, become outraged. It was as if he
could not decide whether to own up or not. The hero of *The
Death Ship* had known these same tensions. He, too, had been
pressed with questions of identity and had been unable to allow
them all to go unanswered. 'I might just ignore their questions
and say nothing. Yet who is he that could stand a hundred questions and answer none?'

The name Hal Croves came up only briefly in our interview
with Luis Spota. He took it for granted that the man he had
tracked down in Acapulco, living under the name Traven Torsvan, was the same man as Hal Croves, who had visited John
Huston. The names Croves and Torsvan and Traven all
emanated from Acapulco, and the photographs 'Fatty' Diaz
had taken of Torsvan showed him to be not unlike the man
snapped unawares on the set of *The Treasure of the Sierra Madre*.
When Spota carried out his below-the-belt investigation it was
only a year since the making of the film and a few months since
Croves's letters to *Time* and *Life*, so he was following a still warm
trail. And I knew that, in the twenty years between Spota's
article and the old man's death, both names, Croves and Torsvan, had been used as alternatives for the same person. Thus,
the evidence we had assembled from the friends and acquaintances of Hal Croves pointing to his being Traven could be
added to the powerful circumstantial case established by Luis
Spota for Torsvan being Traven.

It was not yet game, set and match – but there was every
reason to believe that the life of Hal Croves held the key to
the works of B. Traven. Nothing we were to hear from Gabriel
Figueroa was to divert us from that view.

13 'It's a Little Complicated'

Gabriel Figueroa lived not far from Spota in the Coyoacan district of Mexico City. We arrived at the address to be confronted by a high stone wall and huge wooden gates, which opened into a large garden laid with lawns and fig trees. As we were led through the garden by a servant, Figueroa emerged from his house and hurried over to offer us a cheerful greeting. He was a short, slightly built and rather dapper man, who I guessed was in his sixties. He had high cheekbones, a grey moustache, and thinning hair. He was carefully turned out in a jumper and cravat and, with his upright walk, could have been the retired head waiter of a grand hotel.

We made three visits to Figueroa in all. Robinson and I went on our own the first time, and spent a couple of hours drinking black coffee with Figueroa, listening to him talk in his lilting Mexican accent about Croves. Two more visits were necessary because the Curse of Traven was still our escort. Emilio had been working like a demon to mend his new American camera and had twice been convinced, in vain, that all was well with it. Ever optimistic, he brought it to film Gabriel Figueroa, a considerable risk as Emilio was already nervous about this assignment. Figueroa had photographed the films made by Luis Buñuel in Mexico as well as several big Hollywood movies, so Emilio would be performing in front of a master of his own profession.

Sure enough, the camera went wrong during Figueroa's first answer and, although we tried twice more, we had to abandon filming for the day. Poor Emilio paced up and down, his eyes turned to the heavens, his fists beating his thighs in an agonised

138

demonstration of grief and embarrassment. He trembled, he apologised endlessly, he shook his head in disbelief. Figueroa did not appear to mind in the least, in fact he was positively amused. The funny thing was, he said, that the last time he had been interviewed for a film about Traven the camera had broken down then as well. That camera crew also had to go away and come back on another day. It was almost, he said, as if there was something trying to stop him telling what he knew. He burst out laughing at this thought.

The Curse may have been obstructive but its powers were distinctly short-lived and, when we returned to Figueroa, we were able to film smoothly enough. One of the first things he told us confirmed that Croves and Torsvan were indeed the same person. Figueroa, who only ever knew the old man as Hal Croves, used to loan him a room in what was now the guest house, outside which we were filming. Figueroa showed us the room, which had later been used by one of his children. Croves stayed there when he made visits to Mexico City from his home in Acapulco. Figueroa remembered one time in particular, just after the *Mañana* article about Torsvan had appeared. Croves arrived in a hurry and very upset and asked if he could stay until all the fuss had died down. The man Figueroa knew as Hal Croves was the man fleeing from Cashew Park. To Figueroa, as to many others, there was also no doubt that this man was the writer B. Traven.

It was through Figueroa that Esperanza Lopez Mateos became the Mexican translator of the Traven books. Early in 1939 Figueroa read *The Bridge in the Jungle* and wanted to make a film of it, so he asked Esperanza, who was his cousin and his sister-in-law (she was married to his brother), to see if she could get in touch with the author. She wrote to Traven through Knopf's and, although she was refused the film rights, Esperanza was fired with enthusiasm for the books and wrote again to Traven, offering to translate his work into Spanish as she considered the Spanish translations in existence to be poor. He wrote back to say that he was not interested in a woman translating his books because he did not believe that any woman could grasp the power and strength of his work. Esperanza was not to be put off and suggested that she translate one of his books for nothing – she chose *The Bridge in the Jungle* – and that if he was not satisfied with her version, that would be the end of it. She translated the whole novel and sent it off. Traven was won over. He congratulated her on her work and said she could publish her text as it stood. That was not all. In the enthusiastic embrace of an isolated and lonely man, he made Esperanza his representative for Latin America, said she could translate all his books and gave her the right to publish them.

As a result of all this the film rights were forthcoming and in the ten years from 1954 to 1963 Gabriel Figueroa worked on four Traven films. He was lighting cameraman on a production of *The Rebellion of the Hanged*, on a portmanteau film of Mexican stories and on *The White Rose*, and he directed a prize-winning film of Traven's short story 'Macario'. For this last, and for *The Rebellion*, the scriptwriter was the author's friend Hal Croves. Neither Esperanza nor Figueroa ever met anyone who admitted to being Traven. They corresponded with the author and with his contact, M.L. Martinez; they met only his collaborator, Croves. Indeed, they became close friends with Croves, guessed that he was really the author and referred to him as such among themselves, but always to him they maintained the fiction that he was merely a representative for the absent Traven.

Figueroa's first meeting with Croves let him know what he was in for. Esperanza was supposed to meet Croves in a café in Mexico City, but on the day of the appointment she felt ill and asked Figueroa if he would go in her place. She told her cousin to look out for a slightly built elderly man, with a long nose, greying hair and a bald patch. When Figueroa reached the café there were few customers present and he quickly spotted the man, who was sitting quietly over a cup of coffee. Figueroa went up to him and asked if he were Mr Croves. He turned round, looked carefully at his accoster and said, 'No.' Figueroa could not be certain that he had approached the right person, so he left the café to find the nearest telephone and called Esperanza, saying that there must have been some mistake. She asked him to describe the man he had seen and when he had done so, she was adamant that this was definitely Croves and told Figueroa to go back and explain carefully that he was her cousin in order to reassure the old man. Figueroa hurried back, but by the time he reached the café again Croves had vanished.

There was always an aura of mystery around Croves. He used to disappear without explanation, sometimes travelling for months down in the jungle in the south; sometimes driving up across the United States' border in his ancient Chevrolet. Figueroa went on one or two of these latter jaunts, when Croves would ferry into Mexico people who were in trouble for their politics in the United States. Croves was not an active member of any political organisation, but was doing his bit to help people who were in a fix – people without papers, perhaps; people who were in the same sort of jam that Gerard Gales had been in.

In all his years of friendship with Croves, Figueroa stuck religiously to the name Hal in his communications with him. In spite of all he heard from Esperanza, who worked closely with Croves on the Traven manuscripts and who accepted him as the author without question, Figueroa only called him Hal. Sometimes he saw people come up to Croves and address him as Mr Traven to see what he would do, but, when this happened, Croves would adopt a fixed expression and ignore them.

Figueroa also believed that Croves–Traven had been the German anarchist, Ret Marut. Groves often denied that he understood German but Figueroa knew that he spoke it well. There was not even much secret about it, for after Figueroa had sent his son to a German school in Mexico Croves used to take the boy aside for German conversation. And Croves was put into a strange ferment when, in the 1960s, the German magazine *Stern* conducted its lengthy search into the history of B. Traven. The chief reporter went to the American cities associated with Traven's birth, Chicago and San Francisco, then travelled down to Mexico interviewing people in the Chiapas and Mexico City. Croves got wind of this project and became nervous. Figueroa reminded us that the Traven books had been banned by the Nazis in the 1930s and that Ret Marut had narrowly escaped death in Germany in 1919. It was his belief that Croves, in the paranoia of old age, had been terrified of long-delayed vengeance from the German right.

The reporters from *Stern* attempted to make an appointment with the frightened Croves, who turned to his friend for help.

He asked Figueroa if he would go to his cousin, Adolfo Lopez Mateos, the then President of Mexico, to request official protection. Figueroa spoke to the President, who passed on a telephone number at which Croves could reach him, if necessary, at any time of the day or night. This helped to calm Croves, but his fears were not completely dispelled. He told Figueroa that it was not being killed that he was afraid of. He was an old man who had lived long enough and he could face death. What frightened him was that he might be kidnapped – presumably to Germany.

When Robinson and I had visited Figueroa before the filming, we had put to him the notion that more than one writer might have had a hand in the Traven books and he had dismissed it with a patient smile. Esperanza, he said, had worked at close quarters with Croves, and she had known that there was only him involved. That was not all she had known. Figueroa adopted a secretive frown and motioned me to turn off the cassette machine with which I was recording our conversation. When I had done so, he lowered his voice and confided to us that Esperanza had known what Hal Croves's real name – the birth name of B. Traven – was. He was not sure whether Croves had told her or if she had found out. He knew that she had it because she had passed it on to him in strictest secrecy. He was far from sure that Señora Lujan knew what the real name was and believed that he was the only person alive who was party to this secret. Figueroa took the responsibility with high seriousness. He had deposited a record of the name in a hidden place, and left instructions for his wife to enable her to reach it in the event of his death.

No, he would not tell us what the real name was. He hinted that we would recognise it as the name of a powerful and wealthy family in Germany around the turn of the century. He even seemed to imply that the surname was an English as well as a German name, and we offered guesses like Smith and Schmidt, Bush and Busch. Figueroa laughed and we could wangle no more clues out of him.

We tried again in front of the camera. There was one name that we had to put to Figueroa: was Traven the son of the Kaiser? He replied, 'I don't believe it, that story ... I know the name of the family and mostly I know the background of the family and all that, so I don't believe that story of the Kaiser.'

Figueroa added that Traven had been the left-wing son of a very wealthy family. It often happened, he said, that the children of the rich were opposed to the capitalist system. In reply to Robinson's questions, he said that the name was not Torsvan and it was not Marut. Perhaps Marut, Mareth, or something like that was the name of the mother?

FIGUEROA: Well, possibly. I don't know that really because ... I have the name of the father but not the name of the mother.

QUESTION: And I have to ask you. Can you tell us the name of the family?

FIGUEROA: No, it's too soon now to say it. It involved a lot of things – politics, families, you know. It's a little complicated. That is why I think it has been ... kept out.

'A little complicated.' Figueroa had hit on a nice euphemism and had given us something to ponder. That evening, as Robinson and I took our regulation two Margueritas before dinner, we went over what Figueroa had told us. Had he been pulling our leg when he allowed us to know that he had the birth name of Traven? We thought not. He had seemed perfectly serious and if he had wanted to make fun of us he could easily have fabricated a tale or slipped us a sensational name which we would have dashed off to pursue. It was probable that he had *a* name but how on earth could we discover if it was *the* name? Esperanza, the source of it, was dead. For the moment, we might as well accept Figueroa's tantalising story at face value. We now had to turn our attention to Señora Rosa Elena Lujan.

We had already made a sighting of her house. When Robinson and I had returned to our hotel after dinner on our first night in Mexico City, it was not late and, as I had noted from a map of the city that we were not far from the Rio Mississippi, we decided to take a first look at the house of secrets. We walked half a mile along the wet pavements of the Rio Panuco until it crossed the Rio Mississippi. I had seen photographs of this street showing a handsome row of sturdy palm trees down the centre, but these were gone. The Rio Mississippi is now a one-way street leading off a motorway and at most hours of the day is enveloped in the noise and fumes of the frenzied traffic. Few cars were about on that damp Saturday evening and we quickly spotted number sixty-one, a little way up to our right on the other side of the street. The treasure chest was waiting to be opened. It was a modern, neatly designed house, of three storeys, presenting a bland and well-protected face to the world. The concrete bands of its balconies, the heavily curtained windows and the large metal double doors added a secretive expression. At last we were coming close to the man we had been trailing. Croves had lived and died here and no one knew more about Traven than he. No one was more likely to be Traven than he. And within this house lived Señora Lujan, the owner of the Traven copyrights.

We did not stand looking for long. We turned and walked back to the Hotel Bristol through the cool night air, for once saying little. We were now tired, slightly drunk and wary of an anti-climax, as well we might be – two pilgrims who had glimpsed the holy of holies for the first time.

14 Mr Torsvan

We paid our first visit to Señora Rosa Elena Lujan on Sunday July 24th, 1977. The metal street doors were opened for us by a short round maid, dressed in black, who led us through a covered passage and into the house. We came into a large room which occupied most of the downstairs. It was closely carpeted, decorated in soft colours and expensively furnished with pictures, ornaments and a large marble dining table. It was not how you might imagine an anarchist's living-room to look and I recalled that many aficionados of the Traven novels were suspicious of the comfortable and elegant life-style of the latter-day Croves. At the back of the room there were French windows on to a small high-walled garden, which was dominated by a huge and rather florid bust of Croves, two or three times life size.

This heroic bust has been an object of interest for the conspiracy-minded. It is described as a head of B. Traven and, as it is not a particularly good likeness of the elderly Croves, some people have guessed that Croves had obtained this authentic head of Traven and stuck it in his back yard to help support his claims to authorship. There is, however, no doubt that the sculptor Federico Canessi took Croves to be Traven and that this was a portrait bust of the man who lived in Rio Mississippi – Canessi was a close friend of Croves and attended his funeral. The problem of the likeness was solved for me when I saw a photograph of Canessi with the bust; it was clear that the portrait was as much like the artist as the sitter. Off the main room was a kitchen, in which the two maids could often be heard shrieking and giggling and, to the front of the house, a small library, into which Robinson and I were now shown.

It was a darkish room with brown walls and black leather furniture, dominated by a large black and white portrait, slightly idealised, of Croves. He gazed out from it at an angle with a noble and far-seeing look. There was also a collection of most beautiful figurines and sculptures, which I took to be the work of Mexican Indians, and, what occupied most of our attention, a wall lined with book-cases holding different editions of Traven's books and works by others on literature and the antiquities of Mexico. I spotted Michael Baumann's book and Judy Stone's, and several other books about Traven. The mass of the material made a telling impression. The last vestiges of doubt about Croves began peeling away, for this was surely the house and library of B. Traven. As if to protect his claim, a cast of Croves's slim and elegant hands sat proprietorially in front of the book-shelves.

After about ten minutes we heard Señora Lujan descend the stairs, and she came in to meet us. We shook hands and introduced ourselves. She was a short, elegant woman with dark hair, dark skin and dark, searching eyes. I took her to be in her mid-fifties (she was actually sixty-two), but she was a woman who had always been attractive and who could pass for almost any age. She was dressed with a calm stylishness in a cream silk shirt and tweed jacket and was at the first, as she was in all my meetings with her, friendly but formal, courteous but a little distant. She had the composure of a rich and successful woman and, with her dark colouring and slightly irregular features, exuded an air of the exotic, which was utterly fitting for the widow of B. Traven.

Some coffee was brought and we sat talking in general terms about our film and the people we had seen so far. Señora Lujan made it obvious that she disapproved of some (Baumann for his scepticisms, Spota for his dirty tricks), approved of others (Stone, Kohner, Hill) and was curious about what we had heard from Figueroa. She told us that there was a world-wide interest in Traven's books, and she was visited constantly by journalists and scholars wishing to know about him or study his works. She asked us to remember that it was not Traven's mystery that was interesting but his books, his greatness as a writer and a man. Altogether too much had been made of the mystery. Her life's work now, she said, was to keep the books

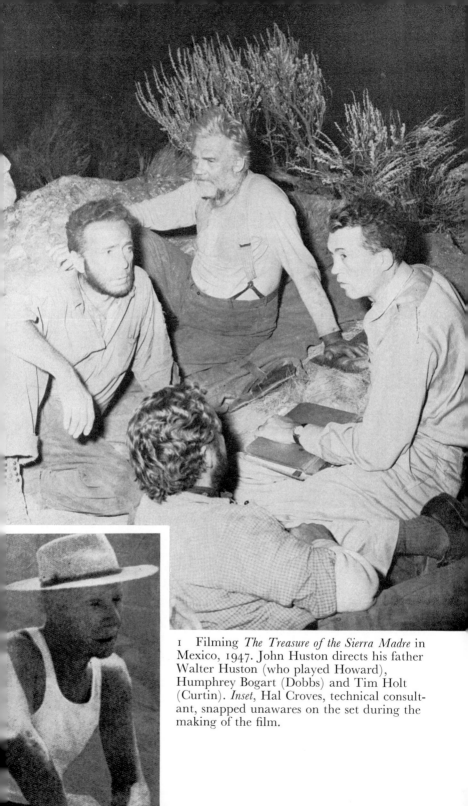

1 Filming *The Treasure of the Sierra Madre* in Mexico, 1947. John Huston directs his father Walter Huston (who played Howard), Humphrey Bogart (Dobbs) and Tim Holt (Curtin). *Inset*, Hal Croves, technical consultant, snapped unawares on the set during the making of the film.

2 Esperanza Lopez Mateos, translator and agent for B. Traven until her death in 1951.

3 The 1930 immigration card of Traven Torsvan, which Luis Spota dug out in Mexico City. It states that Torsvan first entered Mexico in 1914 at Ciudad Juarez on the Texan border and that he had been born in Chicago in 1890, making him 40 at the time of issue.

4 Filming *The Rebellion of the Hanged* in Mexico. In the foreground, back to camera and wearing dark glasses, is the scriptwriter, Hal Croves. The cameraman was Gabriel Figueroa, in centre without shirt.

5 and 6   Luis Spota corners El Gringo one afternoon in Acapulco, 1948.
'You are a son of a bitch. I am   'Why do you follow me? ... Why
not B. Traven.' Torsvan turns   don't you leave me in peace?'
away from Spota and the camera   Torsvan (right) tries to lose the
as Fernando Lopez signals to the   persistent Spota.
photographer.

7   Paul Kohner (right) and his wife, Lupita, meet Hal Croves shortly
before the old man's death. Kohner was certain that Croves was B.
Traven: 'He knew very well, as far as I was concerned, the game
was up.'

8   Part of the study, 'the bridge', in the house on Rio Mississippi, with the death mask of the man who called himself Hal Croves. Above it is a portrait of Ret Marut by the artist F. W. Seiwert, sent to Señora Lujan by Marut's former secretary.

9   Rosa Elena Lujan at home in Mexico City.

in print and bring the inspiring message they carried to as many people as possible. In an unobtrusive but effective way she let us know that we were dealing with a woman of substance and position, gently insinuating into the conversation something of her own history: her study of art, her upbringing in a prominent Mexican family, her wealthy if imprudent first husband, her friendship with the leading artists and political figures of Mexico.

As Señora Lujan answered our questions, she often slid from one aspect of her husband's life to another, or from describing an incident in his history into describing an adventure from the books. It was as if the life, the works and all the tales about Traven were part of one seamless story. At times she was almost rambling as she drove on through inconsistencies and omissions; at others the words came haltingly as she monitored them to step round potential traps and deny contradictions. Behind everything she said was a fervent belief in the value of the works. She was determined to say or do nothing which might discourage us from talking about, writing about or filming the story of B. Traven and his books.

Before we left to take Señora Lujan out to lunch, she led us up to the second floor of the house to see her husband's study, which she had kept much as he had left it. It was a bright room with windows all along one wall, from which the old man had liked to feed the birds, especially when there had still been palm trees in the street outside. This room contained hundreds more copies of Traven's books in English, German, Russian, Swedish, French, Italian and many other languages, sometimes with several copies of one edition. There were also volumes from the old man's library, works on folklore, Eastern religion, architecture, sculpture, archaeology and anthropology. And there, at the far end of the room, sandwiched between books and surrounded by small Indian sculptures and earthenware pots, was the bronze death mask of the man who had lived and worked here, the man I now had to accept as B. Traven. It was the face of a very old man with hollow cheeks and a large nose. The sunken eyes were closed and oblivious to the intrusions of these enquiring strangers. The Señora saw us gazing at this dignified head of her husband, and told us that within the family he had always liked to be called by the nautical term

'Skipper'. She herself had been the 'first mate' and her two daughters by her first marriage, Elena and Malu, the 'second and third mates'. Her husband, she said, had been a sailor and had loved the sea, and she unnecessarily reminded us of the connection with the story of *The Death Ship*. These names had begun as a game for his stepdaughters but he had taken it all seriously, referring to the study we were in as 'the bridge', always saying 'going below' rather than 'going downstairs'. You had to co-operate to look after the ship, he had said, and you had to do the same with a house.

I looked out of the windows of the bridge across the busy traffic of the street below. Directly opposite was a restaurant, the front of which was built as a life-size replica of an old sailing-ship. This must have pleased the old man. He surely had felt at home here, looked after by these attractive and loving women, able to run his own little ship according to his own rules with an obedient and trusting crew. After all those bossy letters, after all those attempts to organise people from a distance, after all the know-all advice which had been ignored, how satisfying it must have been to skipper this handsome little brig.

Malu, the Señora's younger daughter, drove us to lunch at the San Angel Inn, a restaurant in an old hacienda on the outskirts of Mexico City. It was full of well-dressed Mexican families out for Sunday lunch, and the four of us sat over Margueritas waiting for a table to come free. Señora Lujan told us that she had first met her husband in the late 1930s, when he was using the name Torsvan. She met him again in 1953 and this time he was introduced as Hal Croves, agent of the famous author B. Traven. She was to translate the film script that Croves had written for *The Rebellion of the Hanged*, and when this was done Croves engaged her to translate some Traven stories into Spanish. Over the next few years, she worked on several stories with Croves, fell in love with him, learned that he was really the author, and in 1957 they were married in San Antonio, Texas.

We moved to our table and a meal of Aztec soup, beef and fresh fruit. As we ate, Robinson and I learned something of the private life of Hal Croves. He was a kind man. He loved the Señora's daughters as his own, played with them, danced with them, educated them, talked to them. At dinner there was always a lively discussion, often political, and when the old man had had enough he would switch off his hearing aid, saying that he could not take on three women on his own. This would lead to more shouting and laughter as the others urged him to turn it back on.

He loved animals. He had two dogs, which would be in his study as he worked, parrots which ate off his plate, and a monkey. He worked late into the night and got up late; breakfast was never before ten. He did not bother about money, and, as he walked everywhere, never carried any. Sometimes he would come home without the evening newspaper because he had not been able to pay for one. As in these small matters of money, so in the large. Quite early on in his relationship with Señora Lujan he assigned all the copyrights of his work to her and they remain with her to this day. When they married, he put all financial matters in her hands, saying that she could do exactly what she wanted, that if she spent the lot in a day he didn't mind, just as long as he did not have to do anything about the money himself.*

If Croves was easy-going with money, he was demanding in other ways. Señora Lujan believed that one of the reasons he took to her so quickly was that she did not ask him questions about his change of name, his real identity or his past. During the whole of their life together, fifteen years or more, she never felt free to ask about these matters. She did not even know her husband's age, and had to guess from the different birth dates he gave her and from her knowledge of him that he was about thirty years older than she was. Croves did talk to her about his past, but it always had to be he who raised the subject and he always chose when to stop. The Señora loved to hear him talk about his life and his adventures, but even when he volunteered the subject, he would tell her to stop prying if she attempted to ask him questions. Señora Lujan only knew what her husband chose to tell her about himself and what she had been able to discover from his papers since his death.

The young stepdaughters learned early that the golden rule

* Esperanza Lopez Mateos had also been put in full charge of his finances. Traven was always desperately keen for his books to be distributed and his message heard, but money never appeared to be a primary concern.

of the household was that no one should ever talk to reporters. Croves took careful precautions to avoid being caught un- awares, always entering the house by the back door in case a newspaperman or any other unwanted or inquisitive visitor had arrived while he was out.

There must have been times when Croves's extreme caution, his suspicion and his calculated mysteriousness placed a heavy burden on the tolerance and good nature of his adopted family, however much they loved him, were mightily entertained by him, or held him in awe. The Señora recalled with laughter some instances of Croves's behaviour which she had borne with stoicism and good grace, but which might have driven many another to distraction. She once went into his study and found him typing in German (she always knocked and went straight in because if she just knocked and waited, he did not answer). Croves had always told her that he did not understand German, so she was surprised to find him typing in the language and hesitantly made some remark about it. Croves turned to her, said firmly, 'I don't know any German', and went on with what he was doing. 'So that,' said Señora Lujan, 'was that.'

Croves spread this deliberate confusion outside the home as well as within it. When he and Señora Lujan were travelling in the state of Oaxaca, looking for filming locations, he decided that they should use false names at an hotel. Why on earth should you ever give your real name, he had asked, who were these people that they should know what your name is? For Croves, names were possessions that you used sparingly. He made up some names for them both and they registered in these at the hotel, before going out to look round the town. When the Señora went back alone and asked for the key to her room, she was unable to remember her new name and had to go off in search of Croves to find out what they were calling themselves.

There was no mistaking the delight that Señora Lujan took in describing her husband's eccentric ways. She enthused about his intelligence, his energy, and several times laid emphasis on what she termed his 'vigour'. We were to know that he was 'a real man', as she put it, right up to the end. She admired his determination to do as he pleased: to stop writing stories in order to work on film scripts, to study the Mayan culture,

to learn the Indian languages, or to explore the pyramids. He
made what he wanted of his life and remained true to his own
vision, and Señora Lujan was proud and happy to have shared
some part of that life. She had learned so much from so 'fascinating' (a word which she used of him often) a man.

Lunch is taken late in Mexico and it was well after six o'clock
by the time we finished and I paid the bill. As we drove back
into the city Señora Lujan touched again on something she had
mentioned before, Croves's fondness for Britain and the British.
I took it as a kind of flattery, a piece of good public relations
for the Traven story, though three points caught my attention.
Croves had evidently wanted to get married in Britain, at
Gretna Green of all places; the Señora had visited London with
him, staying at an hotel near Marble Arch (this could have
been when the fleeting visit to the offices of Jonathan Cape took
place); and the name Hal Croves was supposed to be made up
from two Scottish names which were in her husband's family.
His grandfather had been of Scottish descent and was called
Croves, and another Scottish branch of the family was called
Halward, from which he had extracted the Christian name
Hal. Further questioning produced nothing more specific.

We drove to Malu's modern apartment, on the other side
of the great Chapultepec Park from the Rio Mississippi. She
had once shot a home movie of her stepfather and offered to
find it for us. The projector was set up and switched on. Malu
ran through two reels of herself and other young Mexicans gam-
bolling on the beaches and in the swimming pools of Acapulco
before she found the right spool. There were more beach scenes
on the front, followed by a shot of a little girl in a garden and
then a group of adults walked self-consciously out of a house.
In their midst was a bony old man in glasses, wearing a woolly
cardigan. This small group milled around for a bit and then
they all walked back into the house, Croves going ahead, his
large bald spot clearly visible, and Señora Lujan waving and
laughing at the camera. It was all over in a few seconds and
we ran it again. I watched Croves closely. He did no capering
for the camera. His large head might have been chiselled from
stone, his expression remained straight and he looked slightly
uncomfortable about the little charade. Malu let me take the
film away to have a copy made.

Next she brought out a cassette recording on which she said there might be a snatch of the 'Skipper's' voice. It began with inconsequential chatter from several people, one of whom was Señora Lujan. There was then a section where some other people began speaking, and here I gradually made out the voice of Paul Kohner. This was a recording taken at that long-delayed first and last meeting between Kohner and Croves. Unfortunately, there was no sound of Croves taking part in the conversation and I was resigning myself to his not being on the tape, when there was suddenly a click followed by a brief clear passage as someone moved the microphone. In a slow, deep and deliberate voice, with an accent which to my untutored ear could have been German or Scandinavian, Hal Groves spoke out clearly. 'I am in a mess,' were the dramatic first words I heard from his lips. He went on, 'not exactly in a mess but I need some advice which perhaps you can give me. Which of the great piano virtuosos composed the Hungarian Rhapsody?' Paul Kohner supplied the answer, 'Franz Liszt'. This had to be repeated for Croves because of his deafness, and as soon as he heard it he raised his voice to Señora Lujan, 'But I told you, and you told me Brahms.'

A discussion about Liszt followed, and then Croves read out a letter he had received from an artist who was asking permission to illustrate a Traven book. I was listening to the timbre of the voice, as much as to what it said. It was a haunting, echoey voice, the voice of an actor, measured in phrasing and varied in tone. There was also a dogmatic ring, as he explained a new contract he had signed for the Traven books to be published by Hill and Wang. This bossy air was partly just the manner of a deaf old man but I fancied that I discerned in it a chime from the B. Traven letters. It was the sound of a man who had plenty of views, who liked to expound them and who wished them to be listened to. There were several interruptions on the tape and the recording ended abruptly in the middle of one of the most interesting passages, when Croves was showing an animated interest in contemporary Germany. He asked Paul Kohner if he was in regular contact with Germany, what political conditions were like there, what sort of a man this Ulbricht was. A very sour man, answered Kohner, but before either of them could explore the topic further, someone had

switched off the recorder and there remained only a dry, elec-
tronic hum.

It was an eerie feeling to sit listening to Traven speak from
beyond the grave and to watch him stutter about the screen
on a home movie. We had been granted a privileged glimpse
of the man's physical form, as if he had passed briefly as a
ghostly presence through the room. We had a sense of him:
a shadow on the wall, a slight disturbance in the air, a dis-
embodied voice asking eagerly about a far-away land. He called
himself Hal Croves, this old man; and Torsvan, and Traven.
We had seen his picture and heard his voice. But who was he?

The following day Señora Lujan showed us some photographs of Croves in his late years. They showed him with his
wife and stepdaughters in cafés and restaurants, in smiling
parties round the lunch table in Rio Mississippi, standing in
a garden, and at the funeral of a friend. There was one of the
meeting with Paul Kohner, which matched the one Kohner
had shown us, and even a sequence showing Croves, in shorts
and beach shirt, clowning with the Señora by the sea. There
he was, a touch scrawny, with the veins standing hard like rope
on his arms, but fit and trim and full of life in spite of his great
age. The Señora was prompted to remind us that he had been
'a real man' to the end. All the photographs were dominated
by his characteristic head: the heavy nose; the high sloping
forehead; the long upper lip, the wide, flat mouth, and the large
ears.

Señora Lujan also showed me some documents from the last
twenty years of her husband's life. With these, with the photographs and everything the Señora allowed me to examine, the
routine was the same. She would go upstairs to her study on the
first floor of the house and return with a selection of papers in
her hand or in a folder. I was never allowed into that study, and
on one occasion was left standing outside while the Señora went
in to fetch something for me and closed the door pointedly. I
had the impression that everything we saw had been carefully
sorted out beforehand and put ready to be brought down to
us. It was a demonstration that we were only to see so much.
Others, I knew, had had a similar experience with Señora
Lujan. What I was unable to make up my mind about
was whether she was protecting a mass of secret, possibly

sensational, material or whether she was simply keeping close tabs to prevent things being lost or stolen.

The documents were interesting. All her husband's official papers were in the name of Torsvan. The very particular Mr Hal Croves, so insistent that his friends call him Hal or Mr Croves, had no official existence. He was really Mr Torsvan, Croves was a name he had tried out on John Huston, written film scripts under and foisted off on all his friends and acquaintances, but he would always have been untraceable under that name. Croves was really Torsvan, the same Torsvan that Luis Spota had discovered in Acapulco – the documents in front of me dispelled any lingering doubt about that. The cunning old man invented the name Croves to use on all his appearances outside Acapulco, and that included the whole of the last twenty years of his life, spent in Mexico City.

Here was the letter, dated October 1st, 1951, informing Mr Traven Torsvan that he had been granted Mexican citizenship as from the following day. His first Mexican citizen's card contained his photograph, his fingerprints and some biographical facts. He was 1·68 m. tall, his eyes were blue and his hair was grey. This tallied with the immigration card, dated 1930, that Spota had dug out (allowing for Torsvan's hair turning grey in the twenty years between the two documents; he had also become a farmer rather than an engineer). The 1951 card still described him as a North American, born in Chicago, but also contained the information that his parents were Burton and Dorothy Torsvan. And there was one strange difference – the date of birth was now given as May 3rd, 1890, not March 5th of that year, as before. It was the same man all right but in those twenty-one years Mr Torsvan had changed his birthday. Señora Lujan could offer no explanation for this.

I picked up a Mexican passport issued to her husband in 1956, which confirmed the birth date as May 3rd, 1890, and the place as Chicago. Height, colour of eyes, and hair were the same as on his citizen's card and his occupation was this time described as fruit farmer. In the passport photograph, Mr Torsvan, dressed neatly in a tweed suit, looked out with a narrow-eyed and suspicious stare. The contemptuous look was directed at the despised officials who would handle this document. It was only to be expected from the man who had wanted 'to bring this business of compulsory passports out into the open'. How it must have irked him to have to apply for a passport, to hand over photograph, signature and thumbprint for some bureaucrat to approve and file away. And yet, even when apparently at the mercy of officialdom, he had managed a small revenge against the presumption of his tormentors. The passport was issued in the name of Traves Torsvan. I noticed that a vaccination certificate and an electoral registration card also had Traves

PASAPORTE.

EXPEDIDO A FAVOR DE:

TRAVES TORSVAN

instead of Traven as the Christian name, and asked Señora Lujan the reason for this. It was quite simple, she said. It was the result of one of her husband's little games. Often when people take down your name and address they mishear or make a spelling mistake and, when you notice this, you correct them. Well, her husband did not correct them. He allowed them to register his name slightly wrongly – and for it to pass, uncorrected, into their records. It was none of his business if a mistake was made. If officials were prying enough to want to know his name it was up to them to get it right, not up to him to go out of his way to help them in their intrusion. And, said the Señora, he had quietly enjoyed the knowledge that he had tricked them into an error and that this might result in confusion. They had a Traves and a Traven; let them sort it out, if they wanted.

It was a trick practised by the author of *The Treasure of the Sierra Madre*: 'Dobbs came to the window, banged his peso upon the table, and said: "Lobbs, for two nights." The clerk took up the register and wrote: "Jobbs", because he had not caught the name and was too polite to ask again.'

The last three items in this batch of papers were three Authors' Guild Cards in the name of B. Traven. The first, for 1952, was unsigned by the author and carried a New York address, care of what I guessed was a literary agency. The other two, 1966 and 1967, had B. Traven, care of R.E. Lujan at a post-office box in Mexico City and, wonder of wonders, were signed with a tiny, almost indecipherable signature. Clearly visible in the squiggle were the all-important initials B.T. My impression was that Señora Lujan wished to impress us with this first file of papers and photographs, and she had succeeded.

The Authors Guild, Inc.

1967   234 WEST 44th STREET, NEW YORK, N. Y. 10036   1967

B. Traven

MEMBER   c/o R. E. Lujan
            Apartado 2701
            Mexico 1, D.F., Mexico

ADDRESS

SIGNATURE

This card identifies a member of
The Authors Guild, Inc. and
The Authors League of America, Inc.   *Membership Secretary*

15 'Such a Fascinating Man'

'Your husband was known as Hal Croves, you were known as Mrs Croves. What relationship was Croves to Traven?'

We began the first of our several filmed interviews with Señora Lujan with this simple and obvious question, and she obliged us with a straightforward answer: 'They were both the same man.'

She added, for emphasis, that her husband had known the books so well that when he was adapting a Traven novel for the screen he would go off for the day to the hotel room, where he worked, without even taking a copy of the book with him. The Señora was a little nervous at the start of the filming and cautious throughout. She sat straight up in her chair and gave her replies with dignified formality. They were brief at first and later grew longer and more expansive, although there was always the feeling that she was rationing what she told us and releasing it only in a carefully tailored form.

We remembered the doubts Baumann and Sanora Babb had expressed about how much the Señora knew of her husband's life. Her manner did little to dispel them. She maintained a fixed and protective smile and her eyes flickered as if she were searching for a catch in every question. Sometimes she would glance suddenly away either from nerves or embarrassment. It was impossible for Robinson and me to tell if we were close to dark truths and bitter secrets or whether there really was nothing else to know but what we were hearing. What we heard was far from clear. She gave equal weight to contradictory accounts of her husband's origins and history and she readily adopted other people's theories about his life. Did she share his taste for devilment and deliberate confusion? Was she continuing his shenanigans out of wifely loyalty? Was she keeping the brew on the boil for the purely commercial purposes of promotion and publicity? Did she embrace every offered explanation in order to disguise her own ignorance of the truth? We could not decide. We admired her for championing her husband's work and for battling doughtily against all attacks on his secrecy. We were irritated by her wilful inconsistencies. We were bewildered by the cloud of vagueness in which our questions disappeared.

The crux of the matter was the question of her husband's name and birth and it was around this that the undergrowth grew thickest. His parents, said the Señora, were Burton and Dorothy Torsvan, as in his passport, but when Robinson asked her if she believed the story that her husband was the illegitimate son of the Kaiser we all became caught in the brambles.

LUJAN. Well, it has been said many times. There were rumours many, many years ago in Germany and it has been published many times. I believe what he told me. I believe my husband. He told me he was Traven, so to me he was Traven Torsvan.

QUESTION. Then how do you account for your husband looking like the Kaiser's other children? The photographs seem to suggest it.

LUJAN. Yes. He looked very much like them and we talked about the Kaiser very much, very often. He had pictures of the Kaiser. He told me many good things and bad things about him. Yes, we discussed him. And the resemblance – it is definite. Yes.

QUESTION. But then does this resemblance convince you that he might have been . . .

LUJAN. It is not a matter of convincing. I mean if he tells you that his parents are so and so. He told me his father was a poor fisherman from Norway, who after lots of difficulty was able to buy with another partner a small ship to go fishing to make a living. And he was drowned in the sea before my husband was born so that he never got to meet his father. And then his mother came to the United States and he was born there.

She neither confirmed nor denied the Kaiser story or any other explanation of his birth. It was as if the circumstance of his birth was not an historical and verifiable occurrence, but something which could be selected and altered, subject to poetic rather than factual truth. He did not want to be the son of the Kaiser, said the Señora, because he did not want anything imposed upon him. He had said to her: 'I can choose my own country; I can choose my own parents.' He rejected the idea of the Kaiser as a father and, for him, that decided the matter.

This was different from the positive account that Señora Lujan had given to Judy Stone, when she had described Croves becoming very excited in Germany and spilling out the news that the Kaiser had been his father. We tried a different tack. Robinson asked whether the Señora thought that her husband had come from a poor, working-class background or from a wealthy, upper-class family. She was sure that it was the latter. His tales about never having been to school were obviously untrue as he was a highly cultured man, who understood eight languages and played the piano and violin. She was able to tell from the way that he ate, dressed and behaved that he was from a good family. It did not sound, we said, as if her husband could really have been the son of a poor fisherman. The Señora simply laughed and said: 'Well, in this life anything is possible.' If you were married to Hal Croves, you had to feel like that.

Croves gave the Señora another story, which was equally at odds with the humble Norwegian version of his background, and which again nodded knowingly in the direction of the Kaiser. According to this story he was the close relation of a famous German woman singer of high birth (Señora Lujan could not remember the name or title but thought she had been a countess). Croves used to show his wife a theatre programme which featured the name of this woman, who, in a Traven-approved gesture, refused ever to use her title, preferring to be known as Frau so and so. This singer was one of a group of musicians who used to perform every year in Karlsbad (now Karlovy Vary in Czechoslovakia), where she met and became friends with the Kaiser and his family. Croves told his wife that his own family used to go to stay with this woman in Karlsbad for holidays. But that was all. The tale stopped just as it promised to reveal something, dribbling away to hints and whispers. With frustration growing we asked Señora Lujan, just for the record, what was her husband's original nationality?

LUJAN. My husband told me that he was born in the United States. He spent his youth part in Great Britain, part in Germany.
QUESTION. Why did he make such a mystery of his identity?
LUJAN. He didn't.

We were going round in circles. The stuff about Britain was new and I suspected that it had been lobbed in to buff up our film, by adding a domestic angle for the BBC audience. I lodged it away all the same. We put it to the Señora that, while her husband might not have disguised his identity from her, he had continuously hidden behind aliases. Maybe, she said, it all stemmed from the earliest part of his life; maybe it was the way he had been brought into the world which had made him this way.

Señora Lujan was quite clear about the fact that Ret Marut had been an earlier identity of her husband's. On her lips the Christian name had sometimes become *F*red and the surname Maru*th* but, yes, her husband had lived in Germany under that name. She enjoyed talking about this period of his life, praising the bravery and idealism of all the leaders of the Munich revolution of 1919. It had been a noble time, a time for men like her husband, who were fighters against injustice. After he had escaped he had been on the run for some years and it was around this time – and here the Señora became a little vague – that he had been a sailor. He had made short trips on various steamers or, as she put it, a trifle glibly I thought, 'on let's say death ships, because he could not show his passport'.

Although he abandoned the name Marut, he was always terrified that the reactionary forces which had taken over in Germany would somehow follow him to Mexico and take revenge. Señora Lujan, like Figueroa, had cause to remember when the *Stern* reporters were on his trail. She woke up one night to the smell of burning and, going downstairs, found her husband burning papers in the fireplace: documents, stories and letters from his Marut days. Only a few papers were saved.

The Señora took us upstairs to 'the bridge', to show us a portrait which hung above the death mask at the end of the room.

It was sent to her after she announced to the world that her husband had been Ret Marut. In Germany, the woman who had been Marut's secretary had read a report of this, brought out the picture, which she had carefully kept for fifty years, and shipped it to the Señora. The drawing, by Franz Seiwert, portrayed Marut, thin faced, dramatically lit and slightly idealised. The long upper lip, the prominent nose and the ear all bore a distinct resemblance to the photographs of the old man.

On the second day of filming we pressed Señora Lujan further about her husband's birth and true name and were soon bogged down again. We did, however, get some more hearsay about the old deceiver's childhood. According to this new version, he told the Señora that he did not spend much time with his parents as a child and ran away from home when still quite young. His father was an impresario, who brought a ballet company to San Francisco, and he himself was born at sea before the ship reached the United States. Hence his feeling that he was a citizen of the world and not of any particular nation. Señora Lujan appeared quite unflustered by the bewildering variety of tales that her husband had spun her. She proclaimed with a defiant loyalty that she did not mind who his father had been; to her these stories were not really contradictions but part of his endlessly fascinating character.

Names, said the Señora, were unimportant to Traven. To me it sounded rather that they were so important that he could hardly bear to own one. They committed you and defined you. He even believed that books should be published anonymously because putting the author's name on the cover encouraged the public to expect a particular kind of book before they had read it. The fame of authorship was something he could manage without. In Traven's story 'The Night Visitor' Doc Cranwell says he has written many books which he has never published and explains why:

'What is fame, after all? It stinks to hell and heaven. To-day I am famous. To-day my name is printed on the front page of all the papers in the world. To-morrow perhaps fifty people can still spell my name correctly. Day after to-morrow I may starve to death and nobody cares. That's what you call fame.'

When a man thought like this, said the Señora, was it any wonder that he changed his name every so often? As a matter of fact, she said, he was about to change it again when he died. Although Croves was a family name of some sort, he was fed up with it and intended taking a new one. He had mentioned several possibilities to her, but had not decided definitely which. Señora Lujan could not remember what the contenders were but was sure that he would have chosen one beginning with D, following Croves in the alphabet, A, B, C, D. I knew of no names beginning with A or B that her husband used so the alphabetical progression did not make much sense. The Señora could not help: 'Well, he didn't tell me exactly the name. Maybe he mentioned the name but I forgot it. That's why we got along so well, because I didn't pay much attention to all those things. You see, if a man tells me, "My name is so and so," that's his name and that's all there is to it. Why should I question him?'

She believed everything and now she fed us with a rich diet of curious snippets, not unaware, we felt, of their publicity value. Sometimes the Señora led herself into tangles, as when she connected the names Gales and Marut, the wind god, and added that the name Torsvan was probably derived from Thor, the Scandinavian god of thunder. In that case, we said, all three names must have been made-up ones, an observation which did not please the Señora. 'You can think what you like,' she retorted, 'his real name was Torsvan.' What she meant was that Torsvan was his official name in Mexico and the name in which she had married him. She wanted no threat to that. Our scepticism over some of these tales must have been visible to her. When she took out a ship's compass, which had belonged to her husband, she was hesitant, almost embarrassed, about trotting out what I took to be her usual recitation, that it was very likely the compass from the actual death ship.

There was really no need for Señora Lujan to labour the significance of the material she possessed. It was a formidable array of documents, articles and also photographs – some of her husband, many hundreds taken by him. Together they comprised an overwhelming body of evidence, albeit circumstantial, that this man was Traven. The papers and photographs we had seen before related to the last years of his life, from 1951 onwards, and now Señora Lujan brought us a folder of material which covered some of his early years in Mexico. There was nothing from the period from 1930 to 1951. During most of those years he lived with Maria de la Luz Martinez and it was quite possible that Señora Lujan had little from this chapter of his life. She may simply have chosen not to show it to us. My curiosity about the gap was outweighed by my excitement at seeing evidence of her husband's activities in Mexico in the 1920s. Even from what she showed us, which I took to be a small selection, it was clear that he was in Mexico calling himself Torsvan from 1925, and that he did the same jobs and visited the same places as Traven.

The earliest two documents in the folder were both from the year 1925 and were the only ones in the name of B. Traven. The first was a notification from the offices of *Vorwärts* in Berlin that they would pay Herr B. Traven of Columbus, Mexico, for his article, 'Where Gods Come From'. It was dated February 7th, 1925, several months before the serialisation of *The Cotton-Pickers*. The second was a letter from the 'El Aguila' petroleum company to B. Traven Esquire of Tampico, thanking him for his request for employment dated August 1st, and informing him that they had no suitable vacancy. All the other documents were in the name of Traven Torsvan.

It looked as though he had called himself B. Traven in Mexico up until 1925 and had thus despatched his first manuscripts in that name. By 1926 he had switched to Traven Torsvan for most purposes but continued to write as B. Traven. He ran these two identities right through until the end of his life, adding a third, Hal Croves, in the early 1940s. The Croves identity was probably introduced to provide a cover for his contacts with film-makers like Figueroa and Huston. So there was B. Traven, novelist and short-story writer, Traven Torsvan, the citizen of Mexico, and Hal Croves, scriptwriter and agent.

The first items in the name of Torsvan were connected with a scientific exploration of the south of Mexico, organised by the government's campaign to combat the locust in 1926. This was the expedition led by Enrique Palacios. Here was Torsvan's identity card for the expedition, complete with a small oval photograph of him looking rather straight-faced in flat-brimmed trilby and bow-tie. Here, also, were various other

papers to do with that adventurous journey: instructions, brief-
ing information and a receipt, signed by Torsvan on collecting
his issue of a mosquito net and grease for his boots.

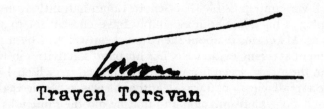

Traven Torsvan

With these papers was the typescript of an article he had
written, setting out the purpose of the trip, which carried the
by-line: 'By our Special Correspondent B.T. Torsvan,' yet
another version of his name.

Torsvan was the photographer for this expedition and Señora
Lujan had boxes of photographs taken by her husband of the
towns, the scenery and, above all, the Indians of the Chiapas
region, through which the explorers passed. They were similar
in subject and style to the photographs in *Land of Spring*, the
one non-fiction book by Traven. The characteristic they shared
was a respect for the dignity of their subjects, whether buildings,
people or the land. Torsvan's cameras and the developing box
he had taken on his many trips to the jungle were still in the
Señora's possession.

I saw a small notebook, which was a diary of a trip to the
Chiapas in 1926, possibly of the official expedition itself. The
entries were pencil-written on lined pages and varied in length.
Sometimes there was a longish description of a journey or a
place; sometimes just a note that he had visited a certain town
or village. One entry confirmed that he was taking photographs
at this time, reading simply 'Developed'. There was nothing
exceptional in the few pages I had time to look at, in fact the
notes were rather dull:

Excursion to the meadows near the mill ... Trip to Arista,
Gulf of Tehuantepec, Pacific Ocean both [?] with motor car
about 75 minutes. Wonderful shore, ideal place for recre-
ation. Has been a harbor, had a railway communication with

Tonala. Broken off and taken away ... 2.30 departure in
motor cars for Tuxtla Gutierrez. Fun [?] on the road. Pictur-
esque road over the Sierra Madre. Oxen carts crawl along
the road by the hundreds. At night they camp and they start
again at 2 a.m. ...

Other papers referred to further long trips to the south. I
saw a pass allowing him to cross into Guatemala for eight days
in 1928; a letter of introduction he was given in San Cristóbal
in 1929, and envelopes and a bank note addressed to Engineer
(Ingeniero) Torsvan in Ococingo in 1930. An inventory of kit
for an expedition included visiting cards, cigars, medicine chest,
cartridges, maps, insect powder and 'one necktie'. A photograph from one trip pictured a Mexican standing guard over
a pile of such equipment under a spreading tree, and another
showed Torsvan's mule, saddled, loaded and grazing by the
roadside.

There were some photographs of the man himself in the
jungle, at ease and smiling in his explorer's outfit of bush shirt,
neckerchief and baggy trousers tucked into lace-up knee boots.
In some he wore a black trilby, in others a pith helmet. From
a large cupboard on 'the bridge', Señora Lujan hauled out
a pair of her husband's long brown boots and a paper bag
containing his pith helmet. She urged me to compare both
items with those in a photograph of Torsvan sitting on a rocky
wall, making a note in his diary. She had thrown nothing
away.

Torsvan's interest in the people and history of Mexico led
him to read widely in anthropology and archaeology, and in
1927 he attended a summer school at the National University
in Mexico City. Señora Lujan still had the receipt for his course
fees of thirty dollars and some photographs of him lunching
with his (mainly female) classmates in a courtyard at the university. His hair was already receding, a large bald spot was
clearly visible in one picture, and he was nattily dressed in a
suit, handkerchief in his top pocket, and bow-tie.

The dandy bow-tie was something he affected throughout
these years. He was wearing one in the photograph on his
identity card for the Palacios expedition, and he was wearing
one again in two more of the interesting documents in the

Señora's collection: a photocopy of the 1930 immigration card
(the one Spota had uncovered), and the original of a game-
shooting licence Torsvan had taken out in 1929. The descriptions on the two forms coincided, apart from a slight difference
in height (1·68 m. against 1·70 m. – not significant) and different
adjectives used to describe the colour of hair (light brown
against sandy – again nothing suspicious). The only strange
point was that the 1929 form showed Torsvan quite fat in the
face, hair greying at the temples, looking well into his forties,
while the 1930 form carried two much earlier pictures, obviously of the same man but smoother skinned and thinner in
the face. Torsvan had cunningly palmed off on the immigration
authorities pictures of himself which must have been at least
ten years out of date.

The material I saw at Señora Lujan's house covered two
periods of her husband's life in Mexico, from 1925 to 1930 and
from 1951 to his death in 1969. The gap in the evidence was
curious but I was not inclined to resurrect any conspiracy
theory. Photographic evidence can never be utterly conclusive,
but to my eye the man who was called Croves and Torsvan
in Mexico City between 1951 and 1969 and who was in Acapulco definitely from the mid-1940s, was the same man who
was called Torsvan in Tampico, Mexico City and the Chiapas
in the 1920s. It was he who had travelled in the wildernesses,
learned the ways of the forest, studied the lives of the Indians,
and noted the exploitation of them in the mahogany camps by
the white landowners and entrepreneurs who were his hosts.
If there had been a plot, if the earlier Torsvan (the real Traven,
say) had died, been murdered or otherwise disposed of, and
replaced by the later Torsvan, then the conspirators had found
a substitute who was not only the same height and build as the
original, but who also looked startlingly like him, behaved like
him and carried on his correspondence with the same extraordinary mixture of boasting, suspicion and kindness. The man who
had lectured Preczang and the Kleins was the man who had
held forth to Spota and Judy Stone; the man who had dodged
Bernard Smith was the man who hid in doorways and tore up
notes from Sanora Babb; the man fascinated by photography
in the 1920s was the man intoxicated by film-making and film
stars in the 1940s and 1950s; the man who had written to Paul

Kohner was the man who met Paul Kohner. It was the same Torsvan throughout.

What of his life before 1925? Señora Lujan had told us that he had been Ret Marut and I asked if she had any papers from that part of his life. When we arrived for the next day of filming, a file was waiting. In it were some interesting documents relating to Marut's acting career and to his part in the Munich revolution, but they were all photocopies given to the Señora by researchers in Germany. I had hoped she would have some original Marut papers brought by her husband from Europe.

The Señora did have a collection of original *Der Ziegelbrenners* which she carefully unwrapped and spread out before us in a brick-coloured fan. Her husband, she said, had carried with him these souvenirs of his previous existence. And there was something else, something even rarer that he had brought from Germany and later given to her as a present. From some tissue

Von

Richard Maurhut

№ 13

1916

J. Mermet Verlag München 23

paper she took a slim green book, a copy of the novel that Marut had written under the name Richard Maurhut. The title was stamped in gold gothic lettering on the pale green cloth binding, *An das Fräulein von S* ... Inside on the title page the copy was numbered, 13, and below was the date and publisher's name: '1916, I. Mermet, Munich.'

'I. Mermet' was Irene Mermet, Marut's girlfriend throughout his time in Munich, who had helped him produce *Der Ziegelbrenner* and who, said Señora Lujan, had fled the city with him in 1919. Mermet had made her way to the United States, and the Señora showed me letters found in her husband's possessions which had been written in 1925 by Mermet in Washington to Marut, now calling himself Traven or Torsvan, in Mexico. With these, as with other papers, I was allowed to handle them but not given time to study them properly. I looked to see how they began and ended. They did not appear to be signed, nor did they begin 'Dear ...'; instead there were two initials at the top which I could not decipher. They could have referred to the date or the place where they were written, but the Señora said that they were a sign used by Marut, Mermet and a group of artists they had stayed with in Cologne.

Señora Lujan spoke fondly of Irene Mermet, feeling an empathy for another woman who had shared the life of this exhilarating, but difficult and demanding man. She had learned from the letters that Irene had at one time been in love with a young Englishman, either of naval family or in the navy himself, a relationship brought to an end by the boy's father. It was not clear whether this sad episode had taken place before or after she was with Marut in Munich. By 1925, said the Señora, she was certainly living in the United States, from where she sent small amounts of money and a typewriter to Marut in Mexico. At some point in late 1925 or early 1926 she travelled south to join him. The reunion was not successful, partly because of his long absences in the jungle, and by 1927 Irene was back in the United States, where she lived for the remainder of her life.

The Señora handed me some photographs of Irene Mermet. They showed a pretty girl with a strong neck, a straight nose, apple cheeks and a lively expression. I was particularly struck by a picture of her out in the countryside, standing with her fists on her hips, a garland of leaves through her arm, and gazing straight at the camera as if ready for anything that life might throw at her. There was, however, no way of being sure that this was Mermet or of knowing where the photographs had been taken. The same was true of two blurry pictures which the Señora said were of Ret Marut in Germany. They were of her husband as a young man, all right, but it was impossible to tell where they had been taken or what the bow-tied young fellow was calling himself at the time. But among the Señora's papers I spotted two items which offered circumstantial evidence that her husband *had* been Marut and that Irene Mermet *had* joined him in Mexico. Again, they were not proof, but they slipped snugly into an already likely story.

They were two certificates of vaccination against smallpox issued in Tampico on February 6th, 1926 – during the time Irene Mermet was supposed to have been in Mexico. As the certificates were given by the same official, on the same day and at the same time (the serial numbers were in succession), two people must have turned up to receive their injections. One certificate was issued in the name of B. Traven Torsvan, of whom we have heard much; the other in the name of I. Traven.

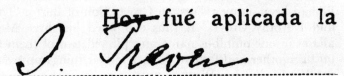

fué aplicada la

(Nombre)

Was this second person Irene, living with Traven as his wife? Her lover was hardly the man to encourage Irene to give her real name, for a start it might have threatened his own cover. The smallpox forms gave no indication of the sex of the subjects, but their ages were given and showed that I. Traven was eleven years younger than B. Traven Torsvan. I knew from some of the Recknagel material that Irene Mermet had been eleven years younger than Ret Marut.

The actual ages given were not the same as those recorded for Marut and Mermet in Germany, but we already had plenty of problems on that score. If Marut and Torsvan were the same man, there were three dates of birth to contend with:

Traven		March 5th,	(immigration
Torsvan	b. Chicago 1	1890	card, 1930)
Traven		May 3rd,	
Torsvan	b. Chicago	1890	(passport, 1956)
Ret Marut	b. San	February	(policecard,
	Francisco	25th, 1882	1908 Germany)

If he was Marut, he must have knocked eight years off his age and chosen a new birthday when he had come to Mexico; no wonder he had shuffled his photographs before deciding which one would go on which official document. Traven Torsvan gave his age as thirty-six on the vaccination certificate, and he would have been just a month short of his *new* thirty-sixth birthday (perhaps he had not even decided the exact day by then). If it was Irene Mermet who had been vaccinated with him, they had *both* simply adjusted their ages by the same amount.

Which, if any, of these dates of birth were correct? Señora Lujan opted for his last official birthday, May 3rd, 1890, and the old man's death certificate, for which she must have provided the information, agreed. This document declared that he had been Traven Torsvan Croves, son of Burton Torsvan and Dorothy Croves. It thus combined his three Mexican aliases in one omnibus name and pinned two of them firmly on his mother and father. Well, it tidied things up even if it was hard to believe. We forbore from raising again the spectres of the Kaiser and the poor Norwegian fisherman.

The same details of his background were legally enshrined in the will of Traven Torsvan Croves, made three weeks before his death. In it, he admitted that he had used the names B. Traven and Hal Croves as pseudonyms, but insisted that his real name was as above. Señora Lujan first read the will in a newspaper the day after her husband's death. He died from sclerosis of the liver and cancer of the prostate gland at 11.20 a.m. on March 26th, 1969, and within an hour the house was full of reporters. The old man's loathing of the press was shown to be justified. They burst in and flooded all over the house asking questions, taking photographs, using the telephone and sorting through papers. One of these vampires must have found the old man's copy of the will and taken it away. Not that there were any surprises in it for the Señora. She was the sole heir.

When we had completed the final shots on the last afternoon of filming, I was left alone with Señora Lujan on 'the bridge'. Robinson had departed earlier to start packing and Emilio's crew were loading the equipment into their van. I helped the Señora put away her husband's boots, his pith helmet, travelling boxes, typewriter, cameras and photograph albums. The afternoon rain was over and the evening sun shone in through the windows from which the old man had once leaned out to feed the birds. The Señora said she hoped that we were pleased with what we had filmed, and that it would all go together well because it was so important that we should lead people to her husband's books. All the business of the so-called mystery was just something the newspapers had latched on to. There was no mystery, only the marvellous books in which B. Traven had fought for justice in the world. He was, she said, just a wonderful man. She looked up at his death mask, which was on top of the cupboard into which we were replacing the photographs. The sun was casting dark shadows in the sunken bronze cheeks. He had not really looked looked like that, she said sadly. By the time the mask was taken his face had fallen and no longer reflected the strength and humour which she had so loved.

The Señora suddenly wanted to show me more things. She went hurriedly round the room opening drawers, taking out books, Indian blankets, cloths and figurines. I felt that it was a final effort to demonstrate to me the variety and vivacity of her husband's life and interests. I was touched by her concern to see him right by us, to make sure that no strangers came and went without feeling the power of the man. At the last drawer she stopped and said that I should have a present to take back for my wife. She took out an old Indian cocoa mixer, a turned and decorated stick with loose rings carved unbroken from the same piece of wood. I had seen modern ones in the tourist shops but this, said the Señora, had been brought back by her husband from one of his expeditions. As I thanked her, she plunged her hand to the bottom of the drawer and handed me a small stone carving of a head. 'Here,' she said, 'this is for you. It belonged to my husband.' I protested at her generosity but she insisted I take it. With her usual firmness and dignity, she pushed the drawer shut and then led me downstairs.

The following morning Robinson and I stopped our taxi on the way to the airport to pay a brief farewell call. We thanked Señora Lujan for her help and her kindness and made our good-byes, which were both friendly and formal. We left the Señora and Rio Mississippi with a distinct feeling that our business was unfinished. We had devoted nearly the whole of our three weeks away from England to thinking and talking about Traven. We had been in his house, we had talked to his acquaintances, his friends and his widow. We had a film about the mystery, but that no longer seemed enough. We had become hypnotised by the black hole at the centre of the story, infected by a rash of unanswered questions. Every certainty we had found had brought only further puzzles.

16 Sand or Gold?

We knew more than most. I was reassured of this by a new dictionary of pseudonyms, which was among the pile of mail and books on my desk when I arrived back in London. Flicking through it past Doris Day (real name Doris Kappelhoff) and Robert Taylor (Spangler Arlington Brugh), I found, opposite the page featuring another fugitive in Mexico, Leon Trotsky (Lev Bronstein), the name of our hero. He was there as Ben Traven, real name 'unknown', born 'about 1886; died ?: The entry read: 'German novelist who lived in Mexico for many years, and wrote several novels during twenties and thirties, one of which, *The Treasure of the Sierra Madre*, was made into a film. His real identity and whereabouts are unknown.'

Equally reassuring was an article which appeared in the *Daily Mirror* about a week after our return. Under the heading, 'Cracking a Legend for the BBC', the *Mirror's* book critic set out to show that we had been wasting our time on 'a costly exercise to unravel the mystery of who wrote *The Treasure of the Sierra Madre*'. He said that we were investigating rumours that Traven was 'a refugee Bavarian Socialist, a renegade American writer called Traven Torsvan and even that he was an illegitimate son of Kaiser Wilhelm', and scoffed confidently, 'There seems to be no reason to think that any of these stories are true.' The indefatigable *Mirror* man appeared to base his article on a call to one of the editors of the *Penguin Companion to Literature*, Eric Mottram, Reader in American Literature at the University of London, who had 'laughed at the thought of there being a mystery about the identity of Traven'. The *Mirror* man concluded that the BBC team 'like the prospectors

in *The Treasure of the Sierra Madre*, may end up not with gold,
but with a lot of dross'. He did not sound overly displeased at
the prospect.

Robinson and I had already begun analysing the strength
of our haul. We had some gold, to be sure; the difficulty lay
in separating it from the ample quantities of sand. On the long
flight home we had tried to fathom out what Señora Lujan had
told us. Robinson inclined to the view that her contradictions
and denials were the result of a straightforward commercial
desire to keep the veil of secrecy lowered, thereby continuing
to attract the attention of scholars and journalists to her husband's works, the copyrights of which she owned. He felt that
behind the deliberate confusions she probably knew about the
origins of B. Traven and was simply keeping them to herself.
She might even be worried that her position as the legal owner
of the works could be called into question by the discovery that
her husband had not been who he had said he was, and that
she had thus been married under a false name.

On the other hand, I believed that there was a great deal
about her husband that the Señora did not know. She had been
close to the old man only from about 1952 onwards, and it
would have been easy for him to ration the portions of his history that he doled out to her. She had obviously adored him
and happily put up with his irritating whims and his peculiar,
even insulting, evasiveness. Yet it would be a blow to the dignity
of any wife, let alone to a sophisticated Mexican woman like
Señora Lujan, for her husband to tell her manifest fibs about
his earlier life, as hers had done, parrying her questions, concealing his origins and thus himself. No wonder that when strangers
came with their questions she might try to disguise the fact that
she knew no more than they about episodes in the life of Traven.
By deliberately baffling us with her answers, I believed that
she had been trying to keep the window on her husband's origins as opaque for us as it was for her. I thought that the Señora
had told us the truth. She had heard all these different tales
from her husband and she had had to make do with them, for
there had been nothing else. She now recited them to us parrot
fashion, aware of the contradictions and inconsistencies, using
them as a screen behind which to hide her own lack of certainty.
I wrote, in a progress report to the Kleins, 'the fog still seems

to descend swiftly when one tries to go back past 1924. Certainly, I remain to be convinced that anyone knows the true details of the birth of Traven/Croves/Torsvan/Marut.'

I did by now believe that Traven/Croves/Torsvan had been the German anarchist Ret Marut, or rather, I was 95 per cent convinced of it. The photographic evidence, which on top of everything else might have clinched this identification, was absent. The only existing photographs of Marut were of stage productions, showing him either as a tiny figure in the distance or covered in heavy make-up, as in the picture of him as an Indian in a production of Peter Pan. All one could say was that the photographs did not disprove the identification. Marut, like the man in Mexico, did not appear to have been a tall man and his head was generally similar in shape. That was all.

The 5 per cent doubt remained. For all the internal similarities that scholars had found between the works of Marut, and the works of Traven and for all the material that Señora Lujan had in her possession, there were still questions. If Marut had become Torsvan he had knocked eight years off his age and, as a man well into his forties, had been able to pass himself off as a man of thirty-five. Torsvan used to shuffle the photographs that he provided for official documents, slipping in some old ones to confuse the authorities. Even so, eight years was a great many to lop off in one go, however pressing the need for disguise, however youthful one's appearance and however great one's vanity.

Thinking back over what Señora Lujan had shown us it was strange that there was nothing which had definitely belonged to Ret Marut himself, which could only have reached Mexico if he had brought it. When she had told us that her husband had burnt most of his German papers, I believed her, but it was a very convenient explanation for the absence of any unequivocal proof. The *Ziegelbrenners* the Señora possessed were rare and the novel even rarer, but they could have been tracked down and bought. Baumann had a copy of *Der Ziegelbrenner* and I knew that other Traven buffs had some. If, say, Traven had not been Marut and had read of the theories linking himself with this mysterious German, he might well have taken steps to find out more about the outlaw journalist whose spirit was thought to be so close to his own. It would have been almost impossible to resist investigating an earlier existence which others had assigned to him. He was obsessive, and would have sought out the writings of this fellow dissenter, a man who was said to share both his outlook and his peculiarities. Over the years he could well have built up a small library of originals. It was a possibility that I could not rule out. The thought even occurred to me that the Señora might have tracked down these publications herself to supply for her husband the provenance which was lacking in the papers he had left behind him.

My first concern on arriving home was to make sure that the film we had shot had come out and that the Curse, which had so artfully armed Emilio Cesar with a duff camera, had not completed his sabotage by attacking the celluloid itself. As it was, he had malevolently escorted Robinson and me home, contriving to make off with my sun-glasses when we changed planes in Miami and smiting Robinson with a mysterious illness. We arrived at Heathrow with me blinking into the morning sun and Robinson groaning and staggering from the plane to a wheelchair, sent out to meet us by the airport doctor. A Mexican stomach bug was diagnosed, but I knew better what had brought my gallant companion to his knees. His recovery a few days later coincided with my first view of the rushes from Mexico. Emilio had done us well. The pictures were in focus, correctly exposed and satisfactorily framed and Pablo had managed to record most of what had happened. I sent a relieved telegram to Emilio offering thanks and congratulations and went off to Suffolk with my family for a week's holiday.

There were too many loose ends for me to begin assembling the film, so I postponed editing until after Christmas and set out on some enquiries of my own. I turned first to the story that Ret Marut had been in London in the 1920s, which I had heard from Baumann and which had been confirmed to me on the telephone by another American writer, Jonah Raskin. I rang the Home Office, and followed up with a written request for access to any material they had on Marut. I also made my formal applications under the American Freedom of Information Act, to the State Department, the FBI and the CIA, for any files on B. Traven, Hal Croves, Traven Torsvan or Ret Marut.

I decided that I should also investigate the story that Traven was the son of the Kaiser. It would provide the most sensational solution to the mystery and there were enough hints and nudges from Mexico to make it worth pursuing further. What was more, I heard that Rolf Recknagel, doyen of the Traven scholars and a man who had been in the field for years before anyone else, was now speculating about this solution. I hoped to visit Recknagel, but it was never possible, for he had an accident and became seriously ill before I could arrange a trip.

A less startling issue but one that I could push on with straight away was the question of Traven's use of German and how it compared with Marut's. I do not speak or read German and ever since Robert Goss had told us that he found Traven's use of the language clumsy and Marut's stylish, I had wanted reassurance that the same person could have written both sets of works. If it were the case that Marut wrote elegant German, whereas Traven was always struggling, this could hardly be so. Baumann found several complicated influences at work in their language and my hunch was that there was some posturing to be found in both their writings. Marut's was a prophetic and revolutionary voice shouting to make itself heard above the drone of the conventional wisdom; he might well have used dramatic constructions and an odd vocabulary to attract attention to his tidings. Traven, in his early books, was writing as an unlettered American and might have affected the syntax and slang that he imagined (or knew from experience) such a man would use.

I found an article by Hubert Jannach of Purdue University, which demonstrated convincingly that Traven's first language was certainly German and that he was at ease writing in this tongue. Jannach compared English and German versions of *The Death Ship*, and found the German by turns tense, rhythmic, naturalistic in its descriptions and revealing of the author's familiarity with the life and culture of Germany. Jannach did not address himself to the Marut writings, so I had the idea of commissioning a purely linguistic, as opposed to stylistic, comparison. I was dimly aware that there were modern techniques of analysing an author's written thumbprint by using a computer to measure the number and regularity of key words, and recognise certain constructions and usages. After some enquiries I found a German-speaking linguist, D.J. Allerton of the Department of General Linguistics at Manchester

University, who was in touch with work in this field. Allerton explained to me that the computer system of linguistic analysis was a specialised, costly and lengthy process which might well not be applicable to the task I had in hand, but he volunteered to make a rough comparison of his own for me. Accordingly, I sent him a German published facsimile of the complete issues of *Der Ziegelbrenner* and a first edition of *The Death Ship*.

Allerton's reply was inconclusive. The underlying thought in diagnosing a writer's style, he said, was that there were several factors involved:

> (i) So-called 'register' – the variation in language used by writers according to whether they are writing a personal letter, a novel, a pamphlet, a scientific report, etc. (ii) So-called 'tenor of discourse' – depending on the attitude of the writer to his subject-matter and reader, whether he is enthusiastic, embittered, jocular, etc. (iii) Purely individual traits of style – the writer's so-called 'ideolect'.

The problem was these were all mixed up, making it almost impossible to determine authorship unless the first two factors could be ruled out and like be compared with like, for example two novels with similar themes or two articles on similar subjects. In this instance a set of political tracts was being unsuitably compared with a novel.

Yet Allerton's comments were more useful to me than he imagined. Nothing he said about the two writers ruled out the possibility that they were the same person. I had quoted to him Goss's claim that Traven's German contained many errors. Referring to his own reading of *The Death Ship*, Allerton replied as follows:

> It is not clear to me what kind of 'errors' he is thinking of. If, as I suspect, he simply means that it is not written in the best prescribed literary High German, then this is obviously true; but it was presumably never intended to be, using a chatty conversational mode of story-telling, such as you might expect a sailor to use. This contains the odd Low German or sailors' slang word such as ... Eimer, 'bucket' for 'vessel' ... I see little or no evidence that it was written by a non-native speaker of German.

10 The actor Ret Marut plays an Indian in *Peter Pan*, Düsseldorf 1912.

11 Elfriede Zielke in 1909, three years before she gave birth to Marut's daughter.

12 Traven's photograph of the house in the jungle in which he wrote 'The Night Visitor'. 'I wrote the novel in this bungalow under the most appalling bodily torment. Mosquito plagues . . . jaguars and lions would come close . . . tarantulas as big as a hand . . . vast armies of big ants.'

13 Members of the 1926 scientific expedition to the south of Mexico, sponsored by the Mexican government. Second from right, with a cigarette, is the expedition's photographer, the 'Norwegian engineer' T. Torsvan.

14 Torsvan makes an entry in his notebook, probably on the 1926 expedition.

15 A page from one of Torsvan's notebooks, beginning May 20th, 1926 in Vera Cruz, with a sketch map of a railway journey via Touala towards Tapachula. In the possession of Señora Lujan.

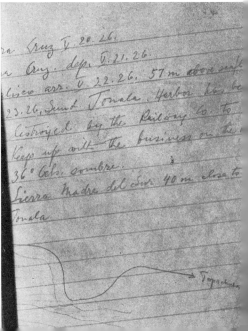

16 Torsvan in jungle kit on the 1926 expedition or soon afterwards.

17 Torsvan's membership card for the Palacios expedition. The government agency behind the trip was the Campaign Against the Locust.

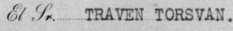

JUNTA NACIONAL DIRECTORA
DE LA
CAMPAÑA CONTRA LA LANGOSTA

El Sr. ___TRAVEN TORSVAN.

cuyo retrato sellado se inserta al margen, desempe-
ña el cargo de MIEMBRO COM.CIENT.EXPL.

Veracruz, Ver., 1° de Mayo de 192 6

EL SECRETARIO,

Vo. Bo.
EL PRESIDENTE,

A DEL INTERESADO

18–20 *Above, and below left*, Torsvan in the Chiapas in the 1920s.

21 *Below right*, identity photograph of Torsvan from his game shooting licence, dated 1929. He appears much older than in the photographs supplied for his immigration card of the following year (see plate 3).

The German of *Der Ziegelbrenner*, he said, was 'thoroughly German', and he noted that it used the rhetorical style of public speaking. Allerton emphasised that he was not a native German speaker and apologised for not being able to give me a definitive answer, but this was not so important. The candidature of Marut remained undented by a linguistic examination.

There was one story I now came across which, if true, damaged beyond repair every Traven theory I had so far encountered. It appeared in the September 1967 issue of the German magazine, *Der Monat*, in an article by one Ernst Fallen de Droog. The piece was poorly argued in its sceptical remarks about Torsvan–Croves, but what commanded the attention was de Droog's eye-witness account of some incidents which took place while he was fighting on the Republican side in the Spanish Civil War. According to de Droog, in the spring of 1937 some new volunteers arrived from Barcelona to join the unit he was in charge of. One of them gave his name only as Ziegel-brenner and was hazy about his nationality, implying that Ger-man, Mexican and American were all somehow correct. His occupation, he said, was simply 'outsider', though in his time he had been a sailor, a beachcomber and, above all, a writer. In the ensuing months this enigmatic recruit displayed a know-ledge of the Munich revolution and its leading participants. He also quoted aloud from *The Death Ship* and referred to *The White Rose* as 'my' book. He obviously intended it to be known that he was both Ret Marut and B. Traven, and this was exactly who de Droog took him to be. On New Year's Eve 1937, in the battle for Teruel, this Ziegelbrenner was with de Droog on an inspection of some forward mortar positions when he was shot and killed by a nationalist bullet. De Droog helped to bury him with his own hands, and afterwards found among his com-rade's few personal possessions some jottings and notes referring to 'my' book *The Cotton-Pickers*. This, concluded de Droog, was how the real B. Traven had died.

This story admitted of four explanations: that de Droog's memory was playing him false about events which had taken place thirty years before; that he was mischievously putting a cat among the Travening pigeons; that the dead soldier, who-ever he was, knew of the tales linking Traven and Marut and took pleasure, as nonentities sometimes will, in pretending to

be the mysterious author he admired; that it was true and that
the man in Mexico was neither Traven nor Marut. There was
no collateral for this story. It stood or fell on the testimony of
de Droog, whom I tried and failed to track down. I doubted
that this was the explanation we had been searching for, not
least because the letters from B. Traven in Mexico to Knopf's
and others had continued well past 1937, with no obvious hic-
cup in frequency or style. The last novel in the jungle cycle,
General from the Jungle, was not published until 1939, and so was
unlikely to have reached the publishers early enough for it to
have been written by the man who fell at Teruel. All this was
without taking into account the authenticity of the final novel,
Aslan Norval, and the short stories which were published in the
1940s and 1950s. Altogether there was plenty to put into the
scales against de Droog's claims. Still, I could not positively
disprove his story and the memory of the shadowy figure, buried
in the Spanish snow, nagged for some time.

Help was at hand. I had followed up my letter to the Home
Office with several telephone calls, in an attempt to speed my
application to see the Marut file through whatever bureaucratic channels it had to navigate. Mr Pearson, the Department-
al Record Officer, was sympathetic and counselled patience.
It was a tricky matter, he said, for an outsider to be given access
to official files and certain procedures would have to be strictly
carried out. Marut had been in trouble with the law in London.
Mr Pearson had found the papers and, as they related only to
this single case so long ago, he thought that I would be able to
see them in the end, but there was no point in trying to hurry
things. In an effort to help, I had provided the Home Office,
as I had provided the American agencies, with a release from
Señora Lujan. It stated that she was the widow of Ret Marut,
that he was dead, and that I had her permission to see any documents relating to him.

On Friday November 18th, I rang Mr Pearson again to see
how matters stood. 'Oh, Mr Wyatt,' he said, 'I've just written
you a letter. You should get it on Monday. I am afraid that
you will not be able to do any filming here in the Department,
but I am pleased to say that I am allowed to show the file on
your man Marut.'

I thanked him for his good offices.

'Yes, I am glad we could help,' he continued. 'It's a very interesting case. Oh, by the way, I have had another look in the file and did you know there is a photograph of your chappie in there? I thought that might interest you.'

I went down to the Home Office that afternoon.

17 An Alien in London

There were strict security arrangements operating at the new Home Office building in Queen Anne's Gate. I had to identify myself, and then I waited to be collected and taken up to Mr Pearson's office. He greeted me and apologised for the length of time that it had taken to deal with my enquiry – it was nearly two and a half months since I had put in my application. He thought I would like to know that my request had had to be cleared 'at the highest level', by which I took him to mean that the then Home Secretary himself, Merlyn Rees, had been asked for his approval. I sensed an air of achievement on Mr Pearson's part, as if a small internal precedent had been set, and whether this was so or not I was genuinely thankful for his efforts on my behalf. The file was awaiting me in the library.

I opened the cardboard folder and my eyes fell immediately on the photograph inside. It was one print containing two likenesses which were obviously mug shots; a full face and right profile, marked with the name Ret Marut and dated December 18th, 1923. These were police pictures taken at that time of the man who was definitely Marut and, at first glance, my heart sank. He had a moustache and was fatter in the face than Traven/Torsvan/Croves in Mexico. I reached down into my briefcase and took out copies of the photographs from Señora Lujan's house. I laid them out on the Home Office desk and compared them with the mug shots. With all the pictures before me, the similarities between Marut and Traven began to assert themselves. The characteristic shape of the large left ear was visible in all the photographs. Marut had the same long, prominent nose, pointing slightly to the right, with one nostril – the

182

left – angled more than the other. The set of the eyes and the creases at the bridge of the nose were the same. The moustache disguised the same long upper lip.

The full-face mug shot had looked unfamiliar at first because Marut was pulling a face, puckering his chin and sucking on his lower lip, in the time-honoured manner of criminals trying to confuse the police. The comical expression he thus produced obscured the usual contour of his mouth. He was dressed in a dark waistcoat and jacket of the same material, a shiny pat-terned tie, pinned collar and what looked like a brand-new tweed flat cap – no bow-tie, but even as an anarchist on the run he maintained a hint of the dapper style I had noticed in the pictures from Mexico. It was the same man all right. For the first time I knew for certain that this strange actor and anarchist journalist had gone to Mexico and become B. Traven. For all the internal evidence recognised by Mühsam and others, for all the work of Recknagel in his studies of the two men and for all the statements of the Señora, this was the final proof of the matter for me.

I examined the folder. It was in the name of:

Ret or Rex Marut alias Albert Otto Max Wienecke
               alias Adolf Rudolf Feige
               alias Barker
               alias Arnolds

It contained, besides the photographs, two copies of Marut's Criminal Record form, signed by the Governor of Brixton Prison on December 20th, 1923.

Prison Register No. 9876
Born – 1882 [On both copies of the form this appeared to
           have been changed from 1872. It had been
           taken down wrongly or Marut had been up to
           his usual tricks.]
       U.S.A.
Trade or occupation – bookseller
Height without shoes – 5 ft 5½ ins
Complexion – fresh
Hair – grey

Eyes – blue
Sentence – deportation
Thames Police Court 17.12.23./Failing to Register.

There was a note on the file that a Deportation Order had
been issued on December 28th, 1923, although no mention of
its being carried out. Some further notes had been added in
1948, presumably when the Deportation Order had come up
for review after twenty-five years. They said in part: 'A German
communist who was recommended for deportation in 1923 ...
In 1924 he left the country as a ship's fireman ...' The Order
had been revoked on April 12th, 1949. So Marut had been no
idle tourist in London. He had been arrested and imprisoned
in Brixton in south London, one of the four big London gaols,
and departed the capital in the stokehold of a ship, a slave to
the furnaces like Gerard Gales, the coal-drag of *The Death Ship*.
The extra clutch of aliases that the London police had
assembled were all new to me and would be worth checking.
Already they answered one small mystery. When Señora Lujan
told me that her husband became tired of the name Croves and
was thinking of changing it, she said that he would have chosen
a name beginning with D as that would make an alphabetical
progression A, B, C, D. She was unable to explain further and
at the time I could see no reason why D should follow. But if
Arnolds and Barker were the precursors of Croves, then the pattern was revealed. For his Anglo-Saxon aliases at least, he had
begun pedantically with A, and worked alphabetically.
I was interested to see that he described himself as a bookseller, which was, I supposed, literally true. His hair was described
as grey, and so it looked on the photographs, as far as one could
see it beneath his cap. In his Mexican documents over the next
few years his hair is described as light brown or reddish. Two
explanations are possible: that he dyed his hair, which would
have been quite in keeping with his obvious vanity about his
appearance; that in Mexico he was able to supply his own description of himself, while in London the police wrote down
their own, less flattering, observations.
With the information I had acquired at the Home Office,
I was able to trace the record of Marut's brush with the law
and his route to Brixton. He was arrested at 1.05 p.m. on

November 30th, 1923, by a CID officer called F. Bickers. The next day he was brought before the magistrate at Thames Police Court, Aylward Street, London E. 1, following into court a string of labourers and seamen charged with being drunk and disorderly. The charge against Marut (his name was written down as 'Marnt' and then altered) was that 'Being an alien, viz: American citizen, did fail to register with the Registration Officer of the district in which he resided'. This was an offence under Article 18 (1) (a) of the Aliens Order, 1920. His occupation was entered in the court register as 'mechanic' and his age as forty-one. As in the Home Office file there was no address. He pleaded guilty and was remanded in custody until December 10th, when he was again remanded, this time for a week. On December 17th, his third and final appearance, he was recommended for deportation and was dispatched to Brixton Prison.

The 17th day of December 192 3								
Name of Informant or Complainant.	Name of Defendant. Age, if known.		Nature of Offence or of Matter of Complaint.	Date of Offence.	Time when		Doctor's Fee, (if any).	Plea.
					Charged.	Bailed.		
Remands								
F. Bickers. C.I.D.	Ret Marnt. 41. (Mechanic)		Being an alien, viz; American citizen, did fail to register with the Registration Officer of the district in which he resided. (1 from 10 12/23)	30·11·23	1. 5 pm.			

The bare record left unanswered such questions as where Marut lived in London, whether he was alone, how he was arrested, how long he was in Brixton, why he was released, and whether he was forcibly put on board ship. I went to New Scotland Yard to see if they had any papers on the case, but they told me that they destroyed files on Deportation Orders about ten years after they were made out. There was no trace either of the detective who had arrested Marut. He could not still be

serving in the Metropolitan Police and there was no police pen-
sioner of that name, so he was almost certainly dead. I did learn
that the initials 'C.O.' which appeared after Bickers's name in
the court register, meant that he was attached to the Commissioner's Office, in other words to Scotland Yard and not to the
local force in the East End. I tried the Port of London Police
in case they had a hand in the arrest but without success.

In *The Death Ship* Traven wrote a page of complaint about
the police in Europe, referring to the police of France and Holland. It now looked as if some of the experience which fuelled
his anger might have come from treatment at the hands of the
British police.

> I have gathered sufficient experience by now to know that
> whenever I run up against certain strange customs anywhere
> in Europe, then I am on my way to a police station ... I may
> sit quite satisfied with myself on a box by the docks, and,
> sure enough, a cop comes up, asks me questions, and takes
> me to the police station. Or I may lie in bed, doing nobody
> any harm, and somebody knocks at the door, and half an
> hour later I am again in a police station.

Was Marut in bed when Bickers called in the early afternoon
of the last day of November? Or was he sitting by the docks?
Or drifting through the busy wharfs and quays of the Port of
London trying to find a ship which would carry him across the
Atlantic? At the Home Office, Mr Pearson's guess was that,
wherever he had been picked up, Marut had probably been
'shopped' by someone. There was enormous suspicion of all
foreigners at the time, especially if they were doing anything
vaguely unusual. A man with a strong German accent, claiming
to be an American, probably making his leftish political
opinions known, would soon have attracted attention to himself
and there would have been plenty of people willing to nudge
the police in his direction. In those days, only six years after
the Russian revolution, the British authorities were easily
panicked by descriptions like 'foreign socialist'. The files of the
period showed that such words were bandied about freely as
a reason for swooping on suspect aliens.

Mr Pearson assured me that I had seen all he had on Marut.

It was not unusual, he said, for there to be so little, as many records were missing from that period. This did not mean, as I had suggested, that they had been carefully weeded to remove any incriminating papers. It had never crossed anyone's mind then that one day these official files might be open to public inspection, so they would not have worried about leaving sensitive material on file. The proof of this, said Pearson, was that there was a mass of compromising stuff remaining on all sorts of subjects. If things were missing from the file, it was because something was done by word of mouth or never properly included in the first place.

Further digging at the Home Office did disclose that the Deportation Order on Marut was signed by the Home Secretary of the time, W.C. Bridgeman, in person, and initialled by his private secretary, H.R. Boyd. Both men were long since dead, Bridgeman in 1935 and Boyd in 1940, and I could trace no one connected with the case who was still alive. The order, however, was never enforced, meaning that Marut must have left the country, to the satisfaction of the authorities, under his own steam. I was not allowed to see the Brixton Prison archives, but I was able to discover that they described Marut as a 'Lithuanian' and recorded that he was 'discharged by order of the court' on February 15th, 1924. His release was signed by the hand of the then Home Secretary, Arthur Henderson, one of the leading figures in the recently elected Labour government. Someone had decided to let him out after he had served a couple of months in gaol. Why?

Given the inconsistencies in the various records in London – Marut was described as both American and Lithuanian; both a bookseller and a mechanic – it seemed unlikely that there was any monolithic plot to let him out because, say, he was specially protected. Had some conspiracy of the establishment been grinding forward on his behalf, surely the biographical details would have tallied? Investigation showed that it was not uncommon in 1924 to let out of prison people who had been sentenced to deportation. It saved money. The prisoners had to notify the authorities of their address outside and they would then be kept under close watch until they left the country. This is what must have happened with Marut. And I knew where he went when he left Brixton. An American researcher,

Professor Charles Humphrey of the University of Southern Colorado, wrote to me to say that he had the State Department documents for which I had applied, and they revealed that Marut lived at 649 Commercial Road from February 15th until April 18th, 1924, when he had sailed from London as a fireman on board a ship called the *Hegri*. Humphrey told me that this ship had been wrecked off Africa and added, excitedly, 'If you will please, check with Lloyd's about the *Hegri* and let me know. I need to know the exact date of the shipwreck, if indeed this ship was Traven's Death Ship, which appears to be highly likely.' I took Commercial Road first.

Commercial Road was a good place to live if you were looking for a ship. It runs through the East End of London from Whitechapel through Stepney to Limehouse, the heart of the dock area in what was then the biggest port in the world. Even now, when nearly all the ships have moved way downstream and much of the life of the district has ebbed away, the seamen's missions remain cast up on the shore as memorials to the time when sailors of every race and tongue passed through here, spending their pay, fighting their fights and changing their vessels. No. 649 is just where Commercial Road passes closest to the river, about four hundred yards north of the sharp loop in the Thames which separates Limehouse Reach from the Pool of London. Ten minutes' walk to the west are the London Docks, ten minutes to the east the India and Millwall Docks, and all along the Thames between lie the riverside wharfs of Wapping and Limehouse.

The house in which Marut stayed at 649 Commercial Road, E. 14 is no longer standing. It was pulled down some time at the beginning of the 1950s and the site is now occupied by a new building, a Danish Seamen's Church. Judging by the houses next door, No. 649 must have been part of an early-nineteenth-century, three-storey terrace, the upper floors of which looked out across the street, over a high wall into the Regent's Canal Dock and beyond that to where the Grand Union Canal enters the Thames. It was a tobacconist's shop run by one Ada Woodbridge, who must have added to her earnings by letting out rooms; the area was full of such sailors' lodgings at that time. I tried hard but failed to find anyone in the district who could remember Ada Woodbridge, or Cyril Woodbridge, who had the shop in the 1930s, and was unable to add anything to the bare fact that this was where Marut lodged for two months after he was released from prison. The house was less than half a mile from the magistrates' court that his case was heard in, so it was quite likely that Marut was living in this vicinity before his arrest, possibly in the same house. The East End was then a centre for anarchists and socialists, and the famous anarchist newspaper *Freedom* was, and still is, published in Whitechapel. It would have been natural for a political refugee to make his way to this district in search of comradeship. If Marut had contacts among radical activists in London he would have been drawn sooner or later to the East End.

I was making little progress tracking Marut down Commercial Road and now turned my attention to the ship that carried him from London – the vessel Humphrey was convinced was the original for *The Death Ship*. In the book there are two death ships. One of them, the ship on to which Gales and his companion, Stanislav the Pole, are shanghaied and on which they are finally wrecked off the coast of West Africa, is British, *The Empress of Madagascar*. Traven makes play with the strictness of English regulations and the consequently greater hypocrisy surrounding the plan to sink the ship for the insurance money. He also slips in one or two jibes and complaints about matters he had some reason to feel sore about. The Captain warns Gales:

It is a very serious offence under the British law to stow away on a British vessel with the intention of entering illegally the British Isles. It will cost you no less than six months' hard labour, perhaps even two years, and deportation.

Although *The Empress* allows Traven to unload some of his resentments against the English and their immigration laws, it is the other death ship, the *Yorikke*, which fills the long central section of the book and on which Traven sets most of the seaborne action, including his almost metaphysical descriptions of work below decks. The *Yorikke* is of undetermined nationality. Only a faded and tattered flag flies above the unpainted stern,

enabling Traven and his hero to identify themselves, and their
own fading nationality, with this fellow vagabond:

> I stopped fishing and I went over to look at the stern. Accord-
> ing to international agreements, the name of her home port
> should have been painted there clearly. Apparently she did
> not want to betray her birthplace. So you're like me, I
> thought, without a proper birth-certificate. Bedfellows, hey?
> Of course there was something painted on the stern. But I
> am sure that only a well-trained archaeologist could have
> deciphered what those spots meant.

No archaeologist was necessary to identify the *Hegri*. At
Lloyd's I looked her up in the shipping register and discovered
that her name was properly spelled *Hegre*. She was a vessel,
1,528 tons, built in 1892 by J. Blumer and Co. of Sunderland
and, in the thirty-two years she had been at sea by the time
Marut came aboard, had sailed under four other names: *Lars-
Lea*, *Follo*, *Ciscar* and *Lissabon*. In 1924 the *Hegre* was owned
by the Bergen Lloyd Company of Bergen, Norway. There was
nothing in the register to suggest that she had been wrecked
nor was there any mention of her in the annual list of disasters
at sea.

I looked up the Lloyd's Lists for the week that the *Hegre* was
said to have sailed from London with Marut on board. The
issue for Thursday April 17th, 1924, reflected the bustling
activity of the City's docks and shipping businesses. The front
page advertised steam passages to every part of the globe. If
Marut had had money enough he could have sailed by P. and
O. to Calcutta; by The Bank Line to Montevideo, Buenos
Aires, Rosario and Bahia Blanca; by The Ben Line to Penang
and Port Swettenham; by the Bibby Line to Rangoon; by
Alfred Holt and Co. to Port Said and Shanghai, or by the Power
Line to Morocco. There were steamers for sale in London, New-
castle, Hull and Liverpool. Captain J.E. Blay was advertising
his services to ship-owners and dealers, 'Transports vessels to
any part of the world ... Provides all things necessary for
voyage'. The *Mauretania* was in repair dock at Cherbourg; business was quiet again in the freight markets; a memorial service
had been held the previous day on board an American ice-

cutter near the site of the sinking of the *Titanic* to commemorate
the twelfth anniversary of that disaster; and Lloyd's and the
Stock Exchange had drawn their third annual football match,
two goals all. And there, in the long list of ship movements
round the world, was the *Hegre*, marked in the river Thames
off Gravesend, heading for Morocco Wharf.

I was about to turn to the next edition of the List to follow
the progress of the *Hegre*, when my eye was caught by the name
of another ship also heading up river past Gravesend on April
16th, 1924. It was a German vessel, the *Trave*, plying between
London and Bremen, and bound in this instance for the
Regent's Canal Dock, the small dock across the street from
where Marut was staying. At the quay there it would have been
visible from a room upstairs at the front of 649 Commercial
Road and there, Marut might well have seen it on his last day
in London. It was an odd coincidence that a ship of this name,
presumably called after the river Trave, should have been on
hand to witness Ret Marut's final departure from Europe. With
that departure, the name Ret Marut disappeared and within
a year B. Traven was born.

If Marut had not spotted the *Trave* from an upstairs window,
he could have seen it, looking back to the entrance of the
Regent's Canal Dock, as he walked down Branch Road and
turned right into The Highway, on his way to the *Hegre*'s
berth. Morocco Wharf was not an enclosed dock but a riverside
mooring at 82–4 Wapping High Street, a narrow thoroughfare
following the curve of the Thames and lined with wharfs and
warehouses. Many of the buildings are now empty, or, like Nos
82–4, pulled down. In 1924 the Morocco and Eagle Sufferance
Wharf was owned by William H. Muller, a busy company of
shipbrokers, wharfingers, warehousekeepers, forwarding agents
and lightermen, who, among their other activities, ran a regular
daily express and parcel service between London and Rotterdam. The *Hegre* dropped anchor there in warm sunny weather
within sight of Tower Bridge. She stayed only a couple of days
and on Saturday, April 19th, her master, Mr Haagensen,
steered her down river past Gravesend, bound, according to
Lloyd's, for Tenerife, via Brixham. The *Hegre* called at that
pretty Devon harbour on the following day and sailed almost
immediately for Lisbon.

The *Hegre* may not have been in the first bloom of youth but she was not the original of *The Death Ship*. She did not sink off the coast of Africa or anywhere else, and neither did she carry Marut to Mexico. On April 25th she sailed from Lisbon for Las Palmas, leaving there four days later for Dieppe, where she arrived safely on May 13th. Somewhere Ret Marut must have transferred to another ship. If *The Death Ship* was literally true, this second vessel was soon to be wrecked. More likely, it was his connection to Mexico.

There were gaps but the picture was filling out. I had tracked Marut through London and knew for sure that he had become Traven. It was time to examine closely what was known about the early years of Ret Marut – the first forty years in the life of B. Traven.

18 'M'

The earliest reference to the existence of Ret Marut is in 1907, by which time, according to his routine police registration, he was already 25 years old. Rolf Recknagel, who painstakingly assembled every particle of evidence about Marut, discovered nothing about this first quarter of a century.

In 1907 Marut joined the State Theatre at Essen, in the Ruhr, as an actor. He worked in the Thüringen city of Suhl in 1908 and the following year was in Crimmitschau, in Saxony, where he met the actress Elfried Zielke, four years his junior. In 1910 they lived near each other in Berlin, where Marut was studying, and together joined the New Theatre of Berlin troupe, in which company Marut was active in the local branch of the actors' association. He and Elfriede made guest appearances in East Prussia and in the towns of Zirke and Pinne in the province of Posen, before Marut joined the Danzig Theatre in September 1911. In Danzig he was chairman and treasurer of the actors' association branch and it was there, too, that Elfriede gave birth to his daughter on March 20th, 1912. The child was known as Irene Zielke. She was to know little of her father, whose relationship with her mother broke up soon after the birth.

In the mid-1960s a reporter traced Irene Zielke, then working as a teacher in East Berlin. She told him that she had heard nothing from her father since she was six years old and that she had no memory of him. Her mother, Elfriede, had told her that he had spoken German with a slight accent, and also some English; that he had been born on a ship; and that the papers of his birth had been destroyed in the earthquake and fire of 1906 in San Francisco. Elfriede also told her daughter that as a child Marut had been a member of a ballet company which had travelled all over the world. He had had a governess from the age of six and his mother, who was Irish, had committed suicide when he was only twelve. In this version of his background, which must have come from Marut himself, his father was English.

There were clear echoes of all this in some of the yarns he had spun to Señora Lujan – the ballet, being born at sea, hints that he had lived in England as a child – and it fitted the information Marut delivered to the German police. The altered registration card had described him as a citizen of England, before it was changed to 'America' after the outbreak of the 1914 war. There was some logic to this if his father were English, yet he himself had been born or registered in the United States. A later police card added the information that his father was called William – an English enough Christian name to go with that peculiar surname of no recognisable nationality. The same document gave his mother's name as Helene Ottarent, about which there was certainly an Irish ring.

From Danzig, Marut moved in 1912 to the Düsseldorf Theatre, where he remained for three years. He cannot have been any great shakes as an actor, for he was still playing tiny parts as waiters and humble retainers, a lack of recognition not greatly to his taste I would imagine.

Muſikanten .. .. {Ret Marut
                                   {Paul Günther
                                   {Joſeph Brucker

Recknagel found a description of him dating from this time. It presages closely the slightly built man who withstood the rigours of the Mexican jungle and who stared out at me from Señora Lujan's photographs: 'Very thin but tough. His body had the toughness of a jockey. He had warm blue eyes and always looked intent. The nose was pointed strong and distinctive – the nose of a tracker dog.'

Marut's bloodhound looks prevented him from being cast as a leading man and his theatrical career was coming to an end. When he moved south to Munich in 1915 he turned his back on acting and became a writer. He had written articles and short stories during the previous three years and now came the novel *An das Fräulein von S ...* , which he wrote under the name of Richard Maurhut. It was published by Mermet – Irene Mermet, the 24-year-old actress who had joined him in Munich. From now until the end of his life, with the exception of the first years in Mexico, Marut–Traven used women friends as his front to the world. They were both a shield to protect him from enquiry, and a bridge to the circle of transactions and strangers with whom an author has to deal and with whom Traven was uncomfortable. Irene Mermet, Maria de la Luz Martinez, Esperanza Lopez Mateos and Rosa Elena Lujan all served loyally in the role.

The first issue of *Der Ziegelbrenner* was published on September 1st, 1917, in Munich. Marut casually boasted to his readers, 'I have got to know practically every country in this world and I have lived for years in many non-German countries.' It was a remark dropped in to establish his credentials as a wise and far-seeing critic of society. There was an anxiety in his yearning to be listened to, which he could only partly disguise with his tone of belligerent independence, a tone reflected in the magazine's sub-title, *Criticism of Current Conditions and Disgusting Contemporaries*. He was offhand towards his readers:

The next issue appears in July. Perhaps. Perhaps even later. Perhaps earlier. Depending on the necessity of baking new bricks. A definite day of issue will not be fixed now nor ever. It wouldn't be kept anyway. We don't need to fix a date and think of this as an advantage not a disadvantage.

Marut, as revealed in *Der Ziegelbrenner*, was hectoring, romantic, capricious, full of exaggerations, obsessive; a man shot through with a desperate idealism. His chief targets were the war, the capitalist war mongers who had brought it about, and the newspapers. He displayed a special venom for the press, and *Der Ziegelbrenner* sometimes described itself as 'for politically mature people who receive no help from the daily press'. It warned its readers that, if they had the good of Germany and the good of humanity at heart, they should steer clear of the major newspapers: 'One has to beware of their editorials as of venereal disease.'

Marut was concerned not with races and countries but with individuals. The magazine contained may emotional reminders of what the war meant to the people involved. The third issue, in March 1918, opened:

> *Chaos*
> Men fall/Men stand/Men die/Men live/Mothers lament/
> Women mourn/Others make hand grenades/Cursing on the
> tramway/Children weeping fills the universe.

Der Ziegelbrenner

2. Jahr	16. März 1918	Heft 3

Chaos

Männer fallen / Männer stehen / Männer sterben / Männer leben / Mütter jammern / Frauen trauern / Andere machen Handgranaten / Fluchen auf der Straßenbahn / Kinder-Weinen füllt das All.

Marut was heavily influenced by the nineteenth-century German philosopher, Max Stirner, whose unique ideas of individualistic anarchism were proclaimed in his book, *The Ego and Its Own*. Stirner believed that personal indignation was the most powerful agent for change. He was against global ideas, rules for all mankind and all institutions, anything which demands a loyalty in conflict with an individual's own wishes and impulses. Each human being should live according to his or her own lights; honesty lay in doing things, including what you did for others, because these things satisfied you. He made selfishness a social force: 'He who loves another human being is richer by that love than he who loves no one.'

It was small wonder that such a creed found a welcome in the heart of Marut. He was to live his life beyond the gates of society, he chose his own rules and at all times, he protected the integrity of his 'self'. *Der Ziegelbrenner* expounded his individualist ideal. 'I want to spread [the word] ... not for *your* sakes, but for *mine*! Only for mine! Only for my own sake do I want to change the atmosphere around me, make it purer, healthier ...' He belonged, he said, to no party or political organisation of any kind.

> I cannot belong to any party because to be a member of any party would be a restriction of my personal freedom, because the obligation to follow a party programme would take away from me all possibility of developing into what I consider to be the highest and noblest goal on earth: *to be a human being*. I do not want to be anything but a human being, just a man.

With so strong a belief in the power and significance of the individual, it was odd that Marut was so shy about standing forth to be seen. There was the weird business of addressing meetings with the lights out, telling readers that he would rather be pissed on by dogs than let them snoop out information about himself, and the provocative warning-off of all visitors. The assertiveness of his voice was in direct proportion to the bashfulness of his physical presence.

In his magazine Marut deployed a wide and detailed knowledge of the Bible. He let it be known that he had studied theology, but had broken it off before, as he put it, he could learn the niceties which would have enabled him to 'pray from the pulpit for the victory of the German Army'. Naturally, being Marut, he had not cut short his studies because he had flunked the examinations; he was forced to quit because he was too challenging, too radical a student: 'I was "removed" during a lecture on account of two "improper" questions and "strictly" forbidden – in Latin – to attend any of the functions of the school of theology.'

This story led scholars to comb the records of German universities in search of any reference to Marut's theological studies. They came up with the name of Charles Trefny, an American theology student who enrolled at the University of Freiburg in the autumn of 1902 and who was sent down by the authorities early in 1903. The university register stated that Trefny had been born on July 2nd, 1880, in St Louis, Missouri, the son of Karl William Trefny. He had previously attended St Xavier College in Cincinnati, Ohio. This fitted Marut quite closely. The nationality was right, and it was a long shot against two American theology students being expelled from German universities around the same time. Also 'Trefny' could have been an early version of 'Traven'.

Investigations in Cincinnati showed that no one called Charles Trefny was a student at either Xavier University or Xavier High School in the ten years prior to 1903, nor was there any inhabitant of the city called Trefny, Traven or Torsvan. This did not matter too much. It would not have been the only time Marut–Traven had invented a background for himself, and Rolf Recknagel and others were convinced that Trefny was Marut.

But the argument is by no means clear-cut. Trefny studied Catholic theology and everything about Marut–Traven suggests that, while he was sympathetic to the teachings of Jesus Christ, he was no lover of the church as an organisation. For instance, in *Der Ziegelbrenner*:

If I say that the greatest rascal and liar during the war was a journalist, I do not forget to add that right after him comes the clergyman. For the representative of Christ on earth there should not be a government – Christ did not know any state, he only knew humanity, he only knew brothers, only children of God.

When Torsvan chatted to Spota at Cashew Park, he was quick to press Spota's friend to convert from Catholicism to the Protestant faith.

Another question mark over Trefny must be the cause of his expulsion from Freiburg. It does not matter that it was not exactly as Ret Marut described, that would be too much to ask. It does matter that it was for something quite out of keeping with even Marut–Traven's peculiar antics. Trefny was in fact arrested by the police for 'immoral activities'. He passed himself off as a doctor specialising in vaccination and, in this guise, carried out examinations on unsuspecting patients. It was the classic Sunday newspaper story of a pathetic young inadequate trying to get close to ladies with their clothes off. This was not Marut's style at all. He appears to have had no difficulty in attracting women by more orthodox methods.

Among the last issues of *Der Ziegelbrenner* published in Munich was one entitled 'The Day is Dawning' (November 9th, 1918), and another headed 'The World Revolution Begins' (January 30th, 1919). Marut's euphoria reflected the turbulent events of a six-month period during which Munich was in the eye of the revolutionary storm and when it must have seemed as if the old order might be thrown off for good. It was Marut's part in the final developments of this time – three weeks of the purest, most hopeless, revolutionary government – that was the cause of his passing through London on the run four years later.

During the last few months of the First World War, Bavaria, and particularly Munich, the capital, was one of the chief centres of German discontent with the continuing and exhausting hostilities. Bavaria always felt slightly apart from the rest of the German Empire, especially from Prussia. It was 70 per cent Catholic, while Prussia was mainly Protestant, and had a far higher proportion of independent tradesmen and land-owning peasants. As the war sapped the resources and spirit of the German Empire, especially from Prussia. It was 70 per resentful about the hardships they believed the Prussians had brought upon them. There was even talk of a separate Bavarian treaty with the Allies. In Munich the desire for peace led the Independent Socialists, implacable in their opposition to the war, to flourish at the expense of the cautious and conservative leadership of the Majority Socialists, the largest party elsewhere.

It was in this atmosphere of agitation and disaffection that a huge peace demonstration took place on the great grass field

of Bavaria Park, in Munich, on the warm sunny afternoon of
November 7th, 1918. An enormous crowd was addressed by
twenty or so socialist speakers, one of whom, Kurt Eisner, had
a dramatic effect. Eisner was a 51-year-old Jewish journalist,
formerly on the editorial board of *Vorwärts*. He urged the
soldiers, who had disobeyed orders to be present, to scatter
throughout the city, win over their comrades, occupy the barracks and seize weapons and ammunition. This they, and much
of the rest of the crowd, did and by the following day Eisner
was head of a government which controlled the city and had
declared Bavaria a republic. King Ludwig III of Bavaria fled
and, away in Berlin on November 9th, in the midst of a general
strike, Kaiser Wilhelm II was pressed into abdication. The
German monarchy was at an end.

Eisner's regime in Munich was, like its leader, eccentric,
idealistic, and chaotic. Eisner himself was a pleasingly bizarre
figure in grey beard, steel-rimmed pince-nez and large black
hat, but support for his regime melted away as confusion grew.
In January there were elections for the Bavarian parliament
and Eisner's Independent Socialists attracted only a tiny vote.
He hung on hopelessly and ineffectually for a few more weeks
before deciding to resign. On his way to tender his resignation
to the parliament, he was shot down and killed by a young,
extreme right-winger, Count Anton Arco-Valley.

The assassination of Eisner brought a wave of mourning for
the man and his ideals, and was followed by a period of even
greater havoc. The Roman Catholic cathedral of Munich was
ceremoniously declared a revolutionary temple; the city went
bankrupt; the citizens suffered from shortages of food and coal
in the extreme cold weather; the beer halls were the scenes of
almost continual political rallies, and there were regular gun
battles in the streets. Ret Marut observed these events as three
factions competed for political power: the Majority Socialists,
who were forced out of the city to set up a Bavarian government
in exile in Bamberg; a Communist group, led by three Russians,
Towia Axelrod, Max Levien and Eugen Leviné; and a band
of anarchist intellectuals under Gustav Landaur, Erich Müh-
same, the poet and playwright, and another poet, 25-year-old
Ernst Toller. Marut was close to this last circle, the 'Coffee-
house Anarchists'. When, on April 6th, 1919, they declared a

'Republic of Councils' (Räterepublik) to govern Bavaria, he
surrendered his natural independence, put aside his suspicion
of all organisations and joined them. This confederation of
workers' and soldiers' councils promised him as loose and as
free an arrangement as could ever deserve the name of government. For possibly the only time in his life, this lone wolf
engaged with others upon a great joint enterprise.

A later warrant for his arrest described Marut as one of the
ring-leaders of the Republic of Councils. While he may well
have been among their number socially and intellectually, he
does not appear to have been among those directing the course
of events. He was a member of a committee set up to disseminate
revolutionary propaganda among the troops, and he sat on a
commission to establish a revolutionary tribunal (he was chosen
as presiding officer according to his own account). He was later
at pains to make it clear that these were not offices that he had
held but tasks with which he had been entrusted. It was not
to Der Ziegelbrenner's taste to hold authority over the lives of
other men. He refused to accept an appointment as Director
of the Press, and became instead one of the censors of the capitalist newspapers and the author of a plan to nationalise newspaper publication. Marut poured scorn on the notion that Germany had ever had a free press. Editors and journalists were
in the clutches of the newspaper owners, who dictated what
policies were pursued. The only freedom which existed was for
those rich enough to be newspaper proprietors.

Marut's brief flirtation with revolutionary action lived on in
his mind when he was writing in Mexico as B. Traven. In the
cycle of Jungle Novels, which chronicles the struggle of the
Indians in pre-Revolutionary Mexico and their uprising
against their masters, Traven urges the need for swift and decisive action. Was he remembering the failures of Munich? In
The Rebellion of the Hanged he praises the Indian rebels for having
none of

> the lamentable deliberations of those men who, in nearly all
> revolutions, speak and orate endlessly – speak, when they
> should be taking action, about the way to carry out their
> resolutions. They talk and talk, and it is these windbags of
> revolution who end by ruining it.

Perhaps Traven was criticising himself. He was neither soldier nor decision-maker. The parts he had played in the revolution, as censor and commission member, were not really true to his character, which inclined him more to stand in the shadows of events, exhorting, criticising, writing. He could never have done what he admired the Indians for doing: taking clear, direct and ruthless action, striking down their enemies in blood. In his books he makes them call for officers to be stabbed, for skulls to be smashed, for millions to be slaughtered and for streams of scarlet blood to be shed. The fiasco of Munich may have made him believe that all this and more was necessary if the poor and oppressed of the world were to throw off their chains. They were not actions that he could carry out and there is an element of self-reproach in his insistence on them. Perhaps he feared that he had been one more of those windbags that the Indians were fortunate to be without:

They had not been contaminated by the deformed and deforming spirit of newspapermen and orators ... Not one of them had ever read a revolutionary article or studied histories of revolutions. They had never attended political meetings or known the significance of a programme.

The Republic of Councils lasted only six days, during which time Munich witnessed a government as dotty, well-meaning and incompetent as any in modern times. It introduced a plan for free money, a plea for new art forms, and a law that no home could contain more than three rooms. A bizarre foreign policy was presented by the Commissar for Foreign Affairs, Dr Franz Lipp, who quickly found cause to declare war on Switzerland. Dr Lipp, it transpired, was genuinely mad; almost his first act on taking office was to send a telegram to Moscow informing the Bolsheviks that his predecessor had taken the key to the office lavatory with him. Before Switzerland could be invaded, almost before the lavatory door could be opened, a new regime under the Russian Communists, Levien, Leviné and Axelrod was in power. The new government raised a Bavarian Red Army and provided it with free food, liquor and prostitutes as well as handsome wages. The soldiers were needed. On April 20th the Majority Socialist government in

Bamberg attacked the revolutionaries, only to be defeated twenty-five miles short of Munich by a detachment of the new Red Army under the command of Ernst Toller.

The Bamberg Socialists now called in the Berlin government, and at the end of April 30,000 Freikorps soldiers marched on Bavaria. The Freikorps were private armies, recruited and commanded by former regular army officers and paid for by the central government. They varied in their professionalism. The force which advanced south to Munich contained some of the newer, least disciplined recruits as well as members of the hardened, crack divisions. The Freikorps surrounded the city and, on May 1st, 1919, moved in to capture it in the face of little serious resistance from the Red Army, which had melted away. On the last night of the revolutionaries' control of Munich, some of their soldiers murdered and mutilated the bodies of twenty hostages, before Toller was able to put a stop to the atrocities. In reprisal the victorious Freikorps unleashed ten days of terror, which far exceeded anything that had occurred under the revolutionaries, who had taken few lives either in gaining power or in exercising it. The Freikorps had killed six hundred or more people in capturing Munich and they now executed or murdered a similar number as the city was 'cleansed'.*

The first targets for revenge were the leaders of the Republic of Councils and Marut was counted among their number. Gustav Landaur, with whom he had worked closely on the Propaganda Commission, was beaten, shot and finally kicked to death; Erich Mühsam, the writer who was later the first to recognise the voice of his friend Marut in the works of B. Traven, was imprisoned;† Leviné was shot by a firing squad; Toller was sentenced to five years.‡ Ret Marut escaped. In the next issue of *Der Ziegelbrenner*, published in December 1919 while he was on the run, wanted for high treason, he gave a

---

* These figures are the estimate of R.M. Watt in his book *The Kings Depart*, on which I have leaned heavily for an account of the Bavarian revolution.

† Mühsam was sentenced to fifteen years but released in 1924 under an amnesty for political prisoners. He was arrested by the Nazis in 1933 and cruelly murdered in Oranienburg concentration camp on July 10th, 1934.

‡ Toller later gained recognition as a talented playwright. He committed suicide in New York in 1939.

dramatic description of what had happened to him on May
1st. It confusingly refers to 'M' in the third person, possibly
to mystify the police, possibly because it was written in part
by Irene Mermet. This account probably exaggerates the importance of Marut's rôle and his coolness in the face of danger,
but it is the only record of his flight which exists and we have
to rely on it.

When the enemy troops drove into the city, Marut was sitting
in the Maria Theresa coffee house on Augusten Strasse, hoping
to meet some of the people attending a meeting of German revolutionary and freedom-loving writers, which was to take place
that afternoon. As he sat there, the Freikorps soldiers machine-
gunned the crowds near the coffee house, and seven people were
shot down, two of them fatally.

While the gunfire continued, Marut helped to carry one un-
conscious victim inside, where a woman doctor tended to the
man's wounds. Marut left the café, but before he had gone more
than a few hundred yards up the street a vehicle, piled high
with weapons and carrying about ten civilians wearing counter-
revolutionary armbands, drew up and stopped him. These
clerks and students recognised Marut as 'the most dangerous
agitator of the Republic of Councils, the scourge of the citi-
zenry, and the destroyer of the press', and ordered him to put
his hands up. He was searched. 'The editorial head of *Der Ziegelbrenner* searched for weapons! If you have nothing better to do,
I suppose that you can search for truffles on bare paving stones
as well.'

His captors began to denounce Marut to the small crowd
which had gathered, saying that he was the main cause of the
bloodshed in Munich and that he was going to get his deserts.
The crowd showed little interest so, instead of bumping him
off on the spot, the troops bundled Marut into the vehicle at
rifle point and drove him off with cries of, 'Now we have really
caught one of them, the most dangerous of them all!' He was
taken to the War Ministry building which, to Marut's scorn,
was full of civilians ('profiteers', 'pimps' and 'hangers on')
swaggering around under the protection of the soldiers. He was
taken to a room at the back of the building, where a guard
waved pistols under his nose. His captors told Marut that he
was accused of various crimes of high treason, for which the

penalty was immediate execution, and urged him to confess.
When he refused, tame witnesses were wheeled in to testify
against him. His request to call witnesses in his defence was
ignored.

His captors took him out of the Ministry, through streets now
full of royalist flags, and into the Residence building, the official
home of the Bavarian kings. Here a lone lieutenant was conducting a court martial, casually smoking a cigarette as he decided whether the prisoner in front of him should go free or
die. Each case took about three minutes, and if there was any
doubt the prisoner was shot. For an hour Marut was held in
an ante-room with many other prisoners, some of them merely
youths and young girls. As they waited, they watched the victims of the lieutenant's hasty judgements being put to their
deaths. Shortly before his case was to be heard, Marut had a
stroke of luck. The prisoner ahead of him began shouting and
struggling with the soldiers who were taking him into the court,
and in the ensuing confusion Marut managed to escape. He
got clean away, thanks to two of the soldiers 'in whom for one
moment a spark of humanity was kindled as they saw what was
being done to the most precious thing a man has, his life'.

Marut fled from Munich and lived in forests, barns and hay-
lofts, hiding from the authorities. He was on the wanted list
for high treason.

256. Marut Ret, geb. 25.2.1882 in San Francisco, letzte Wohnung: Clemensstraße 84 III:
war Mitglied des Propagandaauschusses und der Kommission zur Bildung eines
Revolutionstribunals.

As he wandered, he talked to small groups in towns and villages, proclaiming the virtues of government by councils as
in the brief, false dawn of the Räterepublik. It was no use, he
wrote, trying to win over vast numbers of people at once; such
swift conversions led only to shallow beliefs and misunderstand-
ings. The only way to spread his conviction that the council
system was the sole pathway to a perfect earthly government
was by talking at length to individuals, filling their minds,
hearts and souls with knowledge of the truth. Behind him in
Munich, the council supporters were being ruthlessly destroyed. One Freikorps commander instructed his officers: 'It's

a lot better to kill a few innocent people than to let one guilty
person escape ... You know how to handle it ... shoot them
and report that they attacked you or tried to escape.' By the
time the Freikorps left the city Munich was set to remain an
ugly and unforgiving political battleground. Adolf Hitler, who
had left Munich in distaste at the onset of the Eisner government the previous autumn, had now returned. He began
to work for the regular army as a political agent and before
long was to meet two like-minded men who were also in the
city: Ernst Röhm, later head of the Nazi S.A., and Rudolf
Hess.

As the future Nazi leaders were making one another's acquaintance in Munich, Ret Marut and his girl friend Irene
Mermet were on their travels. Irene had also been arrested,
but she had been quickly released and had then joined Marut
in flight. Their trail is difficult to follow. They probably moved
from Bavaria to Vienna, and certainly, by the late autumn of
1919, they were living in an attic in Berlin, where they provided
shelter for another fugitive from Munich, Erich Wollenberg,
one of the commanders of the Bavarian Red Army. Wollenberg
later remembered Marut coming to sit on his bed at night and
relating his idealistic visions of a better world. By day, Irene
made little rag dolls, which Marut sold on the streets of Berlin.
They moved on to Cologne. The left bank of the Rhine was
still occupied territory, and many radicals sought refuge there
from the German authorities or used it as a staging post to slip
across the border into Holland. It was also the city that Irene
had been born in. She and Marut had met the Cologne artist
Franz Wilhelm Seiwert when he had visited Munich, and now
that they were in his city they made contact with him and the
group of artists of which he was a member, the Kalltal
Gemeinschaft.

The fugitive couple returned to Berlin in June 1921 and
stayed with another comrade from the Ziegelbrenner days
Goetz Öhly. They borrowed Öhly's passport and left the city
only a day before the police came to search the house. Öhly
received a letter soon after saying that the passport had been
lost. Marut and Irene went back to their artist friends in
Cologne and it was from there that they published, on
December 21st, 1921, the final issue of Der Ziegelbrenner, illus-

trated by Franz Seiwert. The last anyone heard of them was that dramatic postcard that Marut sent to the imprisoned Erich Mühsam at the end of 1922: 'In a few hours' time I shall board a ship to take me across the Atlantic. With that I shall have ceased to exist.'

He had not ceased to exist. He had not even disappeared from Europe as he had intended. Instead he turned up in London in 1923: forty-one years old, without a passport, without a country. I had word from Charles Humphrey in America suggesting that in the meantime Marut had managed to cross the Atlantic – to Canada, where he had been refused entry and put on a ship back to Europe. Hence his unplanned arrival in England. It was not until his departure from London, in April 1924, that he had truly vanished from Europe and the identity of Ret Marut had finally ceased to exist.

Given that the *Hegre* was not bound for Mexico, it is impossible to know if Marut had by now decided on that country as his final destination. It is likely. Mexico was always a land to disappear in, it was far away and little known, and in the early 1920s it glittered with distant hope in the eyes of those European radicals who had witnessed the collapse of the German revolutions. In 1911 the dictator, Porfirio Diaz, had been overthrown by a largely peasant revolution under the slogan of 'Land and Liberty'. Since then a series of regimes had been trying to establish a new and equitable order. The revolution continued. A man of pure ideals and ingenuous optimism, like Marut, could look to Mexico as a land where ancient wrongs were being righted, where there was a chance to build the Utopia he believed men were capable of creating.

If, when he was in the East End of London, Marut had seen the latest issues of the anarchist monthly, *Freedom*, he would have been reminded of the opportunity that Mexico offered. In August 1923 it reprinted an American article about the Mexican struggle:

The revolutionary world, habitually exhausted by never-ending contests on its home battlefields, has but the dimmest conception of how important is the role that Mexico has been compelled to play.

Life has sprung up again, invincible.

In December *Freedom* returned to the subject of revolutionary Mexico where, Marut could have read, there was a need for those who could tend the beacon of rebellion. He could continue his work.

> The picture presented [by Mexican activity] is one that, as we conceive, can scarcely fail to impress the reflective reader. That the Spirit of Revolt is flamingly awake seems to us beyond dispute ...

In Mexico, then, Marut could be both safe and useful. As a hiding place it did not disappoint him. A Mexican port provided the camouflage of hundreds of rootless ones like himself. He described it in *The Cotton-Pickers*, the 'starving immigrants, if not Hungarians, then Austrians, or Germans or Poles or Czechs. The port was swarming with them'.

Of his exact route from London to Tampico, the Gulf port that B. Traven first wrote from, there was no evidence. Nor was there as to when he and Irene Mermet parted company. I had previously assumed that she had travelled directly to the United States. But if Marut attempted and failed to get into Canada, perhaps the two of them journeyed there together and only she was allowed to stay. He had lost Goetz Öhly's passport, which he had been hoping to travel on, and I knew from the London episode that he had not acquired another. Irene Mermet was not wanted for treason and so could presumably travel quite openly on her German papers and could have entered Canada or the United States in the normal way. It is likely that there was a forced parting. Whatever story they concocted to explain Marut's lack of papers to the Canadians must have failed. Irene was clean and decided to remain in Canada the immigration authorities pointed Marut back across the Atlantic.

Irene Mermet was definitely in the United States in 1924. A letter Judy Stone received from Santa Fé, New Mexico supplies the evidence.

Dear Miss Stone,
    In reading your article, 'The Mystery of B. Traven', in the September, 1967, issue of *Ramparts*, I noticed you

remarks as to a certain Irene Mermet. I suspect that this is the same Irene Mermet that my wife and I became friendly with away back in the early '20s in Greenwich Village, New York. How my wife came to know her I am not certain. All I know is that she brought Irene home with her one day and she stayed with us for a short while pending a job of tutoring with a wealthy family that was in the offing. I remember this part of her story as to escaping from Germany. It seemed that she and a companion(s?) left Germany in a small boat headed for England. They were caught in a storm and were stranded on the coast of Holland. I remember her saying, 'I'll never forget waking up on the shore in the morning and there in a half-circle around us stood a herd of cows peacefully chewing their cuds and watching us!' If she told us anymore as to how she got out of Holland and to America, the story is lost in the mists of 45 years.

At that time she gave us two colored early cubist drawings, and though I do not recall the name of the artist, they are signed 'FWS 23'. I have three of her letters to us, two of which were addressed to my wife who was in the theater under the name of Dora Malet at that time (she died in 1927) and one to me in Detroit, Michigan, where I had gone on a job. These are dated July 30th, 1924, October 18th, 1924 (to Dora Malet) and March 28th, 1925 (to myself). The first letter came from St Jovite, Canada, where the family had gone for the summer, and the second and third were from Washington, D.C.

When Irene took the tutoring job, it was only to be temporary as she then wanted to live in New York and planned to take up quarters with us at 51 Barrow Street where we had taken a whole house. However, due to circumstances – both with us as well as with her – this never materialized. There was an interesting note tacked onto the letter of July 30th, 1924, in which she said, 'My friend I spoke of as another prospective for a room will not be able to take advantage of it *during this* winter because he is lying sick with malaria in the South Sea Islands.'

In her letter of March 28th, 1925, she wrote in part, 'I have a very busy and exciting time behind me and am now in full preparation to clear out for Mexico, maybe Argentine.

I am entirely sick of civilizations and try to get away from it as far as possible. I am sorry that you are so far away. There is very little chance to see you before I leave for the wilderness.'

Sincerely yours,
GEORGE MCCROSSEN

There is little doubt that this was the same Irene Mermet, and that the drawings were by F.W. Seiwert. The date on the pictures presents a problem because it indicates that Irene was still in Germany in 1923. If the famous postcard to Erich Mühsam really was sent from Rotterdam at the end of 1922, Irene must have been left in Germany on her own. But if the date was remembered wrongly and the card was actually sent in 1923, it is possible to construct a story which keeps them together. Recknagel has recently found evidence among the effects in Mexico City that Marut and Irene planned to travel by train from Trier to Luxembourg as late as July 1923. That may not have taken place and they could both have been with Seiwert in Cologne early that year before trying to reach England in the small boat. (There is no reason for Irene to have made up this part of the story.) They were washed ashore in Holland and made their way to Rotterdam, one of the busiest ports in Europe, where they might hope to find a ship to take them across the Atlantic. If they sailed from there to Canada, Marut could have been turned away and recrossed the ocean in time to be arrested in London in November 1923.

The friend that Irene Mermet spoke of as another likely roomer in McCrossen's house was surely Marut. The reference to the South Sea Islands sounds like a deliberate cover for the truth. Irene had by now learned that Marut was not coming to New York because he had been deported from England and had made for a country where they were less fussy about papers than the United States. It is not impossible that he sailed the long way eastwards round the world, but he was almost certainly in Mexico by July 1924 and all the early evidence of his presence places him in or near Tampico, in the state of Tamaulipas – where you would arrive on the Atlantic route. It was from Tamaulipas that he wrote his long letters to Preczang at the Büchergilde, describing and boasting of his hardships, letters which were suffused with the intensity of his new experiences.

Irene's letter to McCrossen implies that it was in the spring of 1925 that she travelled south to Mexico to be reunited with Marut, now transformed into B. Traven and Traven Torsvan. She had not seen him for at least eighteen months. The reunion may well have been joyful at first, but it did not survive the strains of a new life, a new continent and new identities. Within two years she was separated from him again, this time voluntarily and for good. There is a story that she returned to Germany for a visit in the early 1930s and told a friend about her months in Mexico. According to this account, Torsvan lodged her in a hacienda while he disappeared into the jungle for weeks or months at a time, returning with manuscripts written on scraps of paper, which Irene had to copy up. It was no way to treat a girl as strong and independent as Irene Mermet. Eventually, she took advantage of one of his lengthy absences and left Mexico to return to the United States. Little is known about her thereafter except that she died in the United States, in the mid-1950s. For thirty years she was the only person outside of Mexico to know something of the secret of B. Traven.

19 Was There Another Man?

Ret Marut wrote the Traven books. Did he write them alone and unaided? I cannot actually disprove the haunting and romantic theory that there was another man in Mexico, whom Ret Marut met and from whom he derived most of his stories, but I see no evidence for such a man and no need to invent him. No one has been able to put a name to this ghost-like 'Erlebnisträger' or 'carrier of experience'. Where he came from and what happened to him is as notional as the evidence for his existence.

The idea stems from the time that Luis Spota cornered the author in Acapulco. Among the several tales that Torsvan tried to fob Spota off with was a story that more than one person was involved in writing the Traven books and that he, Torsvan, was only one of them. Many Traven followers seized on this story because it provided an explanation for what appeared to be an insoluble problem. Traven always said that he could only write from his own direct experience; he always claimed to be an American; in his early books, which had a powerful autobiographical flavour, he wrote in the first person as if he were an American. All this was impossible to equate with Ret Marut writing the books on his own. Although Marut might have been technically American, as he claimed, he did not have the American background that Gerard Gales paraded in *The Death Ship* and *The Cotton-Pickers*. Nor could he have written all the books from his own experience. *But* if Marut worked from stories, possibly even rough manuscripts, provided by an itinerant, socialist worker from the United States, he would have been justified in everything he said because the name B. Traven would have concealed a *joint* identity.

This ingenious theory also provides the answer to another question: could Ret Marut have written the books in time? Even when it was thought that Marut had reached Tampico some time in 1923, there were several sceptics who said that it was simply not possible for anyone to have digested enough of life in Mexico and produced the books as quickly as Marut would have had to do. Now that it is evident that Marut could not have had his first glimpse of that country much before the middle of 1924, this argument is strengthened. The first B. Traven stories reached the offices of *Vorwärts* in Berlin in the spring of 1925, so they must have been written and despatched within six to eight months of Marut's arriving in Mexico. Over the next five years, six more books were published and one of them, the non-fiction work, *Land des Frühlings*, hinted that Traven's association went back many years before Marut could have got there.

The first-person storyteller and the strong whiff of authenticity in the early books added fuel to the belief that the only way that Marut could have written them was by mining the experiences of someone else's life. This other man, so the argument runs, was the 'real' Gerard Gales and it was his adventures which Marut chronicled in those early works. It was not surprising then that the books began to flow easily from Marut's typewriter, for the stories had already been lived by this other American; Marut was transcribing material provided for him by a 'carrier of experience'.

The overwhelming appeal of this hypothesis for many Traven fans is that it allows their hero to tell the truth. If all his pronouncements about writing from experience, coming from the Midwest and so on related to a *dual* identity, then they could be true for one half of the partnership and the other half could still be Ret Marut. In the same way, it casts in an honourable light all those denials that Traven made in the last twenty years of his life. When the old man told Huston or Spota or Judy Stone or any of his friends that he was not the author B. Traven, he was not telling a barefaced lie but displaying a punctilious honesty. He would not admit to being the author because he was only the *co*-author. To have taken the whole

credit for the works himself would have been to deny the contribution of that anonymous American who had supplied the
essential ingredients. So the 'Erlebnisträger' hypothesis has
it.

Some students of the Traven works have even attempted to
differentiate between the character of Marut, as revealed in *Der
Ziegelbrenner*, and the character of this mysterious American, as
revealed by the narratives of Gerard Gales. It is possible, some
claim, to divine the presence of two authors of the Traven books
from the mixture of philosophies that the works exhibit:
Marut's is individualistic, based on the thoughts of Max
Stirner; the American's, more communal and syndicalist.
These two strains compete in the Traven books as Ret Marut
injects his own reading and beliefs into the more simply socialist
stories of the untutored American.

I can find not one shred of evidence that this 'carrier of experience' ever existed. Everything that has been written about
him has been supposition, introduced in order to plug gaps in
our knowledge of Traven or to explain away his lies and decep-
tions. Those who have loved and been inspired by his writings
have been unwilling to face the fact that a noble writer might
also be an incorrigible liar. Within Traven two powerful obsessions were in conflict. His passion for anonymity strained
against his determination to make himself heard. To cover the
resulting cracks he told lies.

The most imposing of the problems for which the 'Erlebnisträger' theory is invoked to provide a solution is the question
of timing. Could Marut have written that much about Mexico
that quickly? But even here the idea of inventing some other
man is by no means the most convincing explanation. It is
appropriate to apply the principle of Occam's Razor, by which
'it is vain to do with more what can be done with less'. A simple
explanation is more likely to be true than a complex one. In
this case it is idle to propose an unnamed, unseen and untraceable person, who passed on his stories and then conveniently
disappeared, when the simple alternative is that Marut was
able to write the books quickly. After all, he was a practised
writer. Over the previous ten years he had published several
short stories and a novel, as well as all his journalism. When
he arrived in the New World for the first time in the middle

of 1924, his antennae would have been extended and his nerve-endings sensitive to the drama and novelty of his experiences. He was alone in an exotic country, alive to circumstances he could previously only have read about or dreamed of. It is hardly surprising that he began to write, and to write quickly.

The first book of *The Cotton-Pickers*, which comprises the stories sent to *Vorwärts*, runs to less than eighty pages in the English language edition. He could easily have written these, and more of the early stories, in his first six months in Mexico. The Mexican settings convince, but there is nothing that Marut could not have written soon after his arrival. The references to politics and the I.W.W. are of the kind that would be second nature to a radical with his ear to the ground and they do not bespeak, as some have claimed, a long and intimate acquaintance with the Wobblies. The second half of *The Cotton-Pickers* ranges more widely. It was written later, in 1925, after Traven's exchanges with Ernst Preczang at the Büchergilde Gutenberg. By then he had travelled more, seen more and heard more.

The first complete novel to be published under the name B. Traven was *The Death Ship*, the content of which owes nothing at all to Mexico. He must have seen something of life below decks on a freighter in order to describe the stokehold of the *Yorikke* so graphically and at such length. It is possible that he acquired this on the journey to or from Canada, or off the coast of Holland and Germany, and that he had drafted, even completed, the book before he had arrived in Mexico. In a letter to the Büchergilde Traven recalled that when he had first heard in the spring of 1925 that his stories were going to be published, he already had 'numerous half-finished manuscripts lying around in a chest which served me as a suitcase, manuscripts which I had written in times of lengthy unemployment ...' *The Death Ship*, or part of it, could well have been one of them. After six months in Mexico Traven was in his own words at 'probably the lowest point in my professional and personal circumstances'. He was in humble employment, separated from Irene, alone and unrecognised. Whether because of the fillip that news of publication gave to his spirits or because of the depression which had preceded it, Marut certainly wrote rapidly in that first year as Traven. He posted the manuscript of *The Bridge in the Jungle* in August 1925, and sent *The Death Ship* the following month. This was not, however, an inhuman speed at which to write.

Much of the argument for there being some other hand in the work has been addressed to the supposed impossibility not so much of Marut's having written, but having lived the adventures in the time available. Some readers have calculated how many months he must have been aboard a death ship, how many months the adventures in *The Cotton-Pickers* would have taken, how many weeks to witness the events of *The Bridge in the Jungle*, and so on. They have added to this the time necessary to mull over the experiences before committing them to paper and multiplied the answer by another factor, computed from back references in the writings. The grand total has then been produced to show that Ret Marut could not possibly have done all these things himself. Of course he did not. He was a writer of fiction and he made things up.

The stories seem real and the locations are convincing because Ret Marut/B. Traven was a good writer. He could make the unfamiliar sound familiar; he could sketch in people and places he had only briefly seen, as if he had known them for years. Writers do this. They take us in with their art. In *Henderson the Rain King* Saul Bellow gave a plausible account of Africa, a continent he had at the time of writing never visited; in *The Siege of Krishnapur* J.G. Farrell transmitted the smell of battle in the Indian Mutiny, making believable – as the good historical novelist must – events he could never have experienced. Those who take at face value Traven's claim that he wrote only of what he had seen do him the disservice of denying him his art. His books may be autobiographical, but generally rather than specifically so. Many of his descriptions of people and places may have been taken from life, many of the incidents too, no doubt. But there is no need to be puzzled because he wrote in the first person about things he could not actually have done. Writing as Gerard Gales was a convenient narrative device, by which he could give a sharp outline and authentic ring to the mixture of experience, invention, acquaintances and half-heard tales, which made up his raw material. Add to this his obvious pleasure in depicting himself as a man who knows his way around the world, a master of anything he turns his hand to, and it is no wonder that it all comes out sounding as if it really happened. Marut could have produced the books in time.

As for the mixture of philosophies in the Traven books, there is no need to invent another mystery man to explain that. The combination of individualism and syndicalism in anarchist writings was quite common then. The Russian and other revolutions had forced anarchists to explore ways in which their individualist beliefs could be used in action. Traven was trying to marry his long-held anarchist ideas with the lessons of the Bavarian revolution, and, simultaneously, apply them to conditions in Mexico. It was inevitable that the offspring of this mixture would not be wholly consistent.

Michael Baumann also believes that some of the Traven work was written first in English and later translated into German by the author. He has found many examples of English and American expressions employed in Traven's German prose. He believes that the source of these may have been the American 'Erlebnisträger'.

I am not competent to judge the nature of Traven's German, but I do not see these English usages as proof of 'the other man'. Baumann himself admits that he uses them in such a way that they do not violate the German and that it must have been a positive decision to leave these Americanisms visible in his prose. I would argue that Traven threw them in to make his writing sound American. If he had truly been working from American originals, he would not have presented English manuscripts to Bernard Smith which were palpably German in shape and texture. And a real Wobbly would surely have managed some more convincing American oaths than the likes of 'What for a thousand devils!' and 'Goldfish in shit!'

All the other difficulties disappear when you allow that Traven's claims about his work might not have been true. He was trying to put people off his scent by pretending that he had lived in Mexico for many years. As a fugitive from a firing squad, he wished to keep his whereabouts hidden from the German authorities, and this fear of reprisal continued long after the amnesty for political prisoners had been declared. Not that he would ever have revealed himself to his publishers and his readers. His mania for secrecy guided his behaviour from his earliest manifestation as Ret Marut to his last days as Hal

Croves. He told lies about himself in his letters to Preczang because he always told lies about his identity. It is idle to attempt to turn these lies into truths by devising the sort of man who would make them true and then pointing to his shadow. There is no evidence for such a person.

One evening, while the *Yorikke* was at anchor off an African port, waiting for cargo and orders, Stanislav told me his story, and I told him mine. The story I told him was not my true story; it was just a good story which he accepted. Of course, I do not know if the story he told me was true. How can anybody know if any story told or heard is true?

The Death Ship

20 Son of the Kaiser?

It was now time to investigate the most spectacular Traven solution: that he was the natural son of the Kaiser. If it were true, it would account for the high secrecy and supply a powerful explanation for his feelings of rejection and rebellion. The Kaiser in question is *the* Kaiser in British mythology – Kaiser Bill, third Emperor of the Second Reich and grandson of Queen Victoria. He was born with a withered arm, became a soldier and grew Europe's most famous moustache, of which he was inordinately proud. He is remembered for sacking Bismarck and for being sacked himself in 1919, after arrogantly leading Germany into the prolonged agony of the First World War.

The story that Ret Marut was the bastard child of Wilhelm II is reported to have begun circulating in Munich as early as 1916. There were several circumstances which encouraged it. In time of war Marut was able to obtain supplies of paper on which to print his subversive journal, and when an opponent of *Der Ziegelbrenner* challenged the authorities about this they replied that they were no happier about it than the complainant but were powerless to prevent it. Was *Der Ziegelbrenner* protected in high places? One issue of his magazine fell foul of the censors, but otherwise he succeeded in publishing a stream of anti-authoritarian, anti-war material with remarkable freedom. After the war he recalled his gratitude to 'the authorities, who were always very friendly and accommodating towards the editor'. Again, why?

There are hints, too, that Marut was a person of some means. In *Der Ziegelbrenner* he twice mentions the 'private fortune' with which he is able to make up the difference, of 'roughly 6,000 marks', between his income and expenditure on the magazine. An article in a Salzburg newspaper described Marut in 1919 as 'not only a writer but a man of property', implying that he was a fair-weather revolutionary. Was it a royal bounty that put this small-time actor in funds? There were other pointers: the apparent ease of his change of nationality from English to American in the police records, and his continued immunity from harassment even after the United States entered the war in 1917.

All these things fell into place in 1966 when Traven made his cryptic remark about being a Hohenzollern, and Señora Lujan told Judy Stone that her husband was the natural son of Wilhelm II. The next year the German magazine *Stern* printed a long article about Traven, claiming that the Señora had told its reporter the same story. A twist in this version was that Traven's mother had been a Norwegian singer, whose first name was Helen. The *Stern* reporter went to Norway to seek any trace of an actress of that name of the right age and in the right place to carry Wilhelm's child. He found no suitable candidates. But *Stern* printed a photograph of the Kaiser's eldest son alongside one of the elderly Traven and commented on the 'striking resemblance'. Señora Lujan reacted as ambiguously to this article as to so many other things. She denied that she had told the German reporter what he had claimed. Yet, when Judy Stone visited her two years later, the Señora was careful to display a photograph of the Kaiser and a copy of the *Almanach de Gotha* in her husband's study.

The Kaiser story had to be taken seriously. In the catalogue to a 1976 exhibition of material connected with the Munich Räterepublik, Rolf Recknagel contributed an article called 'The Last Mystery about Marut–Traven', in which this doyen of Traven followers outlined the theory of royal parentage. He offered a possible biographical sketch.

Are there any connections between Ret Marut–B. Traven and Prince Wilhelm, later Kaiser Wilhelm II? From 15th September until 1st December, 1883, the *Nouvelle Revue* in Paris carried a *chronique scandaleuse* about life at Wilhelm I's court in Potsdam, written by Count Paul Vaseli (probably a pseudonym). The then 24-year-old Prince was reported to have many affairs, to neglect his wife, Princess Augusta Victoria of Schleswig-Holstein (born in 1858), and to have come under the spell of a dangerous mistress at that time.

This mistress was probably Helene Mareth, an Irish-born actress, who lived in Pennsylvania and had toured North America with a company before turning up at the court in Potsdam in 1880. Her illegitimate son was thought to have been born at the beginning of 1882. He was looked after by a governess and spent his childhood in the castle of Cronthal (in Taunus), in Brandenburg and in Hanover. Wilhelm's father, Crown Prince Frederick, knew about this child, who was christened Alfred William, through his wife Victoria, the former Princess Royal of Great Britain and Ireland. The enmity between the Prince and his parents had grown considerably. After the death of Wilhelm I on 9th March, 1888, Frederick III reigned as Kaiser for only 99 days, and on 14th June, 1888 as Frederick lay dying in the New Palace in Potsdam, the building was surrounded by soldiers, each door guarded by sentries 'on the express orders of His Imperial Majesty, Crown Prince Wilhelm'. The palace was searched for the diaries of Frederick III and for the letters of his wife, Victoria. But this plot was thwarted: already, some weeks before, the diaries and letters had been safely deposited in the Royal Archives in London ... the late Empress Victoria was sent to Cronthal.

In the meantime, Helene Mareth had returned to North America with her son, and her name could be found as 'Maret' and 'Mareth' in the programmes of German theatres of various towns (e.g. Cincinnati, Ohio). Her son, Alfred W. Mareth received his training with an emphasis on ballet ...

Some time after the turn of the century, said Recknagel, the company returned to Germany, where Alfred W. left it to take up his studies.

It was only (in 1915) that his mother, who later lived in London and Wales, revealed to him the identity of his father ... Ret Marut received considerable financial remuneration under the condition of silence about his origin.

I tried to test this story from a different standpoint. Instead of starting, as a Traven buff might be expected to, with Marut and trying to find clues which connected him to the German royal family, I examined the life of the Kaiser to see if the known facts about him could encompass such a rumour. A new researcher, David Turnbull, had joined me on the project and together we began reading biographies of the Kaiser and approaching historians who had studied this period of German history. Norman Stone* of Jesus College, Cambridge, came to lunch with us in London; we travelled to Brighton to visit John Rohl,† Reader in History at the University of Sussex; we spoke on the telephone to Lamar Cecil‡ of the University of North Carolina. Neither they nor any other historian we talked to, had heard of the Marut story or of a mistress called Helene Mareth. All of them were sceptical of the tale. They did not consider it especially significant that Marut managed to keep his magazine going. Many such publications were produced on a shoestring at this time and he would not have needed a rich benefactor. Also, when magazines were distributed by subscription, there was nothing to stop their saying what they pleased; the censors could do little about it. Der Ziegelbrenner would not have required a powerful protector to ward off the authorities.

Friedrich Wilhelm Viktor Albrecht von Hohenzollern was not yet the Kaiser at the time he was supposed to have impregnated Helene Mareth. His grandfather Wilhelm I, King of Prussia and Emperor of Germany, was still on the throne; his father, Frederick, was the fifty-year-old Crown Prince, awaiting his turn in power, and Willy himself was cutting a dash as a captain in the Foot Guards and taking lessons from Bismarck in how the country was run. In 1880, soon after his twenty-first birthday, the young Prince Wilhelm became secretly engaged to Princess Augusta Victoria of Schleswig-Holstein-Sonderburg-Augustenburg, Dona to her family. She

---

* Author of *The Eastern Front, 1914–17*, Hodder and Stoughton, 1975.

† Author of *Germany Without Bismarck: The Crisis of Government in the Second Reich, 1890–1900*, Batsford, 1967, and editor of the letters of Count Philipp Eulenburg.

‡ Author of *The German Diplomatic Service, 1871–1914*, Princeton University Press, 1976.

was three months older than her fiancé and, in spite of the impressive-sounding family name, was considered in princely circles to be not quite out of the top drawer. Imperial objections to the match only hardened Wilhelm's resolve. He was an immature young man but apparently devoted to Dona, and eventually he had his way. The wedding took place, amid great pomp and splendour, in Berlin on February 26th, 1881. The young couple began their life together in Potsdam, the summer home of the kings of Prussia. Wilhelm continued with his army career.

Ret Marut's registered birth date was February 25th, 1882, so if Recknagel's hypothetical account was true (and he seemed to support that date) the child must have been conceived in May or June 1881. This was within three or four months of the young prince's marriage and while he was surely doing his utmost to provide for a legitimate successor. (The first child of the marriage was born on May 6th, 1882.) All accounts agree that Dona was devoted to her husband from the first, but there is some disagreement as to how faithfully Wilhelm returned her love. She was not an exciting or a beautiful woman. She had few interests, knew nothing of the affairs of state and her conversation was limited to chatter about clothes and children. Princess Daisy of Pless described her as 'like a good, quiet, soft cow that has calves and eats grass slowly and ruminates'. She bored Wilhelm and, after the birth of the first of her seven children, she made little attempt to recover her figure. This is not to say that he was looking elsewhere for female company as soon after his marriage as the summer of 1881. In his own book, *My Early Life*, Wilhelm looked back with pleasure to his time as a young officer in Potsdam. He recalled the busy days and the happy evenings he had spent playing cards, chess and billiards with his brother officers, evenings which would conclude with beer and sandwiches and 'lively talk, salted with harmless wit and frank fun' before the young bloods retired to an early bed. Were there some evenings when Willy found time to squeeze in some less wholesome amusements and when the bed that he retired to was not his wife's?

Wilhelm not uncommonly behaved rudely and inconsiderately to Dona; he was often away from home on duty; he had a taste for pornographic pictures, and he liked to have the company of women, who would listen to and sympathise with his problems. In spite of this, his biographers have generally believed that he was not a womaniser, concluding that his strong sexual appetite could well have been satisfied by his wife. In his authoritative biography, *The Kaiser and His Times*, Michael Balfour states that the lack of solid evidence of Wilhelm's infidelity 'is certainly remarkable when one considers how many people would have liked to catch him erring'. Some historians suggested to us that any extra-marital amusement on Wilhelm's part was as likely to have been with members of his own sex as with women. There were strong rumours that he was attracted to men. He was noticed to have the habit of pinching the cheeks of young boys and of slapping his colleagues playfully on the bottom. There was also his close friendship, which began in 1886, with the glamorous figure of Count Philipp Eulenburg, an artist and a diplomat, who certainly was bisexual. Nothing is proven.

Of the people we consulted, John Rohl had the most detailed knowledge of Wilhelm II's private life, of which he had made a particular study. He was doubtful of the Mareth story, pointing out that there was no theatre in Potsdam in the 1880s. The mysterious actress could have performed in Berlin, which was very near, but there was no question of her simply 'turning up' at the court in the manner suggested. Rohl did believe that Willy had had affairs with women during the 1880s. There was evidence that Willy visited a brothel in Vienna early in the decade, and that a woman in Strasbourg tried to blackmail the German government by claiming to have had an affair with him. Bismarck investigated this allegation, found it to be true and sent his son to Strasbourg to retrieve the letters that Wilhelm had written to her. Another possible mistress was a girl called Ella Roche, whose parents claimed she had slept with Wilhelm, and the young prince was in the habit of making mysterious, and quite unnecessary, overnight stops at a particular inn on the short journey between Berlin and Potsdam. Another tale referred to a mistress and an illegitimate daughter living in Potsdam. One historian told us interestingly enough that none of the supposed mistresses of the Kaiser's were ever German women – they were all American, English or French. Helene Mareth, as an Irish American, fitted into this pattern of rumour. None of the above stories had any direct bearing on her or Marut, but they did show that young Prince Wilhelm probably looked for sex outside his marriage and that he may have begun doing so quite early in his married life. In May 1881 Wilhelm and his wife travelled to Vienna to attend the wedding of Crown Prince Rudolf to Princess Stephanie of the Belgians. The coupling with Helene Mareth, if it did take place, must have happened soon after his return to Potsdam, in order for the child to have been born almost a year to the day after Wilhelm's own wedding. He would not have been the only royal prince with a natural son in America. According to Judith Listowel in her book *A Hapsburg Tragedy*, Rudolf had an affair with an illegitimate daughter of Czar Alexander II, producing a child who was brought up in the United States.

In Recknagel's proffered account of the early life of Marut–Traven, royal offspring, he referred to the child being brought up in the castle of Cronthal in the Taunus region and being taken to America by his mother by the time Wilhelm became Kaiser in 1888. None of the historians we consulted had heard of any castle of Cronthal and their unanimous opinion was that Recknagel must be referring to the castle near Kronberg in the Taunus hills. This was the house that Wilhelm's mother bought soon after the death of her husband. But if this was the castle where the child spent his first years (and it seems the only candidate) there are two snags. Firstly, it must mean that the royal family took some responsibility for the little boy, looking after him, providing a home and a governess. If this were so, he would probably have been given some suitable title and it is extremely unlikely that, having taken him on board in this way, they would then have allowed his mother to disappear with him when he was five or six years old. Secondly, his grandmother did not buy this castle until after Helene Mareth is supposed to have gone back to America, and the dowager Empress did not move into it until 1893, by which time the young Marut would have been thirteen years old and well advanced with his ballet classes in the United States.

I was intrigued by Recknagel's claim that Frederick III's diaries mentioned Traven's birth, and that this was why Wilhelm sealed off his parents' palace and had it searched before his father's body was cold. Wilhelm certainly moved with crude

haste when his father was dying. He prevented his mother from
leaving the New Palace, he had every incoming and outgoing
telegram intercepted and examined, and, in the full dress uniform of the Hussars, he personally supervised the search of his
parents' rooms. His mother, the outgoing Empress, later wrote
that he had been looking for evidence of liberal plots against
the constitution. Wilhelm was a traditionalist. He was fiercely
opposed to the reforms his father had favoured, and he also suspected his English-born mother of passing information secretly
to Britain. Our historians agreed that Wilhelm had been
searching for papers of political significance rather than any
potentially damaging personal documents.

The Empress and her husband had sought to hide some documents from their son. A year earlier they had visited England
for Queen Victoria's Jubilee, and Frederick had taken with
them three boxes of papers, which he had deposited at Windsor.
Then, on the morning of June 14th, 1888, less than an hour
before Wilhelm arrived to imprison her in her own house, the
Empress smuggled out some further papers. These, containing
Frederick's diary for the previous ten years, travelled via the
British Embassy to Queen Victoria at Balmoral. There is a note
in the Queen's journal for June 17th that she had received 'some
papers which Fritz had desired should be put in my care'. It
was in these documents that Recknagel suggested the birth of
Alfred William Mareth was recorded. I thought it was unlikely
on the face of it that Wilhelm's parents would have known
about any illegitimate offspring. Even if he had been on good
terms with them it was something he might well wish to hide.
As it was, he was at odds with them personally and opposed
to them politically. He was unlikely to have confided in them
in such a matter.

I telephoned the Royal Archives at Windsor to ask if I could
see the diaries of Frederick III and was told that they had long
since been returned to Germany. The Archives did, however,
contain letters written by the Empress to her mother, Queen
Victoria. They were not open to research, but the archivists
checked their index and assured me that there was no reference
to any natural child of Kaiser Wilhelm II.

On the advice of the people at Windsor, I tried some foreign
archives. The State Archive in Berlin could only tell me what

I already knew, that there was no mention of little Alfred William in any of the published sections of Frederick's diary. The East German Ministry of the Interior informed me that there was no reference to the birth in the State Archives of Merseburg and Potsdam. Dr Anton Ritthaler of the Hohenzollern Archive in Hechingen could find no reference to any Irish actress connected with the court at Potsdam. He explained with more than a hint of weariness:

> You should know that people have often looked for traces of illegitimate children of Kaiser Wilhelm II but always without success ... It is hardly conceivable that evidence of any illegitimate offspring would not have come to light ... In the period 1881–3 I think that any connection with this lady, especially in Potsdam under the eyes of his young wife and the whole court would be doubly difficult to believe. But these are only suppositions.

After a long delay, because he had been ill, I received a reply from Wolfgang, Prince von Hessen, the Kaiser's nephew, who lives still at the Empress Frederick's castle near Kronberg, Schloss Friedrichshof. He wrote:

> The diaries of Kaiser Frederick III are not in the possession of my family any more. They have never been in Windsor either. The information you received must be based on a misunderstanding. What the Royal Archives in Windsor did contain for a certain period of time after World War II were the letters written during her long life by Queen Victoria to her daughter, Empress Frederick. In the meantime, however, these letters have been returned and are now in our archives in Kronberg.
>
> The diaries of Kaiser Frederick were part of the estate of the Empress Frederick, which was inherited from her by my mother, Margaret von Hessen, Princess of Prussia. At the request of Kaiser Wilhelm II the diaries were loaned to the Royal House Archive in Berlin in or around 1910. The Royal House Archive was at that time in Monbijou Castle, which is to-day in East Berlin. As far as I know much of the castle was destroyed during the war. Whether or not the diaries

still exist is not very clear. Several years ago we put this question to the East German Government. We did not, however,
receive any answer. Personally I do not think that the diaries
do or did contain any important facts which are not yet
known to to-day's historical researchers.

At every turn we were left clutching at the air. There were
no proper clues to substantiate the Mareth story and yet, like
all such rumours, it was almost impossible to disprove it. While
Turnbull and I chased along the Kaiser trail, we also kept in
mind Gabriel Figueroa's claim that he knew Traven's real
name and that it was a very well-known one in both Germany
and Britain. We asked our historians which powerful families
had been prominent in both countries, and one name was put
to us again and again: Battenberg, the original and German
version of Mountbatten. I wrote to Earl Mountbatten of Burma
explaining about the Kaiser rumour and asking if the true
family connection of Marut–Traven could have been the Bat-
tenbergs. He thought not.

> From what I know of my most extensive family, I should have
> thought it was in the highest degree unlikely that Kaiser
> Wilhelm II was the father.
> As regards the Battenbergs, it has long been believed in
> the family that the only one who had an illegitimate child
> was my own father who fell madly in love with the beautiful
> Lillie Langtry and under King Edward VII's overall friend-
> ship, had an affair with her which produced, as the world
> now knows, a daughter.
> This was a true love child and I am convinced that my
> father never had an affair with anybody else and produced
> an illegitimate child. In other words I just do not personally
> think that it is likely that this man was the illegitimate son
> of some great family. Why should he have been?

Mountbatten encouraged me to write to his friend Arnold
McNaughton, editor of *The Book of Kings*, and a man who, he
said, knew more about the Royal Family than anyone. I did
so. McNaughton had never heard of Mareth nor of anyone like
her. Nor did he know of any natural children of the Kaiser.

It was difficult, he said, to identify any royal bastards for certain, unless they were acknowledged by their father, like the 354 offspring sired by the extraordinary King Augustus I of Saxony. McNaughton believed that Wilhelm had been faithful to his wife. He was able to supply one small footnote, that the Count Paul Vaseli, author of the scandal sheet which had helped fuel Recknagel's tale, was indeed a pseudonym, behind which lurked a woman, Princess Catherine Radziwill. Otherwise, McNaughton could only pass me on to another researcher, Ian Kilburn. Kilburn had spent years tracing illegitimate lines but had never come across the Mareth story or anything like it. He felt that it would be impossible to substantiate any such tale unless the child had been acknowledged.

I was fairly sure by now that the Mareth story was a projection of what might have been. It could just about be sustained as an unlikely hypothesis, when viewed from the direction of the Traven mystery, but it disappeared into the light when you looked back at it from what was known about the Kaiser.

We made a final despairing attempt to find some trace of Helene Mareth. Unfortunately birth records in Ireland were not organised centrally for all the years in which she might have been born. But no one at all was born with the name of Mareth in Ireland during the ten years after a central register was introduced. For good measure we checked births in England and Wales. No one called Mareth was born in any of the years which would have enabled Helene to be of child-bearing age in 1882. We tried theatrical archives in the hope of finding some references to Helene Mareth performing. According to Recknagel, she toured the United States as an actress before arriving in Germany and returned with her son to perform there. And she was supposed to have appeared in London and in Wales. She was as elusive as an actress as she was as a mistress. The Mander and Mitcheson theatre archive in London had no record of her, neither had the theatre collection of the New York Public Library nor the comprehensive *New York Times* index of actresses. Recknagel said she had performed in German theatres in the United States, and specifically mentioned Cincinnati. The Cincinnati Historical Society were unable to find any hint of her existence. Recknagel reported that the shadowy Miss Mareth had lived in Pennsylvania. The Historical Society of Pennsylvania, the Union League of Philadelphia and the Philadelphia City Archives all failed to find a trace of her in any capacity.

Helene Mareth was nowhere to be found. The Kaiser, if he had any illegitimate children, hid them with enough cunning to fool all the historians of his life. The legitimacy or otherwise of Traven's birth remained as much a mystery as everything else about it. Traven cast himself off from his birth name like the hero of *The Death Ship*.

So I abandoned my good name. I think it was anyway only my mother's name, since it had never been clear if my father had really added his name or not. I severed all family connections. I no longer had a name that was by right my own.

Traven adopted new names and dropped them the moment they became a hindrance. They fell like a spoor behind him; faint, confusing and deceptive. Marut had not led to Mareth and on to the Kaiser. The scent had died in the nostrils. But the spoor was there to be read, and Traven could never have allowed for the Freedom of Information Act.

21 A Confession

The Central Intelligence Agency was the first to process my application under the Freedom of Information Act. It was easy to see why: the Agency had almost nothing to tell me. A bored-sounding letter from the CIA's Information and Privacy Co-ordinator informed me that, 'We found only one item, a 26-year-old document in which an author was looking for a translator for Mr Traven's works. This is hardly germane to your request for material for Mr Traven's biography.' He sounded as if he would prefer to be co-ordinating something altogether more central to his nation's destiny. He added that there were one or two other documents in the file but they had originated with the FBI and the State Department and that I should approach them. I already had.

I wrote three times to the FBI during the autumn of 1977 and in return received one acknowledgement but no documents. The State Department were quite helpful but could let me have nothing until Señora Lujan had given them the go-ahead and, in spite of my reminders, she was slow to send them permission. Early in 1978 I travelled to the United States on other BBC business and, while in Washington, I called on the FBI.

Washington is a city with more than its fair share of ugly and cold-hearted buildings and the Bureau's new headquarters fits sweetly into the dishonourable tradition. The small reception area extends no welcome and, on my visit, was presided over by two well-fed young men, pleased with themselves as only the uniformed can be. My assigned contact, Agent Ed Grimsley, however, was friendly enough. I was not allowed in

past the barrier; he came down to see me, bringing an envelope
of material. He said he was sorry that there was not more and
suggested that I try the National Archives across the road. I
did and was lucky. The assistant, to whom I explained my purpose, whisked me in to see the Chief of the Diplomatic Section,
Dr Milton Gustafson, who had traced Marut documents for
an earlier enquiry. Gustafson questioned me about my
researches and promised to dig out everything he could find
by the next day.

When I had completed my other appointments I went back
to my hotel and examined what Agent Grimsley had given me.
The photocopied documents had been painstakingly edited to
remove all references to cases other than the one covered by
my application. Some pages were left with only one line referring to Traven; others resembled a school test paper, studded
with gaps where all the proper nouns were left out. The batch
of papers related to the 1950s and early 1960s and contained
mostly warmed-up second-hand information.

The FBI was interested in Traven because his books proclaimed a strong radical message and were popular in leftist
circles. What shone out of the documents most clearly was that
FBI agents were keen to find work for themselves. They wished
to be seen reporting on something. Several pages related to a
foreign publishing house in Chicago, which in 1951 was said
to have 'substantial communist connections'. Two mitigating
factors were that there was 'no agency relationship involved
in transactions with foreign sources and' (the seal of approval)
'profit motive dominates'. The FBI man religiously listed all
the books this firm published in Hungarian, among them works
by Dickens, Tolstoy, Mann, Zola, Twain, Hugo – and Traven.
In 1955 another agent with too little to do spotted *The Rebellion
of the Hanged* on the list of a leftist book club in San Francisco
and filed a report. In the mid-1950s there were one or two
reports from Mexico which mentioned that 'Harold Groves'
(sic) was connected with the filming of one of the Traven
books.

It was reassuring to see how confused these agents could
become. 1956 brought a buzz of activity, when a strange advertisement in the personal column of a Texan newspaper
mentioned B. Traven and was followed up by a card to the

newspaper written in Russian. Agents scurried to and fro, fingerprints were taken, and secret inks searched for, before it became clear, even to the FBI, that this was part of a harmless literary game played by some college students. 'B. Traven' was not the code to start the Russian invasion.

Finally, there was a long report from the American Embassy in Mexico about the controversy surrounding the film of the 'anti-American novel *La Rosa Blanca*, by the celebrated and mysterious Bruno Traven'. The Embassy was worried that this story of the ruthless attempts by an American company to appropriate Mexican oil would create bad feeling against the United States. The first secretary, who wrote this report, concluded that B. Traven was probably the pseudonym for a group of collaborators led by Esperanza Lopez Mateos and including Hollywood scriptwriters. He seemed chiefly attracted to this notion because it linked Traven to the presidential family. From the FBI, that was all.

When I returned to the United States National Archives, Dr Gustafson greeted me with a thick wad of photocopied State Department documents and wished me good luck. A quick glance showed me that, unlike the FBI papers, all this material related to the Ret Marut period of Traven's life, where mysteries remained to be solved. And, also unlike the FBI stuff, it promised to tell me more about Traven than it did about the agencies reporting on him. I returned to my hotel and settled down to read it.

The kernel of these State Department papers was a correspondence which emanated from the American Embassy in London early in 1924, while Ret Marut was in Brixton Prison following his conviction at Thames Police Court. Marut told the British authorities that he was American, and this was why his case came to the notice of the United States' Embassy in January 1924. But some items in the file were dated as late as 1927 and others stretched back as far as 1915, when as this new evidence showed, Ret Marut first volunteered his existence to an American official. This twelve-year period in Marut's life produced some risky moments for him. The apostle of secrecy was called on several times to offer an account of himself and his history.

The earliest document in the file was a copy of a letter, dated

July 6th, 1915, from the Department of Public Health in San Francisco to Ret Marut at the theatre in Düsseldorf. Marut had asked for a copy of his birth certificate.

> Subject: Birth record inquiry
>   Ret Marut
>
> Sir,
>   Replying to your communication of June 3rd, relative to the matter mentioned in the foregoing subject, will state that owing to the destruction of all the birth records of the City prior to April 18th, 1906 I am unable to comply with your request. No provision in law has ever been made for the restoration of certificates so destroyed, and the best that this office can offer is the following statement which is self explanatory:
>   'This is to certify that all the birth records of the City and County of San Francisco, State of California, prior to April 18th, 1906 were destroyed in a general conflagration on April 18th, 19th and 20th, 1906: therefore this office is unable to furnish a certified copy of the birth record of Ret Marut, said to have been born in the City of San Francisco on the twenty-fifth day of February 1882.'

By 1915 Marut had it in mind to visit the United States (for the first time?) and was seeking some evidence of his identity. It was in 1915, too, that the country of his citizenship was altered from 'England' to 'America' on his police registration card. I no longer suspected a conspiracy over this change. He may well have achieved it simply by claiming that there had been a mistake and that the wrong country had been entered in the first place (as perhaps it had). After all, his birth place was down as San Francisco.

The copy of this Health Department letter was on file because Marut took it with him when on March 8th, 1917, he presented himself to the American Vice-Consul in Munich and asked for an American passport. The first batch of documents were the result of this meeting. Marut might well have felt that it was then or never. The United States had broken off relations with Germany a month before – the American consular office was housed temporarily in the Spanish Consulate in Munich – and

war between the two countries looked imminent. (It was declared on April 6th.) Marut told the American Vice-Consul
that he had once had a proper birth certificate and 'other
papers' but they had unfortunately been destroyed by a fire
in December 1910 in Pillkallen, East Prussia, in the farthest
corner of Germany. He claimed that he had applied for an
American passport on two previous occasions; the first at
Barmen in November 1914, when the consul had not asked him
for any proof of his American citizenship and had advised him
that he did not need a passport unless he was returning to the
United States; the second time, in July or August 1916 (or
1915) at Cologne, where the American Consul had again
advised him 'to save his two dollars'.

These two earlier requests for a passport sound like Marut's
attempt to build up a circumstantial case for his American citizenship. If he had tried previously, it was most likely that he
had been told to furnish some proof of his American birth and
been sent packing. His letter to San Francisco was a long shot
that failed and now, still without proof in 1917, he was having
another go before war spoiled his chances, possibly for ever.
Whether or not he was telling the truth about the interviews
in Barmen and Cologne, there was no mistaking the source of
the first chapters of *The Death Ship*.

For a long while he looks at me with dull eyes. He does not
know what more to ask. He drums the desk with his pencil.
Then he says: 'Well, I cannot give you a passport, and that
is all there is to it. Sorry.'

'But why, sir?'

'Upon what proofs? Your statement that you claim American citizenship is no proof. Personally, I believe that you are
American. However, the Department of Labor in Washington, to which I am responsible for making out passports
and other identifications, does not wish to know what I
believe and what I do not believe. This office in Washington
accepts only unquestionable evidence and no mere belief of
a consul abroad. If you bring proper evidence, it will be my
obligation to issue a passport to you. How can you prove that
you are American, that I am obliged to spend my time on
your case?'

So, on March 8th, 1917, Marut filled in an American passport application form for the first time. He gave the usual details of his birth and stated that his father, William Marut, had also been born in San Francisco and had died there in 1901. He himself was studying philosophy in Munich, living at Clemensstrasse, 84. He had last left the United States in 1904 and had no address in that country, but intended to return there within the year. He was described as thirty-five years old; five feet seven inches tall; forehead, medium; eyes, blue-grey; nose, broad; mouth, medium; chin, oval; hair, brown; complexion, fair; face, oval. In the absence of any proper identification, Marut filled in an affidavit form 'to explain protracted foreign residence and to overcome presumption of expatriation'. The affidavit said that he had last lived in the United States in 1901, as against 1904 on the passport form. Both documents were filled in on the same day and I suspect the inconsistency is due to a typing error. In the affidavit Marut stated that he had arrived in Munich in November 1915 (which was true), that he had visited France and Spain, as well as Germany, and now wished to return permanently to the United States within three months. He was travelling in Europe while studying philosophy and political economy. He did not pay American Income Tax because his income was below three thousand dollars per year.

Because he was unable to provide any references in the United States, Marut attached a memorandum giving the names of people in San Francisco, who he said would know him. He clearly had a bad memory for addresses and supplied only vague directions.

1) Ret James Chambers (or Champers, or Chambears). My father told me I got my Christian name from him. He lived in one of the streets to the left of the Market Street (coming from Blue Mountain) between City Hall and Ferry and between the border of the Chinese quarter and the Market Street.
2) John Carpenter, he was a commercial friend of my father, he lived in the third or fourth street behind the Mint, coming from Blue Mountain.
3) Dick (Richard?) Jawcelf, clerk at a printers; he was a friend of mine and lived with his mother.

4) Mrs Jawcelf (Christian name, I believe, Elinor); she was a widow. If I wanted to visit them I had to go along St Patrick, behind it, coming from Market Street.

I am convinced when I am in my native town there I shall meet many friends of mine and many acquaintances of my parents. But it is very difficult – even quite impossible – to remember all men and their homes which I knew, after this long time, especially therefore, I got about a hundred new names and addresses in many other countries and towns during this time.

(signed) RET MARUT

The consul added a note: 'Marut claims that his mother died during his infancy and he does not remember where he lived in San Francisco.'

The bare bones of the application itself might have passed muster but this memorandum sounded pretty feeble. I was sure that Ret Marut was a pseudonym and dismissed his claim that 'Ret' came from a family friend, whose second name he could not remember. He did know the names of a few streets in San Francisco, but here was a man of thirty-five saying that he could not remember what his home address had been when he was twenty. I tested my own memory of people and places that I had not seen for fifteen years. I could remember addresses that I had stayed in for only a few weeks or months, yet Marut could not remember his family home. I could remember the names, occupations and addresses of people that I had not met or heard of for twenty-five years; Marut offered only a meagre list from a mere fifteen years back. I did not believe that he had come from San Francisco. If he had really spent his childhood in that city he would have remembered much more.

Marut's encounter with the consul was echoed clearly in *The Death Ship*, where the consul was similarly curious.

'Know somebody in the States who has known you since you were a boy?'

'I think there ought to be lots of people who ought to know me.'

He took up a pencil and got ready to write down names

and addresses. 'Will you, please, name any of these people who have known you for a long time – let us say fifteen years or so?'

'How could I recall any of them, sir? They are all people of no importance. Just plain people. Working folks ...'

'Have you a permanent address back home?'

'No, sir. I could not pay for one ...'

'Your mother still alive?'

'I think so. But I do not know for sure.'

In real life, the Vice-Consul who interviewed him was nearly as sceptical as I was. He reported to Washington:

In my opinion the statements made in the foregoing application and affidavit require such confirmation as may be possible to obtain in San Francisco ...

Applicant's memory seems to fail him badly and his manner of replying to pointed questions is reluctant and not convincing. These indications, together with the fact that he speaks English with a remarkable foreign accent, considering his claim to have resided in the United States up to his twenty-second year, prompt me to question that he is entitled to the protection of the Government of the United States.

The application was routed via the Spanish Embassy in Berlin and the Spanish Legation in The Hague, and reached Washington a few days before the United States declared war on Germany. The answer was communicated to Marut on the last day of the month. He was not recognised as an American citizen and he would not be granted a passport. This was not to be Marut's last brush with consuls, a breed he took some revenge on.

These guys sit at their desk, scratching and filing and polishing their fingernails and smiling crooked at you if you want something from them – maybe a paper to help you along They feel so very superior to us working men. Easy to feel great a hundred miles away from real life.

The Death Ship

For the time being Marut directed his anger into another channel. Four months and one day after the news of his rejection, he published the first issue of *Der Ziegelbrenner*.

If Marut was not an American, it was open to him to apply for a passport from his true fatherland. He could have left Germany and he could have entered the United States on any properly issued passport. The thought of seeking German travel papers must have crossed his mind, as it did Stanislav's, the Polish sailor in *The Death Ship*. 'With such a passport in hand he could even emigrate to God's own beloved country, and he would be received at Ellis Island with a brass band and all the sirens singing. Yes, Sir!'

Marut's desire to keep his identity a secret was too great for him to take the risk and, having begun to call himself an American, he decided to stick to it. By the time his name next appeared in the American records his options were limited. The events of 1919 had made him a wanted man in Germany, and he had no alternative but to claim the protection of the United States once more.

In January 1924, during Marut's first month in Brixton prison, the American Consul in London received a letter from McElroy and Reid, a law firm of Washington D.C., which had been retained to establish the citizenship of Ret Marut and which was confident it could find people who would vouch for his American birth. The Consul wrote to the State Department asking if it could issue an emergency certificate of registration so Marut could be deported to the United States, 'although his ordinary place of residence for some considerable time has been Germany'. There was no hint as to who had engaged the lawyers on Marut's behalf. My guess was that it was Irene Mermet. Nowhere in the thick State Department file was there any mention of her. She was not picked up by the police in London. She did not appear to have made any protestations about Marut's arrest nor to have interceded in any way to help him. From what I knew of Irene, who was an intelligent and energetic woman, loyal to Marut, she would surely have made her voice heard if she had been in London at the time. I believed that she was already in America, employing McElroy and Reid to prise her lover out of the clutches of the British prison service and deposit him in the land they had both set out for.

Before the American Consul in London received a reply from Washington, another cadre of the American diplomatic service took a hand in the case. This new turn was marked by a letter sent from London on January 22nd, 1924, which was the central pivot of the whole dossier. It was from Boylston A. Beal in the Embassy to Norman Armour in the Under-Secretary of State's office in Washington. I will quote it in full.

Dear Norman:

A rather mysterious case has been brought to my notice by one of our friends in the Special Branch. He came to see me a few days ago concerning a man who claimed to be an American, passing under the name of RET MARUT and in possession of German Police papers stating that he was born in San Francisco in 1882. This man came under the notice of the Police as being intimately mixed up with Communist circles here and is now detained on the ground of failure of registration. They now tell me that he has confessed that his real name is HERMAN OTTO ALBERT MAX FEIGE, and that he was born at Schwiebus, in Germany, in 1882. It is believed that he was in the United States in 1918 but whether he has ever acquired American nationality is doubtful. He landed in this country last summer and was allowed to pass through as transmigrant on his way to Canada, but he was sent back from there as his papers were not in order. I wrote unofficially to the Embassy in Berlin to see if they could give me any information, and they wrote back saying that they had made inquiries of the political police as well as the local authorities in the town of Schwiebus and could apparently get no information concerning him.

There is a suspicion here that he was connected with espionage in America at the time of the War, and he also may have been concerned in destructive work there.

I am enclosing his photograph. You will probably notice a very strong likeness to a well-known German. It does not look to me like the face of a man who says that he is the son of a potter and a mill hand in Schwiebus. I am told that he is well acquainted with that town which makes it apparent that he has had some connection there, and it seems strange that the authorities in such a small place know nothing of him.

If you have anything really important on this man, would you be good enough to send me a cable, as it is a case in which I am interested and about which the Police here are completely mystified.

Yours ever,
B.A.B.

The attached photograph showed Marut looking a little younger than in the police photos in the Home Office file. It must have been a picture that he supplied himself. He was wearing what looked like a three-piece corduroy suit, with a wide tie, and he was staring directly out with a proud, almost regal, demeanour. It was true, he did not look like a man from humble origins, but who on earth was the 'well-known German'? Examining the picture again, there was no denying a similarity to some of the photographs of Kaiser Wilhelm II. Was this the person Beal had in mind? He was only implying that Marut had the aura of one who was high born, but it was truly strange that he should express himself as he did.

The letter also confirmed that Marut was in touch with leftist groups in London and that this was how he had attracted the attention of the police. I was interested to learn that Marut passed through Britain on his way to Canada – possibly with Irene Mermet, but again no mention of her. And here was another, and significant-sounding reference to the name Feige. I had first come across it at the Home Office, where it was allied to the Christian names Adolf Rudolf; here, he was calling himself Herman Otto Albert Max. It appeared to be another alias since there was no record of any such person in the town he was supposed to have come from. I could find no reference to Ret Marut acting in Schwiebus, but it was quite possible that he had visited the town and made use of his memories of it when questioned by the police. It was worth noting that this was the first time Ret Marut conceded that his name and his attachment to San Francisco were false; the use of the word 'confessed' hinted at a prolonged interrogation by the London Police. Marut never realised that the English police were passing on what he told them to the American officials. He continued to pretend to the U.S. Embassy that he was just a fellow from San Francisco trying to get back home.

The suggestion that Marut was in the United States in 1918 surprised me. He had neither an American nor a German passport to travel on, he published three issues of *Der Ziegelbrenner*, comprising some 110 pages, in 1918, and everything else known about him placed him in Munich throughout that year. The 'espionage' and 'destructive work' were out of character as well. He was passionately anti-militarist and would hardly have been working behind enemy lines as part of the German war effort. Besides, he was always a writer, a critic, a preacher and above all an individualist. He would not have spied or planted bombs on behalf of any organised leftist conspiracy. At the beginning of 1919 he wrote in his magazine, 'I cannot belong to any party, because I see membership of any party as a restriction of my personal freedom.' And I could not imagine him tearing himself away from Munich just as a revolution was coming to the boil. I did not think that he could have or would have been in the United States in 1918.

A few days after Boylston Beal had sent this letter, he received further news about Marut from the American Embassy in Berlin, where H. Dorsey Newson had been in touch with the German political police. They knew nothing about Marut calling himself Feige, wrote Newson, and were 'extremely anxious to ascertain his whereabouts'. The German authorities intended to investigate Schwiebus to see if anyone called Marut or Feige had been born there. They knew about the San Francisco identity and passed on a physical description of Marut which fitted closely with the other available, although it described his hair as 'dark', as opposed to the 'brown' of his previous passport application, or the 'grey' of the criminal record form in London. But three details linked pleasingly with later episodes of his life: 'fast gait' as described by others in Mexico; 'large bald spot', visible on the Croves photographs, and 'slim hands', a cast of which I had myself seen in Señora Lujan's house in Mexico City.

The story in the file continued. In Washington, Norman Armour took up the enquiry, and wrote asking about Marut to the Director of Military Intelligence and the Commissioner General of Immigration. Neither could trace him as either Marut or Feige. Armour wrote again, adding extra information from the German authorities; still they turned up nothing. The

22   The Mexican passport issued to Traves Torsvan in 1956. It said he was born in Chicago, May 3rd, 1890.

23   T. Torsvan, also called Hal Croves, and his wife, Rosa Elena Lujan, on a beach in Mexico in the 1960s. He was full of vigour to the end.

24 and 25   Croves and his wife lived in Mexico City for the twelve years of their marriage, from 1957 till his death in 1969. *Above*, Croves, lunching with his wife and stepdaughter, adjusts his glasses as the camera shutter opens. *Below*, out to dinner in the 1960s.

26 The mug shots of Ret Marut found at the Home Office in London. This was Marut on the run in December 1923, when by his own admission he was 41 years old.

27 The register at Thames Police Court in East London recording Ret Marut's first appearance there on December 1st, 1923, the day after his arrest. After being twice remanded in custody he was recommended for deportation and held in Brixton Prison.

IN THE METROPOLITAN POLICE DISTRICT.

Register of the Court of Summary Jurisdiction sitting at _____Thames_____ Police Court.

The _1st_ day of _December_ 1923

Name of Informant or Complainant.	Name of Defendant. Age, if known.	Nature of Offence or of Matter of Complaint.	Date of Offence.	Time when Charged.	Bailed.	Doctor's Fee, (if any).	Plea.	Minute of Adjudication.	Time allowed for Payments and Instalment
M. Ryman 386ᴴ	Peter O'Reilly 31 (Labourer)	Drunk & disorderly	30·11·23	10·55 pm		10/6	G	40/- a 21 days n.g.a.	
W. Paradine 177ᴴ	Jack Peley 20 (Waiter)	Drunk & disorderly	30·11·23	8·50 pm	3am 1·12·23	10/6	G	B.O. £5 6 mo	
W. Beadle 117ᴴ	Edward Stevens 32 (Labourer)	Drunk & disorderly	30·11·23	8·20 pm			G	40/- a 21 days	7 days
A. Hayward 314ᴴ	Archibald Moore 39 (Labourer)	Drunk & disorderly	30·11·23	10·35 pm	7·30 am 1·12·23		G	10/- a 7 days	7 days
B. Smith 986ᴷ	Frithjof Aberg 28 (Fireman)	Drunk & disorderly	30·11·23	10·30 pm		10/6	G	10/- a 7 days	n.g.a.
A. Porter 362ᴴ	Hugh Dow 27 (Seaman)	Drunk & indecent	30·11·23	10·15 pm			G	10/- a 7 days	
F. Bickers C.I.D. O.O	Ret Marut (mechanic)	Being an alien, viz: American Citizen, did fail to register with the Registration Officer of the district in which he resided.	30·11·23	1·5 pm			G (Court)	Rem a 10 Dec	

W. V. Orin

28 Friedrich Wilhelm Viktor Albrecht von Hohenzollern, 1859–1941. Kaiser Wilhelm II.

29 Photograph of Ret Marut in the U.S. State Department files. 'You will probably notice a very strong likeness to a well-known German.'

30 and 31 Picture of Marut probably taken while he was still in Germany. He was on the run after May 1st, 1919, accompanied by his girl friend, the former actress Irene Mermet, (*below right*) who was his partner in publishing *Der Ziegelbrenner*.

London Embassy belatedly discovered that Marut also called himself Albert Otto Wienecke and passed this on with the plaintive, but understandable, apology, 'It seems difficult to get any definite information about this man'.

Armour also wrote to the Director of the Bureau of Investigation, William J. Burns, who in turn circulated his agents in various American cities with all the information from London. In Chicago, Seattle, Washington D.C. and New York, the agents' questions drew a blank. In San Francisco an exhaustive search among radical groups and the German community failed to find anyone who knew or had heard of Marut. In two cities, though, the enquiries did produce results of sorts. The Portland, Oregon, office turned up the case of a German alien called Herman Feig, who had been arrested in Minidoka County, Idaho, in August 1918 for a violation of the Espionage Act. The alleged offence was that Feig was driving a wagon load of hay away from his colleagues in the fields, when he concluded a conversation about the war with the parting shot: 'The Kaiser is going to rule the world and I am proud of it. The war is not over yet.' These were hardly the sentiments of Ret Marut or B. Traven, and also this Feig claimed to have been in the United States for seventeen years. The matter was soon sorted out. A photograph of Marut was hurried out to Idaho, where the local sheriff reported that the man Feig they had tangled with was not the man arrested in London. He added that the photograph looked more like one of the witnesses against Feig, a man called C.H. Coburn, who was 'as unAmerican as they get and an I.W.W.' That sounded more like Traven. Suppose our quarry had been in America in 1918, calling himself C.H. Coburn, meeting a German called Herman Feig, whose name and nationality he stole for future use? It was easy to invest every detail with pregnant meaning and to chase blindly after every scent. How could Marut have got to and from Idaho in 1918? What on earth was he doing there? If he was Coburn, why was there no mention of his strong German accent as there was of Feig's? It was a wild idea.

The FBI report from Los Angeles carried more weight, at least at first sight. Agent Kosterlitzky reported that he had shown the photograph of 'Feige alias Marut' to 'well-known Germans of Socialistic tendencies', and that they had identified

REPORT MADE AT:	DATE WHEN MADE:	PERIOD FOR WHICH MADE:	REPORT MADE BY:
LOS ANGELES, CAL.	3/27/34	3/27/34	F. KOSTERLITZKY /N

TITLE AND CHARACTER OF CASE:
HERMAN OTTO ALBERT MAX FEIGE,   -----   ALLEGED COMMUNIST.   61 - 4952
alias RFT, MARUT.   PROVED

FACTS DEVELOPED: Attention Mr. Hoover-No.2
At Los Angeles, Cal.   Los Angeles File 135/3179

him as a man who appeared in Los Angeles in the latter part
of November 1918, and who attended several socialist meetings
at the old 'Turner Hall' on Main Street. Two witnesses, one
of them an elderly actor, said they remembered the man as a
self-confessed Marxist, who was very reserved, made no friends
among the socialists and never attempted to address the meetings. Both of them believed that he had come from Mexico to
Los Angeles, and both evidently remembered that he had disappeared from the city as abruptly as he had arrived. If all this

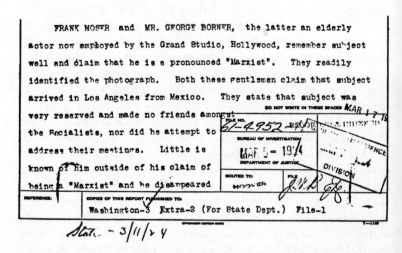

FRANK MOSER and MR. GEORGE BORNER, the latter an elderly
actor now employed by the Grand Studio, Hollywood, remember subject
well and claim that he is a pronounced "Marxist". They readily
identified the photograph. Both these gentlemen claim that subject
arrived in Los Angeles from Mexico. They state that subject was
very reserved and made no friends amongst
the Socialists, nor did he attempt to
address their meetings. Little is
known of him outside of his claim of
being a "Marxist" and he disappeared

FILE NO. 61-4952

BUREAU OF INVESTIGATION

DEPARTMENT OF JUSTICE

ROUTED TO: HOOVER

Washington-3 Extra-2 (For State Dept.) File-1

State. - 3/11/x4

were true, it was a breakthrough in the Traven story. It would
mean that he was in Mexico well before 1924, that he insinuated
himself into the United States and was then able to travel back
into Germany. Someone suggested to me that perhaps this man
Feige in Los Angeles was the 'other man', the shadowy 'Erlebnisträger', whom Marut then met afterwards in Mexico. But if
the two witnesses identified the photograph correctly, it was

Ret Marut who must have somehow been on the West Coast of America in 1918.

I was inclined not to believe this identification. I could not disprove it, nor can I now, but I thought that I detected the sound of an agent or his informants being deliberately 'useful'. It was the kind of helpful information which would present either party in a favourable light and which could not be denied or checked. The man the informants said they remembered had left no friends, no contacts, no name, no trail of any kind, as they were careful to point out. Possibly they mistook the photograph for somebody else. Either way, it would surely not be the only time in the history of the FBI that agents or informants 'helped' themselves and their masters in this way. I could not believe that Marut was out of Munich in November 1918. It was the month that Eisner came to power, the beginning of the longed-for revolution. Marut brought out a major issue of *Der Ziegelbrenner* in that same month, and published two more editions, comprising 120 pages, in January 1919. Whoever it was, if anyone at all, that the two informants spotted at the meetings in Los Angeles, it was not likely to have been Ret Marut, who was otherwise engaged.

The Bureau of Investigation, now in the charge of Acting Director, J.E. Hoover, called off its search for information about Ret Marut following the news from the London Embassy that Marut had sailed from Britain 'on the Norwegian Steamship HEGRI'. While the correspondence hummed between London, Berlin and Washington and while agents combed American cities for any sign of his droppings, Marut, oblivious to all this activity, had been allowed to walk out of Brixton prison on the fine clear morning of February 15th. He was also unaware that the Special Branch had handed over to the Americans the little that they had been able to find out about him, and just over two weeks later he called at the Consular Office of the American Embassy, seeking to register as a native citizen – still Ret Marut, born in San Francisco. On his application form, he now claimed that he had last left the United States in 1892. He had been in Australia and Europe 'as Seaman, Play Producer, Teacher Dramatic School Düsseldorf – with two short visits as seaman in 1896 and in 1901' before arriving in London (from Canada) on August 19th, 1923. At the bottom

Form No. 225 A—Consular.   NOTE.—One copy only of this form should be sent to the Department.
(February, 1916.)

APPLICATION FOR REGISTRATION—NATIVE CITIZEN.

Consular No. ....

Department No. ....

I, *Ret Marut* ...., hereby apply to the Consulate

.....of the United States at .... for registration as an American citizen.

I was born at *San Francisco, Cal.*, on *Feb. 25, 1882*
                                        (State)   (Month and day.)   (Year.)

My father *Wm. Marut* .... was born on .... *1855 (?)*
                        (Name.)   (Month and day.)   (Year.)
San Francisco, Cal. ....; [emigrated to the United States on or
        (City or town.)   (State or country.)

.... ; I ....; resided...........years uninterruptedly, in the United States, from l..............

.... at ....; was naturalized as a citizen of the United States before

.... Court of ...., at ....

.... I ...., as shown by the Certificate of Naturalization exhibited herewith, and
                                                    (Certificate must be exhibited if applicant was born abroad.)

now reside at ....

I last left the United States on .... *892* arriving at *London England*
                                                                                    (Town, province.)

on *Aug. 19, 1923* ...., where I am now residing for the purpose of
        (Country.)

...., on behalf of ....
        (Occupation.)   (Name, nationality, and address of firm, corporation, or other organization represented, if any.)

I have resided outside the United States at the following places for the following periods:

Australia .... from .... to ....

and Europe .... from *1892* .... *date*

as Seaman, Play Producer, Teacher Dramatic School in 1896 a
Düsseldorf— .... two strong visits as Seaman *1901*
.....Residence at *6 Hypotenplatz, Düsseldorf, Ger.*, but I am now residing
London— having been released from Brixton Prison on Feb. 15, 1924.

I desire to remain a citizen of the United States and intend to return thereto permanently to reside and perform the duties

of citizenship within ....years, or when *no intention*

---

of the form he signed the American Oath of Allegiance. There
was a space for the applicant to state when he intended to return
permanently to the United States and perform the duties of
citizenship. I noted that Marut had entered the words 'no
intention'. Someone in the Embassy must have let him know
that they were allowing him to apply for citizenship merely as a
formality. He was not going to be accepted as an American
and they did not want him trying to get into the United States.

Ret Marut was forty-two years old, stateless, subject to a

OATH OF ALLEGIANCE.

Further, I do solemnly swear that I will support and defend the Constitution of the United States against all enemies, foreign
and domestic; that I will bear true faith and allegiance to the same; and that I take this obligation freely, without any mental
reservation or purpose of evasion: So help me God.

R. Marut
(Signature of applicant.)

[SEAL.]   SUBSCRIBED AND SWORN to before me this *3* day of *Mar* ...., 19 *24*
[No fee.]

Consul ....of the United States at ....

The applicant's personal description is as follows:

Age, *42* ; height, *5* feet *7* inches; color of eyes, *Blue* ; color of hair, *dark brown grey*
complexion, *fair* ; distinguishing features or marks, ...

* Evidence of the applicant's birth in the United States or that of the person through whom birth in this country citizenship is claimed must be submitted.
If applicant's birth is not legally recorded, baptismal certificate or affidavits of two reputable persons (preferably American citizens) should be furnished, or,
if those also are not obtainable, the applicant should give names and address of two or more reputable persons in the United States who have knowledge of

deportation order in Britain, wanted for treason in Germany and *persona non grata* in Canada and the United States. In the course of time he would take his revenge on these nations in his books. For the moment, in March 1924, he made one final and, for him, desperate attempt to satisfy American official requirements: he supplied a life history, taken down in four pages of longhand by an Embassy scribe. A photocopy of it lay in the State Department File.

Applicant is the son of William Marut and Helene Marut (née Otorrent) and was born he says in San Francisco, Cal. in ... He ran away from home when he was ten years of age, having signed on as a Kitchen* boy on a ship bound for Australia (1892–summer). After 5 or 6 weeks he left there, Sydney, and proceeded to India. Then to Singapore and from there to Rotterdam finally (1895). From there on another ship to India and after 18 mos. cruise returned to Rotterdam (1897). Then to Germany and on another boat from Hamburg proceeded to Rio and from there to Frisco and returned to Rio (1899). From Rio to N.Y. and having changed there proceeded to Rotterdam (1900). Stayed in Rotterdam waiting for another boat (1901). Then to Germany remaining [?] short and from there to Vienna where he took up the study of languages. Later he obtained position as actor in Vienna and later became full fledged actor under the name Lainger (1907). Then to Germany, Berlin, where he opened theatrical agency, thence to Frankfort [sic] where he obtained work as actor and translator throughout Germany. Then to Dantzic [sic] as actor to 1912. From 1912 to 1915 at Düsseldorf Play Producer. 1915 to 1919 at Munich, P.P. and actor and teacher of languages and dramatic art.

[In the margin] Made applic. join Germ. Army but after *Lusitania* was sunk withdrew his applic.

In April 1919, left Ger. for Austria on acct. of Revolution, following profession of actor and teacher of languages. Run until 1922. From 1922 to date has been in Switzerland,

* The word 'chicken' is crossed out. Marut dictated this history and his German accent may well have been the cause of the mistake.

Austria (interpreter). Return to Swit., Holland, to Copen-
hagen, Denmark, thence to Canada, leaving about July, was
rejected there and returned to England where he was
(arrested) on Nov. 1923. Never arrested before except in Düsseldorf in 1914 as a suspect, was released same day. Father
and Mother dead. Has relative in U.S. but does not know
where.

Was released from Brixton on Feb. 15, 1924 at direction
of Home Secretary. Now residing 649 Commercial Road, E.
Has in his possession a Personalausweis Nr. 1061 describing
him as a citizen of the U.S. issued by the Police President
at Munich on January 18, 1918.

Never served in any army, but was a Pacifist.

Has released from Brixton on Feb, 15, 1924 at direction of Home Secretary. Now residing 649 Commercial Road, E, Has in his possession a Personalausweis Nr, 1061 describing him as a citizen of the U.S issued by the Police President at Munich on January 18, 1918. Never served in any army, but was a Pacifist

Some of this was true: about Danzig and Düsseldorf and not
being allowed into Canada. Some of it was lies: about his birth
and parents, and about what he was doing in Munich – there
was no mention of writing and publishing *Der Ziegelbrenner*. I
had no way of knowing if he was telling the truth about being
a seaman for nine years. The claim that he ran away from home
at the age of ten echoed the version of his life that he put about
thirty years later in the *B.T. News Reports*. That later rendering
said that he had earned his own living from the age of seven,
that his only schooling was the school of life and that he was
at sea when he was ten. Perhaps they were both true; perhaps
neither. It was interesting that for so many years he carried
a memory that he had been alone in the world and in charge
of his own destiny since childhood. It was an echo which was
to reverberate once more.

I did not believe that Marut had ever volunteered for the
German army. That little tale was dragged in so that he could
ingratiate himself with the Americans by displaying his horror
at the sinking of the *Lusitania*. Many American civilians died
when the Germans sank this passenger liner in 1915. One confusing aspect of Marut's deposition was his reference to the
Bavarian revolution. The scribe's handwriting was difficult to
decipher on this point, but it seemed to say that Marut had
left Munich on account of the revolution and was then on the
run. That was all. It was not quite clear as to whether he
had fled to avoid the revolution or because it had ended. The
mention of him being on the run suggests that he admitted
being a fugitive or, possibly, that the American officials told
him that they knew that the Germans were still pursuing him
and why. But the deposition said that Marut had left Munich
in April. Had he in fact slipped out of the city before the Freikorps had invaded, before the destruction of the Republic of
Councils? He could hardly have forgotten the dates. It was on
May 1st, 1919, that the hostile troops had attacked Munich. It
was on that same day that he had, according to his own dramatic account, been captured in the street, been nearly executed
and then escaped. Why, then, did he say he had left in April?
There was no reason to lie to the Americans. They apparently
knew that he was wanted for treason, and it would make no
difference to them which day he had fled on. The possibility

had to be accepted that he had left Munich on April 30th or even earlier; that the famous and dashing description of his adventures on May 1st was not true. It would not have been out of character for Traven to have made it up, placing himself at the centre of the stage for literary effect. He was a writer, not a historian. If his memorable account of May 1st was true in spirit but not in fact, so be it: 'How do I know whether the story Stanislav told me was the story of what he had experienced in fact, or whether it was the reflection in his mind of what he believed he had experienced?'

Marut's transcribed life story opened no doors to him. He left London, and the State Department closed the file. No one even bothered to attach a formal rejection to his application for citizenship. They did not appear to have taken it seriously. However, two and a half years later there was an interesting postscript. Boylston Beal, who was still sniffing out subversives, wrote to Washington about three Americans in London, Anna Isabella Hunkins, Hazel Hunkins and Charles Thomas Hallinan. Hazel and Hallinan were living at the same address, 11 Belsize Square. Hallinan was a journalist of the left and had formerly been Secretary of the American Union Against Militarism. One of the connections that brought him to the attention of the Embassy agents was that in November 1923 he had been a contact for 'a mysterious German named Ret Marut or Barker or Arnolds'.

According to the report in the file, the Labor Bureau in New York managed to arm Marut with a letter of introduction to Hallinan, as someone who might help him reach the United States. In this letter Hallinan was described as 'thoroughly in sympathy with all that you are interested in', and the New York contact sent the sum of thirty-four pounds to Hallinan for Marut's use. Once again I thought that I detected the presence of Irene Mermet acting as Marut's American agent and conducting these arrangements on his behalf. Hallinan had given Marut some help, but he had evidently declared to the American authorities that he knew nothing which could support the claim for nationality.

This 1926 letter from Beal also reported that Marut had been shielded in London by Sylvia Pankhurst, younger daughter of the suffragette leader, Mrs Pankhurst, and a strenuous cam-

paigner against the First World War. She and Marut shared
strong anti-military sympathies and they might well have been
in touch before he ever arrived in London. Sylvia was living
in the East End at this time. According to Beal, she and her
friend, Nora Smyth, protected Marut because they feared that
if he were sent back to Germany he might lose his life.

In the two and a half years since Beal's first dealings with
the Marut case, he had learned nothing more about the
man's identity. All efforts by the American and German authorities to trace Marut's provenance had failed, Beal concluded
his letter in December 1922: 'It is felt here that although Marut
was assumed to be identical with one Albert Max Feige, a German, his identity has never been absolutely established.'

There were just a couple more papers on the Hallinan case,
which by documenting a report from a State Department
'Special Agent' to the 'Special Agent in Charge', who passed
it on to the 'Chief Special Agent', revealed the poor quality
of research and the shallowness of judgement in this bureaucracy of spies. This report produced an alias for Marut of Herman Otto Albert Max SDIGE. It was clearly a misreading of
a longhand rendering of FEIGE: an error made abundantly
obvious by the lack of any mention of Feige in a list of names
used by Marut. The same agent concluded simple-mindedly
that: 'The common interest between him [Hallinan] and
Marut was Communism pure and simple.' Marut was always
assiduous in avoiding any political party and on several
occasions ruled out the Communists in particular; Hallinan
was also never a Communist. The sympathy between the two
men stemmed from their shared abhorrence of war, especially
the First World War.

You ought to know what America has achieved in the one
hundred and fifty years of her existence. How fast she works
to surpass even Imperial Russia with passports, visés, restric-
tions of free movements. Limitations and moldiness everywhere. All the world over, in consequence of the war for
democracy, and for fear of communistic ideas, the bureaucrat
has become the new czar who rules with more omnipotence
than God the Almighty ever had, denying the birth of a living person if the birth-certificate cannot be produced, and

making it impossible for a human being to move freely without a permit properly stamped and signed.

The Death Ship

The documents ended their story. There were no more papers on Ret Marut, who had succeeded in slipping out of sight of agents and spies. I closed the file in my Washington hotel room and looked at my notebook. I knew much more about Marut: his attempts to prove himself an American, the stories of his childhood, his contacts and his interrogations. And I had a mass of new leads to follow when I returned home: the Pankhursts, Hallinan, the London police again, the new names. One of them might lead me behind the wall of deception by which Marut had protected his true self. His capacity for secrecy was unending. A glance at any moment of his existence found him playing the same game and not even his desire to leave Germany and to reach the United States tempted him to wash off the make-up.

I was finished with my business in Washington and now had to fly on to Chicago and the West Coast. For a few extra pounds I could fly home via Mexico City and pay another call on Señora Lujan.

22 As Far as I Could Go?

My head was still buzzing with the disclosures in the American documents when I arrived again in Mexico City. This time, seeking inspiration from the ghostly encounters of the past, I stayed at the Reforma Hotel, where the bashful Mr Croves had first manifested himself to John Huston. I rang Señora Lujan to confirm my appointment and she welcomed me like an old friend.

I knew that since my last visit she also had received copies of the documents I had seen in Washington, and the few new scraps of information that she gave me were consistent with but did not go beyond what was in the official files. The Señora had recently been in Germany, where she had donated a number of paintings and drawings by Franz Seiwert to a museum in Cologne. She talked eagerly about this trip, on which she had been fêted as the widow of B. Traven, and properly thanked for returning the pictures to their country of origin. She told me that after Irene Mermet and her husband had left Cologne, it was Irene who had maintained communication with Seiwert. She had brought Seiwert's pictures down to Mexico and left them with Traven when she went back north across the border. The Señora showed me the catalogue of an exhibition of Seiwert's work which had been mounted a week or so previously in Cologne. It contained reproductions of many of the pictures that she had given: cartoon-like drawings of factories and workers, sketches of single figures, portraits (some of Marut). The works in her gift had been executed between 1918 and 1923 and to a layman's eye the style seemed influenced at different times by Picasso, Klee and Munch.

The only time that Señora Lujan mentioned the American files was when I asked her if one of the aliases her husband had given in London could have been his true name. She would have none of it. She said that Recknagel had checked the Wienecke identity and there was no one of that name. She gave the impression that Recknagel had also ruled out the name Feige and the town of Schwiebus, but when I put them to her specifically I was almost certain that I detected a momentary ripple in her usual calm. I watched her face carefully as I spoke the names. Her eyes flicked casually away (too casually?) as I offered Feige; her expression remained composed (too composed?) as I followed with Schwiebus. There was no further response and the moment was past.

Before arriving I had asked Señora Lujan if I could see some more of her husband's papers. She had a varied and, I was sure, carefully selected folder of them ready for me. They ranged from the German period to the last years of his life, many of them making no particular sense to me then or now. Among the more interesting items was a copy of a letter from Señor Don B. Traven written in poor Spanish to the Customs at Columbus, Tamaulipas on December 12th, 1924. It was about some of his clothes that the Customs still held. Although this copy was simply for his own reference, he had obsessively rubbed out his signature and the names of the countries where the impounded clothes had been made. I was just able to make out what he had written: the signature was Traven; the clothes had been made in Germany, Switzerland and Austria.

The Señora allowed me to look at some of Traven's notebooks dating from his first few years in Mexico. They were written in English and the dates were recorded in the American manner, with the month first. One was like the notebook I had seen before, a sparse diary of his travels in 1924, containing only bare notes like: 'Arrived 7.30. Mr. S. alright. The rest of the family seemed not or at least indifferent ... Nice place. Wants hard work. Nigro in hut. Staying with three cotton pickers. Two Mex one nigro. Night horrible. No sleep too many mosquitoes.' Another book appeared to record the dates on which he had dispatched his stories to Germany.

In another, I found the sketch of a story idea. His tangles with the bureaucrats preyed on his mind as he sat, plagued by the discomforts of the jungle: 'Arnold [a name he had made use of in different circumstances] been obsessed all his life with papers, passports, certificates, election tickets, tax receipts. Arrive in Heaven. First words he hears, "Where is Your Certificate of Baptism?" "I lost it." "You go back and get it".' On another page was a little homily to himself.

> Don't preach,
> Don't teach,
> Talk plain,
> Entertain.

In a sheaf of papers, which carried rambling and unconnected thoughts written down in a longhand suggesting that he was an old man at the time, I came across a strange line: 'befuddled mind   BEFUDDLED MIND   PANKHURST SYLVIA'. It appeared to be by Traven. Nothing else on the page offered a hint of explanation. Perhaps the old man had been struggling to recall events and confederates of long ago, expressing irritation with himself and jotting down what he could remember. I wondered if I was being teased by Señora Lujan. I was sure that she would not have let me see the reference to Sylvia Pankhurst before she knew that I must have come across the name in the State Department documents. I was allowed to see only what was on the periphery of what I already knew. I was sure that the Señora herself was still discovering things about her husband, slowly trying to piece together the full story from the books and papers that he had left behind. She was paying out the line to me only so far as she had untangled it herself.

There was one more quite inexplicable item. It was a cutting from *The Times* of London, dated December 19th, 1928. The headline read: 'PRINCE HAS COOKING LESSONS IN KITCHENS OF BERENGARIA.' The article recounted how 'Prince George had a cookery lesson to-day in the kitchens of this Cunard liner … His concern over the illness of his father was obviously greatly increased by the less hopeful bulletin he received by radio from Buckingham Palace last night.' The Prince referred to, was the later George VI. I asked Señora Lujan how her husband had obtained this clipping and why he had kept it, but she had no idea. Perhaps she had included it in the papers she showed me hoping that, because I was English, I would be able to shed some light on it. I could not.

I took Señora Lujan to a restaurant in the nearby Avenue Reforma for lunch. We had lots to drink. Such was the sophistication and gallantry of my approach, that I ignobly hoped to fracture the Señora's defences with a quantity of wine. She talked about her children and I talked about mine; we talked about Mexico and about England; we talked about writers and, eventually, towards the end of the meal, I charged head on at the ramparts. I said that when Robinson and I had departed from Mexico six months before we had argued between ourselves about how much she knew of the mysteries of her husband's life. One of us had believed that she knew all but wished to keep it to herself; the other that she knew little more than the rest of the world and chose to disguise her ignorance. Which of us had been right, I asked. To my surprise, she did not repeat the assertions that there was no mystery, that the books were all-important and so on, but her response was equally enigmatic. She simply burst out laughing, raking the restaurant with her eyes, allowing them to settle anywhere but on mine.

I flew back to London and began editing the film. Robinson and I had already thrashed out a story line, and I now turned this into an editing script, which I placed in the capable hands of Geoff Botterill, one of the BBC's senior film editors. I arranged to do some further filming at Brixton and in the East End to cover the London episodes; if any other discoveries grew out of the information in the American files, I would have to tag them on afterwards.

As the editing got under way Turnbull and I began to follow up the leads from Washington and to make a final sweep through everything we knew. We had a little more time for this than we had expected, for my old friend the Curse of B.T. put in a final appearance, reminding me of his existence and introducing himself to newcomers. With the film now in the cutting room he sensibly chose the editor as his victim, and only a few days after starting work on the film Geoff Botterill fell off a ladder, broke his ankle and tore his hand. We had to adjourn the editing. Turnbull and I strode bravely on, turning our attention to the long list of names we now knew that Traven had used.

For our own peace of mind we had already checked San

Francisco on the off-chance that someone might have discovered a store of records which had escaped the fire of 1906.
No one had, nor was there any sign of Ret Marut in the register
of delayed births. During his years in Mexico Traven used the
names Torsvan and Croves and always gave Chicago as his
place of birth. We had two birth dates during this time, March
5th, 1890, and May 3rd, 1890, probably as a result of a confusion at some point over whether the day or the month came
first in 5.3.90. The American convention is to put the month
first.

We checked the Chicago records for both these dates, for
February 25th, 1882 (Marut's registered birth date), and, on
an even longer shot, July 2nd, 1880, which was the date of birth
given by the theology student Charles Trefny. The Clerk of
Cook County sent us certificates stating that no record could
be found.

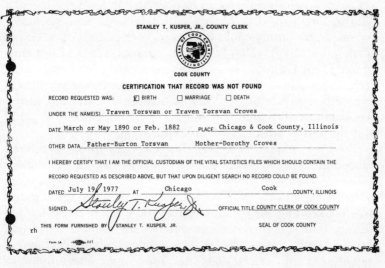

STANLEY T. KUSPER, JR., COUNTY CLERK

COOK COUNTY

CERTIFICATION THAT RECORD WAS NOT FOUND

RECORD REQUESTED WAS: ☒ BIRTH ☐ MARRIAGE ☐ DEATH

UNDER THE NAME(S) Traven Torsvan or Traven Torsvan Croves

DATE March or May 1890 or Feb. 1882 PLACE Chicago & Cook County, Illinois

OTHER DATA Father-Burton Torsvan   Mother-Dorothy Croves

I HEREBY CERTIFY THAT I AM THE OFFICIAL CUSTODIAN OF THE VITAL STATISTICS FILES WHICH SHOULD CONTAIN THE
RECORD REQUESTED AS DESCRIBED ABOVE, BUT THAT UPON DILIGENT SEARCH NO RECORD COULD BE FOUND.

DATED July 19 1977 AT Chicago , Cook COUNTY, ILLINOIS

SIGNED _Stanley T. Kusper Jr._ OFFICIAL TITLE COUNTY CLERK OF COOK COUNTY

THIS FORM FURNISHED BY STANLEY T. KUSPER, JR. SEAL OF COOK COUNTY

rh

Form 1A

Trefny had given his place of birth as St Louis, so we tried
there also, offering the names Trefny, Marut, Torsvan and
Croves against all the acknowledged birth dates. By an eerie
coincidence the woman who replied to us was a Mary Ann
Lujan. It was not compulsory to record births or deaths before
February 1910, she said, and she could find nothing in her
files under the names provided. Ret Marut's first recorded

nationality was English, so Turnbull went down to St Catherine's House in London to check the whole of the years 1880, 1882 and 1890 for any of the names. He found only the birth of a Mary Croves in 1882, but not even the wildest Traven rumour had ever proposed a sex change in the saga.

We now had Arnolds, Barker, Feige and Wienecke added to the list and I sent Turnbull round the route again, looking for any of these in the same places and on the same dates. He added his own search through the birth columns of the *San Francisco Chronicle*, but once again there was no sign of any of the names. All the names Traven chose were strange-sounding and rare. With the old rumours that he was a Scandinavian in mind, we looked up the telephone directories for Stockholm, Oslo and Helsinki. There was not a Croves, Marut, Traven or Torsvan between them. Nor were there any in Munich or Düsseldorf. In Chicago there were two Travens and a Marut, and we wrote off to them without reply. In San Francisco itself there was a Marut, Dr Edward L. Marut, with whom we made contact. No one in his family could have been connected with a Marut birth in the city in 1882, because his grandfather had not emigrated to the United States until about 1910. He had originated from the southern part of Poland, where the name Marut was evidently not uncommon. We found another Marut in London whose family also came from southern Poland. Once more there was no sign of kinship with Ret Marut, later B.T.

The Feige I found in the London telephone directory offered more hope. The family had lived in the Breslau area of Germany (now south-west Poland) and seven children were born there in the 1880s and 1890s. Two or three became lawyers, another was a baker, and one got into trouble and was sent to the United States. This black sheep, despatched to another continent by his family, might have accumulated enough feelings of resentment and rejection to develop Traven-like obsessions about his parents and his country. But, if he had, they had not metabolised into the Traven books. On further enquiries, I found out enough about this lost brother to prove that this Feige family housed no Traven.

What about the Feige family which Traven claimed to come from in Schwiebus? The German police had found no trace in 1924 but, if we were reduced to picking out names from the

London telephone directory, we might as well go through the formalities of an enquiry, as we had with San Francisco. Schwiebus remained German after the Treaty of Versailles but became part of modern Poland at the end of the Second World War. It is now called Swiebodzin, in the province of Zielona Gora. Through the British Embassy in Warsaw Turnbull discovered where the records for Schwiebus would be kept, if they still existed after the fighting of the Second World War, and wrote off. The Embassy warned him that he might have to wait a long time for his enquiry to be processed and that it was not unheard of for such letters to be lost.

Stumbling upon a Feige in London today and thinking again about Marut's first claim to be English, encouraged us to trawl all the British birth records for the 1880s. Turnbull trudged wearily to St Catherine's House and, after another day's hunting, returned with a lone but interesting catch: there was a Feige born in England in the 1880s. What was more, his Christian names were Alfred (as in Alfred Mareth) and Otto (one of the names Traven had admitted to the police). And he was born in West Ham in East London, not more than a couple of miles from 649 Commercial Road. We acquired a copy of the birth certificate. The child's full name was Alfred Otto Williams Feige, born September 1st, 1889, at 39 Rosher Road, Stratford. His parents' names were Ellen Feige, formerly Brooks, and Herman (another of the names Traven had admitted to the police) Otto Williams Feige, a warehouseman.

CERTIFIED COPY OF AN ENTRY OF BIRTH

		REGISTRATION DISTRICT West Ham
1889.	BIRTH in the Sub-district of	Stratford in t

Columns:— 1	2	3	4	5	6	
No.	When and where born	Name, if any	Sex	Name and surname of father	Name, surname and maiden surname of mother	Occupation of father	Signa resic
	First September 1889 39 Rosher Road	Alfred Otto Williams	Boy	Herman Otto Williams Feige	Ellen Feige formerly Brooks		

I drove down to West Ham. Rosher Road no longer existed, but a map at the local library showed that it had been part of what was then a poor area, bounded by Stratford High Street and Carpenter's Road, and backing on to Abbey Creek. The Feiges must have rented rooms at 39 Rosher (sometimes spelled Roscher) Road, since the house was not owned by them. From the West Ham Registrar, I obtained a copy of the Feiges' marriage certificate, which revealed that Herman Otto and Ellen's wedding had taken place at West Ham Parish Church on March 15th, 1889, less than six months before the birth of their child, Alfred. Hardly an unusual occurrence and not the illegitimacy I had expected to find at the Traven birth, but it might well have caused discomfort in the family and thereby to the young boy. The marriage certificate produced an echo, which, however distant, seemed charged with meaning in the absence of other clues to Traven's birth. Herman Otto recorded the profession of his father as 'engineer'. Had 'Engineer Torsvan' really been Feige, adopting his grandfather's occupation in Mexico and giving his father's names to the police in London? Here, at least, was the beginning of an explanation of the Traven identity. Had it not been for a later revelation, I might have been carried away.

In the meantime, I wanted to find out more about Traven when he was in the hands of the police in London in 1923–4, in particular the circumstances of his 'confession'. The Home Office informed me that they had no more papers on the case, I was unable to trace the arresting officer, Bickers, and Scotland Yard told me they had nothing. The case had been handled by the Special Branch, an arm of Scotland Yard established in 1883 to gather domestic intelligence. The Branch had always taken a particular interest in Irish matters and in the activities of foreign anarchists and socialists in Britain. In 1924 there were about 120 officers in the Special Branch, two of whom were discovered under the stage of a Communist Party meeting in April of that year and were forced to flee, leaving their notebooks behind. It would have been instructive to examine the notebooks of the officers who had interrogated Marut, but Special Branch records on individual cases are subject to a long hold of seventy-five years before they are released for public scrutiny. I managed to make a private enquiry through a contact with access to past and present Special Branch records. This person confirmed that there was nothing in the department's files under the names Marut or Feige.

It occurred to me that the American officials who had handled the case might have some memory of it. Boylston Beal was the most involved but he had died and the only one of the correspondents I could trace was Norman Armour, who had dealt with the Washington end of the matter. I wrote to Armour in New York. His wife replied on his behalf, explaining that he was ninety years old and unable to write himself. He had been assistant to the Under-Secretary at the time but had no recollection of the Marut case.

Turnbull followed up the reference to Sylvia Pankhurst. He spoke to her son, Dr Richard Pankhurst, who had not heard of the Marut case but thought it quite feasible that his mother would have helped in the circumstances. She had had contacts on the European mainland and had possibly made a brief visit to Germany while Marut was still there. Turnbull found someone to go through the Pankhurst papers in Amsterdam. There was nothing about our man.

I was interested in Charles Hallinan, the radical American journalist, who helped Marut when he was in London. The files commented on his proximity to Anna Isabella and Hazel Hunkins, although what they were thought to be mixed up in was not clear. If he was alive, Hallinan might still be in London and, on the off-chance, I looked him up in the telephone book. He was not there but, when I flicked through the Hs to find Hunkins, I was lucky: Hunkins-Hallinan, H., was there – just around the corner from the Belsize Park address where Hallinan was living in 1926. I rang the number. A woman with a slight American accent answered and, when I had explained the purpose of my call, she told me that she herself was Hazel Hunkins, the widow of Charles Hallinan. I made an appointment to meet her for tea at her club in Mayfair a few days later.

Mrs Hunkins-Hallinan was a lively and attractive woman in her seventies, who thought it a great joke that the State Department agents had kept a dossier on her and her husband. She was a small woman whose demeanour suggested a bird-like energy and I was not surprised to learn that she had been a prominent campaigner for women's rights in America and had recently returned to Washington to be honoured for her work. She told me that Charles Hallinan had been a newspaperman with the *Chicago Herald* before becoming Secretary of the American Union Against Militarism. He had later gone back to newspapers with the *New York Post*. She had never heard of Ret Marut and, when I put to her the suggestion I had heard from another Traven searcher that Marut had stayed with Hallinan in London, she said this was impossible. She had married Hallinan in 1920 in America and had come to London with him as his wife in the same year, so it was not all that clever of the American agents of the Special Branch to have spotted that Hallinan 'appeared to be among the residents ... of the same block of flats' as Hazel and her mother, Anna Isabella. By 1926, when the intelligence men made this knowing observation, she had three children all born in London during the previous six years. Mrs Hunkins-Hallinan said that she had naturally been busy at home over these years and that if Marut had stayed with them in 1923, she could hardly not have noticed. She had a clear memory of that period, dating by the ages of her children and by the timing of her move to Belsize Park in the autumn of 1923.

I showed her some photographs of Traven – the London police photographs and some other pictures taken when he was in his thirties and forties. She did not recognise him nor could she remember hearing any of his other names that I put to her. Mrs Hunkins-Hallinan could not remember her husband mentioning Sylvia Pankhurst or Nora Smyth, but he had known many conscientious objectors in the United States and his contacts in London might have been in similar circles. She did recall the names of Boylston Beal and Ray Atherton, another official at the Embassy, but she did not know anything about her husband's dealings with them. Nothing that Mrs Hunkins-Hallinan told me contradicted the report that her husband had aided Ret Marut and I was not inclined to doubt it, but I was disappointed that she was not able to confirm it from memory or supply any telling corroboration.

As I was leaving, however, she gave me one of those scraps of information which signified little and proved nothing, but which vibrated unmistakably. I wanted to check that her husband's name was Charles Thomas Hallinan, as I had seen it written. Yes, that was it, she said, but of course everyone had called him 'Hal'. I smiled to myself as I thanked Mrs Hunkins-Hallinan and said goodbye.

Perhaps it was almost too good to be true. But why shouldn't Traven have remembered the name of one who had helped him in London, when he needed to rechristen himself twenty years later? He had adopted the name Hal Croves to introduce himself to the visiting American film-makers. It was a name which was both distinctive and authentic, a name which might have allowed him to pay private tribute to one American who had not asked him too many awkward questions.

The film editor, Geoff Botterill, was back at work and 'The Mystery of B. Traven', as I had decided to call the film, was approaching its final shape. I shot the extra sequences with Robinson in London. All that remained was to work out a concluding tribute to Traven as a great writer, whose origins – the source of his obsessions – he had successfully lost beyond recall. I still might be able to touch in a detail here and there. There were no more leads to follow but continued sniffing on the trail in London might identify an unfamiliar scent. That apart, I had run the story to ground. Or so it seemed.

Somewhere in eastern Europe a piece of paper that proved otherwise was being slipped into an airmail envelope.

23 A Letter from Poland

Stanislav wrote a letter to Poznań, asking for his birth-certificate. He waited for one week. No certificate came. He waited two weeks. No answer. He waited another week. The certificate still did not come. He had sent a registered letter and put in two hundred and fifty billion marks to cover the expenses. All this was of no avail. No certificate was sent and no answer either.

The Death Ship

On a Monday morning in the spring of 1978 I received a telephone call which heralded the climax to our quest. It was from Turnbull. I had not seen him for a while, since I had all but finished editing the film and he had moved on to work in a different part of the BBC. He came quickly to the point. 'You know some months back the British Embassy told me where to write to for Polish birth records?'

'You never had a reply, did you?'

'One's come this morning.'

'They have sent you a letter?'

'No, they have sent me a birth certificate. For Feige.' Turnbull is a phlegmatic young man, but I could detect over the telephone that even his pulse rate had been raised by this unexpected twist. He said that he would bring the document over at lunchtime.

I tried to get on with some other work, but it was a long morning as I waited for Turnbull to arrive with this windfall. This was the first time that any of the names or birth places connected with Traven had ever produced any corroboration.

No other alias attributed to him or adopted by him could boast
a copy of that most hated of documents, a birth certificate. Just
once, it seemed, he had failed to cover his tracks.

Turnbull came early to my office, looking justifiably pleased
with himself and holding an airmail envelope, from which he
took the certificate and handed it to me.

POLSKA RZECZPOSPOLITA LUDOWA

Województwo .... Zielona Góra ....

URZĄD STANU CYWILNEGO w .... Świebodzinie ....

Odpis skrócony aktu urodzenia

1. Nazwisko .... Feige ....

2. Imię (imiona) .... Hermann-Albert-Otto-Maksymilian ....

3. Data urodzenia .... dwudziestego trzeciego lutego tysiąc
osiemset osiemdziesiątego drugiego 19 1882

4. Miejsce urodzenia .... Świebodzin ....

5. Nazwisko i imię .... Feige Adolf-Rudolf ....
   (ojca)
   .... zawód .... garncarz ....

6. Nazwisko rodowe (ojca) ....

7. Imię i nazwisko rodowe .... Hermina Wienecke ....
   (matki)
   .... zawód .... robotnica ....

Poświadcza się zgodność powyższego odpisu

z treścią aktu urodzenia Nr .... 57/1882 ....

.... Świebodzin ...., dnia 24 stycznia 197 8 r.

Miejsce na opłatę skarbową	**KIEROWNIK** Urzędu Stanu Cywilnego
	Jerzy Wysocki

Pu-M-8 zam. nr 1920/DW/On
ŁZG Zakł. Nr 3 w Pab., zam. .... szt. f. A5, piśm. sat. kl. 3

It was a standard form printed in Polish with details of the individual typed in and those details were close enough to what Marut had told the police in London for me to let out a whoop of joy. The certificate recorded that the child Feige had been born, as he had said, in Swiebodzin (formerly Schwiebus). The Christian names were Hermann Albert Otto Max, distinctly similar to the Herman Otto Albert Max of Marut's London confession. The confession had given only the year of birth, 1882; here was the exact date, February 23rd, 1882 – two days before the date of birth that Ret Marut had always admitted to. How pleasing that the child's father was down as Adolf Rudolf Feige and his mother as Hormina Wienecke. Pleasing, because I knew that two of the aliases Marut had used in London were Adolf Rudolf Feige and Albert Otto Max Wienecke.

I hurriedly rang the BBC reference library, where there was a Polish–English dictionary, to decipher the two remaining pieces of information: the parents' occupations. Marut had told the police that his mother had been a mill-hand and his father a potter; the form said 'robotnica' and 'gancarz'. 'Robotnica' had two meanings, said the lady in the library: unskilled worker or factory worker. And what about 'gancarz'? I asked. There was only one meaning, she replied. It meant 'potter'.

For once in his life Traven had given a name which could be traced: there really had been a Hermann Albert Otto Max Feige. On the face of it, we had caught him out at last and tracked down his beginnings to a distant corner of nineteenth-century Germany. But was Feige our man? An uncomfortable thought framed itself. I remembered the novel *The Day of the Jackal*, in which the assassin assumes the identity of someone he knows to be dead and obtains papers in that name. John Stonehouse used a similar method to equip himself with phoney passports prior to his staged disappearance. Had Traven done the same? When he was arrested in London, did he finally 'confess' to a name that he had in fact borrowed from an old acquaintance or comrade, or from a childhood friend; someone, perhaps, that he knew to be dead or otherwise untraceable? According to the police he had known something about the town of Schwiebus. Had he merely visited it?

Two things persuaded me that it was not a borrowed identity

and that we had hit upon the true birth name of Traven. Firstly, he had been able to tell the police in London what the occupations of the Feige parents had been forty years before. The certificate said 'factory worker', a general term which would encompass the more specific 'mill-hand', and 'potter' was absolutely correct. If they were not Traven's parents but someone else's, it was unlikely that he would have remembered their jobs from so long ago. And then there was his use of the name Wienecke as an alias. It was another long shot that he would have known the maiden name of a friend or acquaintance's mother from forty years back. I thought of my own friends and acquaintances. There were one or two from childhood whose parents' jobs I could remember; if not the jobs they were doing at the time of my birth, then the jobs they held at the time I knew their children. In none of these instances did I also know the maiden name of the mother. In fact I could not remember, if I had ever known, the maiden name of any friend's mother. Traven had known the mother's maiden name and the full name of the father because, surely, they were his own parents.

It was strange that fifty years before the German police and political police had searched for a man bearing this name and found no one. They had reported that no such Feige was known in Schwiebus. Now, from that same town half a century, a world war and a change of nationality later, he turns up in response to a straightforward approach to the district registry. That was a mystery in itself. We had to go to Poland. With luck we might find out more about Hermann Albert Otto Max Feige, and possibly begin to track him through the years to see if he would collide with or melt into our knowledge of Traven's time as Ret Marut.

It would be fitting if Traven had come from a town which had changed its name and its country, as Swiebodzin had. It is now in western Poland, just over forty miles from the East German border. I made arrangements with Polish Television to use a film crew from their station in Poznan, and for a researcher to make some enquiries in Swiebodzin before we arrived. Robinson, my assistant Jane Lush, and I flew to Warsaw, where we completed negotiations with Polish TV and picked up a Polish friend of Jane's who had volunteered to translate for us. We flew on to Poznan. On the evening of Saturday, April 8th, we arrived at our modern hotel in some excitement. We were one short step now from the birth town of Traven.

In the dark we had seen little enough of Poznan itself, but while there was no time to explore the city, it was more than a mere staging post. It was the home of Stanislav Koslovski, the Polish sailor, Gales's friend and fellow sufferer, in *The Death Ship*. Stanislav was born in Poznan, or Posen as it was called when part of Prussia, and went to school there until he was fourteen.

All instruction was given in German, but he knew a little Polish from his parents, who spoke it occasionally, mainly at church service. The German Poles, it seemed, had the idea that the Lord would not understand them if they addressed him in German.

When he left school, his parents wanted to apprentice him to a master tailor. Stanislav had other ideas. 'A couple of hundred stories in imitation of Cooper's *Last of the Mohicans*, sold at a dime apiece, and another couple of hundred sea stories and pirate yarns, had ambushed his spirit, and he ran away from home ...'

Was there as much Traven autobiography in Stanislav as there was in Gales? Had Traven come from near Poznan and had the dream of adventure, which ambushed his spirit, swept him to Berlin, Düsseldorf and Munich, from the fastness of the Polish plain?

I telephoned our Polish researcher, Lidia Owczarzak, after dinner. She had some good news for me. She had visited Swiebodzin and discovered that the Town Hall records contained details not only of Feige's birth but also of his parents' wedding. Fearing that Hermann Feige had died in infancy or childhood, that Traven had known of this and, like the hero of *The Day of The Jackal*, made use of it in constructing an alias, I had asked Lidia to search for a death certificate for the boy. Happily she had found no indication that young Feige had not survived.

The following morning Lidia joined us early at our hotel. She was a woman in her forties and, when not serving as a re-

searcher for visiting firemen like ourselves, was actually a producer with the local television station. She spoke good English
and worked hard and intelligently for us, although always
worrying that she was not translating well enough or that her
arrangements would go wrong.

Two taxis arrived to ferry us the seventy miles to Swiebodzin.
We set off past the thick grey slabs of apartment buildings on
the outskirts of Poznan and broke into the open country along
a tree-lined empty road which led straight on to Berlin. The
landscape spread threateningly wide on either side, the open
fields tramped flat by the advances and retreats of many armies
in many wars. Occasionally we passed a sturdy red-brick farm,
where the peasants and their horses laboured slowly over
their crops. Where it was able to, the road skirted the thick
black forest; now and then it plunged unavoidably through
the gloomy depths of it. This was the home of witches, wood-
choppers and wolves, the heart of the continent.

This land – though part of the ancient cradle of Poland –
had known many proprietors over the past six hundred years.
The Kings of Poland, the Margraves of Brandenburg, the
Counts of Silesia and the Kings of Prussia had fought for,
treated for and procreated for the right to hold sway here. From
the mid-eighteenth century it was part of the Prussian kingdom,
later the German Empire. The old mixture of Germans and
Poles was altered by German colonisation under Bismarck,
when the Polish language was persecuted and the culture of
these territories forcibly Germanised. At the end of the First
World War Poznan and most of the province of Poznania
became part of the new state of Poland. In border areas the
local populations decided by plebiscite whether they wished to
belong to Poland or Germany. As a result, Schwiebus, as it still
was, found itself a mere fourteen miles inside the German
border.

The various territorial dispensations of the Treaty of Versailles ('that masterpiece of the overwhelming stupidity of brilliant statesmanship') produced in Traven a particular irritation,
over and above his usual sensitivity in all matters touching on
nationality. He was especially aggravated by the requirement
for inhabitants of certain areas to opt for one country or
another. No less than three of the sailors on the *Yorikke* suffer

from being born in disputed territories. Paul, born in Alsace, is shunted back and forth by the French and Germans because he was away from home too long to have declared a preference for either country. Kurt, from Memel on the Baltic coast, also failed to adopt a country under the regulations of the Treaty of Versailles. In consequence Kurt is 'neither German, nor a citizen of this tiny little worm of a new nation that does not know and never will know, what to do with herself' (Lithuania). And most tellingly, in the light of our unfolding discoveries, there is Stanislav, born in Poznan and harassed because he too failed to declare his nationality as the Treaty laid down.

Schwiebus eventually became Swiebodzin in Poland at the end of the Second World War. It is a pleasant, modest town of some twenty-five thousand inhabitants, many of whom came here from the Polish territories lost to Russia in 1945. Our excitement as we entered the town was tempered with apprehension. If we were wrong in our researches, we would now find out. We parked in a wide avenue and walked through some narrow streets into a clean, attractive market square, which was paved and for pedestrians only. It was Sunday morning and we had the bright square to ourselves as we walked across it to the grey stone, nineteenth-century Town Hall.

Lidia had arranged for the registry office to be opened up specially. The mayor, a young and cheerful man who offered us every possible courtesy and assistance, was waiting for us. He introduced his registrar and an elderly citizen, who was in attendance to read the elaborate German script in which the old records had been kept. I made our introductions through our interpreter and, after a few halting compliments all round, our attention was directed to a large black-bound book on the table. A label on its cover read clearly, '1882. Geburts-Register'. Even I knew by now that this meant 'birth register'.

The excited registrar ceremoniously opened the register as if executing a manœuvre of the greatest delicacy and skill and laid in front of us entry number 57.

It was filled out in a black spidery handwriting which made it difficult to decipher anything but the odd word, and the elderly citizen was ushered forward to break the code. He translated carefully into Polish, which was then written down and further translated into English, a slow process forcing us to be patient but aiding accuracy. There were surprises.

Entry number 57 had been made by a midwife called Joanna Korhale, née Deutschmann, on February 28th, 1882. She had attended at the birth of a child on February 23rd to Hormina Wienecke, an unmarried factory worker of the evangelical religion, at the home of her father, the cloth-worker Carl Wilhelm Albert Wienecke.

The baby had been born at ten o'clock in the morning and named Hermann Albert Otto Max.

Hermann Albert Otto Max

erhalten habe .

This was not all. Alongside in the margin, the registrar of the time had added a handwritten note, dated May 30th, 1882, which read:

> Today, in the presence of the undersigned registrar, an agreement took place between the potter Adolf Rudolf Feige, living in Finsterwalde, and the petitioner Hormina Wienecke. The aforementioned has acknowledged paternity in relation to the child born to the latter as registered opposite. The above petition allows them to get married.

If this was Traven, he *was* born out of wedlock after all, and he was three months old before his father returned to claim him and marry his mother.

The present registrar hurried out and returned with the book of marriage records for 1882, which he opened at entry number 25. Adolf Rudolf and Hormina had married here in the town hall on the same day that the addendum had been entered on the birth record. Adolf Rudolf was a native of Finsterwalde, born there on May 23rd, 1860, the son of Gottlob Feige, a weaver, and his wife Joanna Wilhelmina, née Reu. Hormina's

Nr. *25.*

Schwiebus am *Donnerstig* ten
Mai tausend acht hundert *sechs* zig und *zwei.*

Vor dem unterzeichneten Standesbeamten erschienen heute zum
Zweck der Eheschließung:

1. der *Töpfer Adolf Rudolf Feige,*

full name was Frederika Dorota Hormina Wienecke. She was
a year older than her husband, born on June 1st, 1859, in
Schwiebus. The name of her father was recorded differently
in the marriage book from in the birth register. Here he was
Wilhelm August Kurt Wienecke and his wife, grandmother to
the three-month-old Hermann, was Frederyke Bogumila, née
Bullarz.

The two versions of the grandfather Wienecke's name were
puzzling, although the first had been supplied not by the family
but by the midwife, who might well have muddled the Christian names. Otherwise, here was the parentage and grand-
parentage of the child B. Traven said he had been. I looked
again at the original birth record of Hermann Albert Otto Max
Feige, the only one of all Traven's names for which a real person
had definitely existed. I could invent ways in which Traven
might have met or heard of this person and made use of the
name. But why Feige? And would he have remembered so
much, for so long? Was it not more likely that he really was
the boy Feige, born to an unmarried woman of humble circumstances in a distant corner of Polish Prussia?

Finsterwalde, where the child's father came from, was eighty
miles to the south-west in what is now East Germany. Presumably Adolf Rudolf came to work in Schwiebus as a potter,
tumbled the cloth-worker's daughter in the hay and perhaps
left the town for some months before returning to make an

honest woman of her. It seemed likely that he was not in Schwiebus as Hormina's pregnancy developed or the marriage would have taken place sooner. Whatever the exact circumstances, they were irregular enough to have planted a seed of resentment or embarrassment within the boy.

The name Feige would not have pleased Traven as he grew up. In German it means 'coward' or 'fig', the latter sometimes with a crude meaning. Lidia suggested that both Wienecke and Bullarz could have been Polish names. When she had been searching through the birth records she had noticed that many Polish names were then spelled in the German manner. Slight changes in the spelling of Hormina's family names produced 'Winecka' and 'Bularz', which were definitely Polish. So it was possible that the boy was German on his father's side and Polish, or part Polish, on his mother's side.

As we chatted with the mayor and Lidia about the likely origins of all the names, I noticed two further references on the bottom of the second page of the marriage records. One had the figure '200' and the year '1895' and I enquired of the registrar what this meant. He waved his hand airily and said that it was just a note and we could learn nothing from it, but I asked him if he would find the birth book for 1895. Reluctantly and with much shrugging of the shoulders, which I took to mean that this was going to be a waste of time, he left the room and came back sulkily a few minutes later with another record book. He put it on the table and flicked through the pages until he reached entry 200, which, he pointed out triumphantly, had nothing to do with the Feiges or the Wieneckes. He looked to the mayor and others for approval. I examined the book myself. He was right about this entry but he had brought in the register for 1885 instead of 1895. I sent him out again and he returned with another black book, which clearly said 1895 on the cover. This time the entries had run out well before page 200, which was blank, though it took only a glance to see that this was the marriage, not the birth book for 1895. At last, the now flustered registrar brought in the correct book and we were rewarded.

On August 5th, 1895, thirteen years after their marriage, Adolf Rudolf and Hormina had produced another son, Johannes Walter Ernst Feige. The birth was registered by Adolf

32 Robinson and the author, holding the birth record book, in town hall of Swiebodzin, Poland.

33 and 34 Margarethe Henze and Ernst Feige, in Wallensen, West Germany, 1978, when (*below*) they identified photographs of their brother Otto.

35 The infant Hermann Albert Otto Maximilian Feige *c.* 1884.

36 Otto Feige's confirmation photograph. Schwiebus (now Swiebodzin) *c.* 1896. The young pastor to be.

37 Otto Feige *c.* 1902 taken in Magdeburg.

38 Ret Marut

39 The Feige parents' silver wedding anniversary, 1907. Otto had
already left home and to complete the group his head was cut from
the photograph in plate 37 and stuck on to the torso of a stand-in,
back row left. Next to him is Erna (1892–1911), then Gertrud (1888–
1951), Willi (1884–1950) and Max (1890–1970). Front row left to right:
Ernst (1895–   ), Hormina (1859–1936), Adolf (1860–1934) and
Margarethe (1893–   ).

40 T. Torsvan

41 Hal Croves

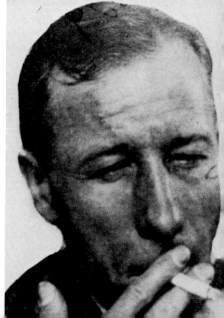

42   Hormina Wienecke, mill hand, and Adolf Rudolf Feige, potter.

43   Torsvan–Croves towards
the end of his life.

44   The photograph from
Time, April 1977, captioned
'Traven in coffin 1969'.

himself, who was now described as a concierge of Bratzerstrasse 13. At the bottom of this page was another reference,
which we would have to follow up elsewhere. It referred forward forty-five years to June 13th, 1940, when this Johannes
Walter Ernst had married, for the second time, in Hamburg.
There was no mention of a first marriage or of any children,
but there was a chance that this Feige would have living offspring who could tell us more about the family. They might
even know what happened to their father's elder brother, con-
firming or categorically disproving that he was Traven.

The Town Hall records had divulged their all: a birth, a marriage and another birth. Sadly, they had disclosed no place of
birth for Hermann Albert Otto Max but they had given us the
address at which the family were living in 1895. Bratzerstrasse
no longer existed, and Lidia had arranged for us to see an old
man who knew the history of the town and who might know
where it had been. Over coffee in the crypt of the Town Hall,
Robinson and I talked with the mayor about Swiebodzin. He
proudly extolled the virtues of this pleasant town and described
how the influx of Poles from the east had been happily assimi-
lated. The citizens worked mainly in light industry and agriculture. Referring to the description of Hormina Wienecke as
a factory worker, Robinson asked what sort of factory she could
have worked in in 1882. The mayor had little doubt about the
answer. Right through the eighteenth and nineteenth centuries
Schwiebus had been famous for its cloth, which had been
exported to Western Europe and to the United States. There
had been many cloth mills in the town, he said, and Hormina
would have worked in one of these. She had been, in other
words, a mill-hand – as Traven had told the London police.
The bare records had known her only as a factory worker;
Traven had known Hormina Wienecke more closely.

We thanked the mayor, his registrar and the elderly citizen
for their help and walked back to the car. The mayor had not
known of any potteries in the town in 1882, but Lidia thought
that the old man we were to visit next might be able to help
us. He lived in a small house on the edge of the town and we
all crammed into his living-room, where an old map was laid
out on the table. He pointed out Bratzerstrasse; it was the wide
street by which we had entered the town and was now called

Poznanskie Street. He confirmed what the mayor had told us about the cloth industry and showed us how the map of Schwiebus was dotted with 'Tuchfabrik' – cloth factories. We asked where a potter could have worked in the town in 1882. Had there been a pottery at that time? There had, said the old man. It had been part of the brickworks, where they had made tiles and earthenware as well as bricks. He turned again to the map to show us where it had been, pointing to a spot close to the main Berlin–Warsaw railway line, which ran through the outskirts of Schwiebus. The area was marked 'Ziegeleien', brickworks. Robinson leaned forward and interrupted. 'Would a man who made tiles in such a place be thought of as a brickmaker?' he asked. We watched the old man as our interpreter translated. He nodded. Robinson said eagerly: 'Would he have been called – a "Ziegelbrenner"?' The old man nodded again. 'Yes,' he said, 'he would.'

The site of the former brickworks was near by. We drove there and found it now a smallholding, guarded by an angry chained dog. The crumbling brick farmhouse looked as though it might once have formed part of the works; we were told that there had been lodgings for the workers among the buildings here. The site was held in the slight curve of the railway which ran alongside. To the east, the tracks led to Poznan and on to Warsaw; to the west, more enticingly to a boy whose mind was ambushed by dreams of adventure and the stage, they pointed to Berlin, eighty miles away. As I walked round the holding I could see few signs of the brickworks though there were many pieces of broken bricks scattered about. I picked some up and slipped them into my pocket. It was just possible that they had been fired by the original of *Der Ziegelbrenner*.

Before we left Schwiebus, we went to look at the house where Hermann Albert Otto Max's father had been caretaker when the boy was thirteen years old. It was a large, pink-painted building, with pilasters and pediments, in a prominent position towards the edge of the town. It now had some municipal function and was empty on this late Sunday afternoon. We wandered round to the back where there was a yard and outbuildings, including a mews dwelling for the likes of a concierge. No one lived there any more and there were no longer Feiges in Swiebodzin.

We set off for Poznan with the late sun pushing shadows of the roadside trees far out into the earth of the fields. We had one more call to make. Lidia had discovered that the last known Feige in Swiebodzin had left some years previously and was now living in a town just off our route back to Poznan. He might know something about the Feige family we were investigating; he might even be a member of it. Thus, we drew up in front of some rudimentary concrete flats at six o'clock on a Sunday evening, and sent our translator in on the comic errand of explaining that there was a party of English people outside who were looking for the relations of a man who had died in Mexico. The rest of us waited by the cars, giggling at the thought of the situation in reverse: of being disturbed after one's own Sunday tea by a group of foreigners searching for the relations of a mystery man. The translator reappeared and summoned us in, saying that the man Feige was at home and would see us.

We followed her inside and into a tiny flat where a man of about fifty, dressed in pyjama bottoms and a jumper, was looking understandably bemused. We said hello and I asked the translator to explain what we knew about the Feiges of Swiebodzin. While she spoke to him in Polish, Robinson and I manœuvred ourselves to get a better view, trying as tactfully as we could to compare him with a photograph of the middle-aged Traven that I was holding surreptitiously in my hand. This Feige was thicker-set and his head was squarer, but he was also quite a short man with a large nose of similar shape to the one with which we were so familiar. Robinson and I stood to one side, nudging each other and whispering until the translator put an end to our imaginings and farcical behaviour. She told us that this Feige had not come to this area until the Second World War and could have no connection with the family of Hermann Albert Otto Max. We left the surprised man to return to his Sunday sleep in peace.

As the cars swept us back to Poznan, Robinson and I debated the Feige evidence. Traven said that his real name was Feige and that he came from Schwiebus; it turned out that he was acquainted with the town and there was such a Feige born there. As Marut he gave February 25th, 1882, as his birthday; Feige was born February 23rd, 1882. He used the name Wienecke as an alias; Wienecke was the mother's maiden name. He used the name Adolf Rudolf Feige as an alias; this was the father's name. Traven was able to say correctly that his mother was a mill-hand although the records only put it more generally as 'factory worker'. He knew the father's trade from forty years before: a potter. Traven called his revolutionary magazine *Der Ziegelbrenner*; this potter very likely made earthenware and tiles in a brickworks in Schwiebus, the town was then a German town and the German for a tile-maker is 'Ziegelbrenner'.

It was not a conclusive case but it was a powerful one. Traven seems only to have revealed the name Feige once, to the police in London in 1923. Yet, as Marut, he named his magazine six years before he ever admitted to the Feige identity, and he gave the date of birth so close to Feige's, from 1907 – fifteen years before. These could have been long coincidences. Or he could have stored details of the Feige identity – the names, the occupations, knowledge of Schwiebus – for at least fifteen years before he made full use of them. Or Traven was Feige. As I looked out of the car window in the fading light, I was not surprised that he had escaped from the oppressive emptiness of this landscape. Here and there it was mellowed by contour or cultivation, but there seemed nothing to stop the land running on like this for ever; there was nowhere to hide. Traven would not have enjoyed the close stare of life in a small town and his spirit would have sought to free itself from the quiet conservatism of this aching space. The car sped on and we began wondering what could have induced Traven to give the police a name and biography which could be traced. If it was not his real name he risked exposure when his lie was checked. If it was his true name, he was breaking the habit of a lifetime.

The American letter in which the name Herman Otto Albert Max Feige appeared spoke of Traven 'confessing' that this was his name, with the implication that he had not given it willingly. There was no suggestion that he had been ill-treated by the police, but it sounded as if his revelation had been a last resort. He might have been 'shopped'. He could have told his name to a fellow inmate in Brixton who passed it on to the officers, who in turn confronted him with it and extracted the full story. But there was no reason for him to have let his name slip in that way.

Above all things Traven wished to avoid being sent back to Germany, where he would face trial and possible execution. On the face of it, this made it inexplicable that he should say he came from Germany but I believed that it provided the key. He might have been persuaded to overcome his lifelong obsession with hiding his identity and to tell the truth, if it was his one chance of avoiding the ultimate disaster, execution. I believe it was the truth that he told the police in London, for he had absolutely no reason to give them yet another false German alias which might cause him to be returned to Germany. There might have been a reason for the truth.

My guess, and it has to be a guess, is that there was a deal. Traven was in prison, faced with deportation and frightened. He wanted to travel on an American passport to join Irene Mermet in the United States, but he was not accepted as an American. He needed help. In return for the truth about who the revolutionary Ret Marut really was, the police in London might have offered not to deport him to Germany. They might have promised to do what they could in the matter of the passport or just to let him out of prison and not stand in his way. As they already believed he was a German and were probably threatening to send him back to Germany if he did not co-operate, he had nothing to lose. The truth was his las chance. It worked in part: he was not deported to Germany and he was let out of prison.

If there was a deal the British police did not play wholly straight with him. By handing over his 'confession' to the United States' Embassy they made sure that he did not go to America. Still, Traven did get safely away from Britain, and he probably believed till the end of his life that the truth about himself was in one ageing file at Scotland Yard and nowhere else.

24 Otto

The final stage in editing a film is the dub, when all the different sound tracks – commentary, interviewees, music and effects – are married together. I had already postponed the date for this once and, after editing in the film we had shot in Poland, I asked Geoff Botterill to hang on for a little while longer. We had thrust one more iron into the fire.

TO PRODUCTION MANAGER NDR HAMBURG
I AM TELEXING YOU THE DETAILS OF THE RESEARCH WE REQUIRE IN HAMBURG. WE ARE TRYING TO TRACE A MAN (OR ANY OF HIS RELATIVES) CALLED JOHANNES WALTER ERNST FEIGE. HE WAS BORN AUGUST 5TH 1895 IN SCHWIEBUS WHICH IS NOW SWIEBODZIN IN POLAND. WE KNOW THAT JOHANNES FEIGE WAS MARRIED FOR THE SECOND TIME IN HAMBURG 4 ON JUNE 13TH 1940 AND THAT THE ENTRY IN THE MARRIAGE BOOK IS NUMBER 456. WE WOULD VERY MUCH LIKE TO INTERVIEW HIM IF HE IS STILL ALIVE OR TO FIND ANY OF HIS CHILDREN OR RELATIVES TO INTERVIEW THEM OR INDEED FIND OUT ANY INFORMATION ABOUT HIM OR HIS FAMILY. THIS IS FOR A TELEVISION DOCUMENTARY FOR THE BBC. THE RESEARCH SHOULD BE DONE BY THE END OF NEXT WEEK APRIL 28TH. REGARDS.
JANE LUSH BBC LONDON

I had asked Jane Lush not to explain the background to our search for two reasons: I wanted to be the first to find a way to the centre of the maze; and if we found any Feiges I did not want them to know why we were interested in them until after we had put our questions – in case it coloured the answers. They might well strain to please both me and themselves by finding connections between their family and a great writer. I was confident that we were right, but if we were not, we should know it.

A few days later I had a message from the German researcher that she had found Feige's marriage record and he had been living in Hamburg in 1957 but there was no trace of him after that, and no sign of any children. Then came another message. She could still find no record of any children, but she had tracked down the 83-year-old Johannes Walter Ernst Feige himself. He was still alive and now living in the village of Wallensen in Lower Saxony. We actually had the telephone number of Traven's brother. I rounded up a German speaker and at six o'clock that evening several of us crowded into my office to place a call to Wallensen. It was to the one person in the world who could confirm or disprove that we had found B. Traven.

When he got through to the number the German speaker calmly explained who we were, that we were researching a documentary and that he was having to translate the conversation as he went along. We proceeded with the questions one at a time, with a pause for each answer to be translated.

Had the Herr Feige we were talking to definitely been born in Schwiebus? He confirmed that he had. Did Herr Feige have a brother? Yes, he was dead. Was he an elder brother? Yes. When had this brother died? About ten years ago. I was amazed. It was just over nine years since Traven had died and I could not imagine how Herr Feige had known about this, unless Traven had kept in touch with the family over the years. I told the German speaker to ask where this brother had died and where he was buried. He did so and the answer sent me reeling. The elder brother, Max, had died there in Wallensen and was buried in the local cemetery. I watched in dismay as the translator's face told me that Herr Feige was rubbing salt into our wounds. This brother had fought in the First World War and had been taken prisoner. He had later returned to Wallensen and worked as a machine operator. So he could not possibly have been in Munich publishing *Der Ziegelbrenner*; he could not possibly have been in Mexico. The translator turned to me from the telephone and said that it was no good, this brother was obviously not the man we were looking for; I must have made some mistake.

I asked him to wait on for a moment before he ended the call. This news meant that somehow I had misread the evidence which we had built up so convincingly. Somewhere we had not spotted an alternative explanation, we had missed a clue or raced on too quickly. It meant that the names and the jobs were just extraordinary coincidences. The father being a 'Ziegel-brenner' was not the telling shaft which pinned the whole story to a time and place, but one more accidental link in a mislead-ing chain of circumstantial evidence. Damn and blast! The translator was telling me that the old man on the end of the line was going to ring off unless there was anything else we had to ask. He was saying that he did not receive many phone calls and did not want to be bothered any more as his wife was very ill.

I could not bear to watch the telephone being put down and accept surrender. I asked the translator to repeat the questions to Herr Feige. Had there by any chance been more than one brother? Yes, there had. Hope returned. In that case, did he have a brother who was much older than he was, thirteen years older: a brother whose full name had been Hermann Albert Otto Max? Ah yes, said Herr Feige, he had. His brother Otto; he had forgotten all about him. Then came a thrilling moment. Before we said anything about what we knew of that brother, Herr Feige volunteered three memories of Otto which removed the last doubts that we had found the true identity of B. Traven. Otto, he said, had left home before the First World War and was never seen again. He had simply disappeared. Herr Feige remembered that in his youth Otto had been a very clever chap. And then he recalled that the family had heard once more from Otto; they knew that he had been in England after the First World War and that the authorities had thrown him out. A clever boy who had disappeared from his family and was deported from England after the First War. The life of Otto Feige held the life of Marut–Traven in an indissoluble embrace.

We ended the call by thanking Herr Feige and promising that we would be in touch with him again shortly – something he did not seem in the least keen on. Nevertheless, we had to visit him. He could tell us what the family had been like, what else he remembered about Otto and he might have photographs. If there was half a chance in a hundred that we were wrong, he was the one man in the world who could prove it. I was fleetingly tempted to avoid the risk, to stand on the cast-iron case we had established and not chance testing it on the man's own brother. If by some fluke we were wrong, Herr Feige might remember Otto as tall or fat or with black curly hair or brown eyes. Or he might recall an instance which would place Otto where Traven could never have been. He was the only person we knew of in the world who could destroy our solution. Against this, I remained sure that we were right, and I would have been driven witless by curiosity if I passed up the opportunity of meeting the brother of B. Traven.

In order to arrange the visit we rang Feige again a couple of days later, only to be driven back by the old man's demands that we leave him alone. It was Traven seeing off Bernard Smith or Klein, or Spota, all over again. Ernst Feige said that we could not go to see him because he was going away for the weekend and did not know when he would be back. (Traven to Smith: 'Last week of August I shall leave for California, Dakota and Wisconsin where I have to see some people, how they are doing.') Ernst Feige said there was no point in coming to Germany, even if he was at home, as he had told the people downstairs that they were not to let us in under any circumstances. (Traven to Klein: 'If you cross the border at San Diego you are still some two thousand miles from the hut that I am living in.') And Herr Feige concluded the telephone conversation with a plea for mercy, saying his friends had told him that since he had been receiving all these strange phone calls he was a changed man. We must stop pestering him. (Traven to Spota: 'You are a son of a bitch ... If you print your story, you will have my death on your hands.')

The similarity in the brothers' attitude towards prying strangers presented me with a problem. It was no use my knocking on Ernst Feige's door, only for him to send me packing. I wanted to talk to him and I wanted him to agree to be interviewed on film. I thought that the best way to approach him was through someone he knew, someone who might persuade him that we were relatively harmless, albeit nosey. I decided to make a reconnaissance and flew to Hanover with a German-speaking colleague, Peter Foges. Such is life's habit of chasing you with your own reflection that we arrived on an evening when the late-night television film in Hanover was *The Treasure of the Sierra Madre*.

The next day we drove the forty miles to Wallensen. It was a morning of mist and drizzle and as we turned on to the road between Hildesheim and Hameln, the clouds steamed out of the dark forests. The steep gables of half-timbered houses lined the village streets and, in the gloom of the morning, the air hung heavy with fairy tale and legend. The twin villages of Wallensen and Thüste lie prettily in a broad-bottomed valley between ranges of high wooded hills. They house about two thousand people between them, Wallensen being the larger.

We drove into its quiet, wide main street and drew up outside the village shop to ask directions to the vicarage. I had decided that our best bet was to throw ourselves on the local vicar, take him into our confidence and ask if he would intercede with Ernst Feige on our behalf. This plan succeeded because we were lucky with our vicar; a moustachioed, slightly built young man, Pastor Heinz Behrends. In the study of his modern house he listened thoughtfully as I explained the background to our mission and described our difficulty with Ernst Feige. He said he knew Feige quite well. The old man was a sad case and he rarely went out now because he had to stay at home with his wife, who suffered cruelly from arterio-sclerosis. This had no doubt contributed to his aggressive stance towards us. The Pastor warned us that it would take more than the box of chocolates we had brought to make Feige change his mind. The Pastor agreed to act as go-between for us. He had a wedding the following day and thought it best if he were to drop in casually on Feige during the week. I was impatient to go then and there, but we were in the Pastor's hands and the interests of his parishioners came first. He was a serious man and I felt that he wanted to digest what we had told him before deciding how much of it he should burden Ernst Feige with. We arranged to ring him at the end of the following week.

We did so and the answer was that Feige would see us. The Pastor also surprised me with a gift which was quite beyond my expectation: Ernst had a sister in Wallensen, a widow called

Margarethe Henze, who had also agreed to talk to us. We flew off again on the morning of May 25th.

This time it was a warm spring day of hazy sunshine as we approached Wallensen and the red tiled roofs shone as bright as a clump of poppies against the young green of the fields. We picked up the Pastor and he directed us to Herr Feige's flat, which was in the sister village of Thüste. We approached it in some trepidation. Outside the house an elderly woman sat still and silent on a bench in the sunshine, watching us without re-action – it was, we learned afterwards, Frau Feige.* Upstairs Ernst was waiting for us, a short, slight man dressed in grey jacket and trousers, fawn cardigan, clean white shirt and tie. A white handkerchief pointed out of his pocket and he had the correct and upright bearing of the waiter he once was.

Our interview was to take place at Frau Henze's house and Feige travelled with us in the car, where I had an opportunity to study him more closely. At first, apart from the height and build, he looked unlike his brother, but I began to notice simi-larities. When he sat down and leant backwards wearing his glasses, he bore a distinct resemblance to the elderly Traven. The hairline and the thin grey hair swept back over the ears were remarkably similar to the Mexican photographs, and the voice had the same quavering assertion that I had heard on the tape recording. Throughout the meeting he spoke much less than his sister and sat patiently with his hands together in his lap.

At Frau Henze's we went through a dark hall into a bright, tidy room lit by two windows. There were many family photo-graphs on view and the cheerful aspect was confirmed by a vase of sweet-scented lilies of the valley in the centre of the table. In the corner a large grandfather clock ticked deeply. Frau Henze, who looked much younger than her eighty-six years, was also short, but stouter than her brother. She had a ruddy, country face with a child-like shine on it and her eyes were startlingly blue. Throughout the two hours we were with her, she talked animatedly, laughing a great deal and at one point becoming quite tearful, though not sad.

We told neither Margarethe Henze nor Ernst Feige about Marut–Traven–Torsvan–Croves before or during our talks

* Frau Feige died at the end of 1978.

with them. They had no notion of what we expected. Indeed, at Pastor Behrends's suggestion, it was not until some time afterwards that we gave them details of their brother's life and the names he had used. Had we been wrong, the story could have been shipwrecked a dozen times on any detail of Otto Feige's life which clashed with what we knew of Traven. But we were not wrong. What we heard from the old couple added colour and chiaroscuro to our picture and erased nothing. The life of B. Traven flowed naturally from the youth of Otto Feige.

And there were the photographs. Photographic evidence can never be conclusive, only suggestive or corroborative, and in this case it arrived only after the identity was proven. But it was exciting. It would have been quite possible that Traven had changed beyond recognition over the years, that the pictures I had of him later in his life bore little or no resemblance to the young Otto Feige from Schwiebus. Many people change dramatically from youth to middle age and it would have done no damage to our identification if it had been so with Otto.

Yet when Frau Henze took out the confirmation photograph of her eldest brother, Otto, and placed it on the lace tablecloth, it was the young Traven who gazed up at us. The challenging stare of B. Traven was already there on the face of the young Otto Feige. A boy of about fourteen, self-contained and immaculately dressed, stood proudly by a rustic seat, Homburg hat in hand. The mouth was slightly flattened, the upper lip long, the left nostril angled more widely than the right. The features which characterised all Traven pictures inhabited this smooth young face. There was, too, a group photograph of the whole family, parents and seven children in all. The father, a small-featured man with narrow eyes and a drooping moustache, sat upright by a table; the mother, Hormina, a solidly built woman with heavy, sensual features, sat stiffly on the other side. At the rear on the left was an odd figure. It was an anonymous torso with a profile photograph of Otto's head cut unhandily from elsewhere and stuck on. The occasion of the group picture was Adolf and Hormina's silver wedding, in May 1907, and Otto's face had to be incorporated by sleight of hand because he had already left home, never to return. Of course he had. 1907 was

the year of the first recorded appearance by the strange young
actor, Ret Marut.

It remained only for us to seek the final confirmation. We
had shown none of our Traven photographs to Frau Henze or
Herr Feige prior to the filming. I now watched apprehensively
as, the camera turning, Robinson took out a folder of pictures
– family snaps from Mexico, identity photos from the Torsvan
documents and the Marut mug shots from London – and passed
them one by one across the table to the old couple. They were
expecting to see pictures of their brother and they showed no
surprise at the likenesses. There was a comment on the Mexican
background and the clothes. Then Margarethe Henze, looking
at the full-face mug shot, exclaimed: 'What a grim face he is
pulling. The chin is like my mother.' She paused for a moment
and cast her eyes over the selection of photographs spread out
on the table. She smiled and nodded: 'Yes, that's him.'

25 'Not Our Son'

From Traven's brother and sister and, later, from three of his nieces I was able to piece together something of the story of the Feige family and the childhood of Otto. He was, as we knew, the eldest child, born three months before his parents married. The reason for this, according to the family, was that Otto's father, Adolf, was in the German army doing his military service at the time and was not allowed leave to marry the woman he had impregnated until after the birth. This explanation is generous to the reputations of both parents and is supported by the dates. Young men were called up for two years' military service at the age of twenty, and if Adolf had joined on his twentieth birthday he would have been released from the army on his twenty-second, May 23rd, 1882. He married Hormina exactly a week later. I have found no clue as to whether Adolf, who would have been in the army for about a year when Otto was conceived, knew his wife-to-be before his military service or whether it was only as a young soldier that he first came to Schwiebus and fell for her.

The technical irregularity of his birth was not the only unusual aspect of Traven's earliest years. His lifelong obsession with the accidental nature of conception and his irritation at being unable to choose his parents may equally well have sprung from the circumstances of his upbringing. For he spent his first years not with his parents but with his maternal grandparents. He was born in the Wieneckes' house near the western edge of Schwiebus and he remained there even after Adolf had returned to marry Hormina. The young couple's poverty was the most likely reason for this arrangement, but the apparent rejection might not have been so easily explained away in the developing consciousness of a young child. Family lore has it that the Wieneckes dearly loved, petted and spoiled their grandchild, who grew up to look upon them as his true parents. Otto's earliest memories must have sprung from this time, when he was the clever and unchallenged object of his grandparents' adoration. It is not clear how long he stayed with the Wieneckes. Frau Henze had no direct memory of all this as she was not yet born at the time and she told me on one occasion that Otto was three and, on another, that he was six years old, when this cosseted introduction to life was ended. I like to think that six years is correct. It imbues with metaphorical truth Ret Marut's tale to Elfriede Zielke, that from the age of six he had been brought up by a governess.

In truth, it was not a governess but his own parents who brought heartache to Otto by separating him from his grandparents. When grandfather Wienecke became ill, Hormina came to take her child home, in spite of the protestations of the old man, who said it would break his heart if the boy was taken from him. The family story says that Hormina promised to return Otto as soon as her father had recovered but the old man went into a decline and died soon afterwards. Otto was as upset as his grandparents by the move and the unhappy repatriation left its mark on him for life. Both Margarethe and Ernst remembered that Otto was always considered as special, a person apart from the rest of the family. The fact that he was a particularly clever boy contributed to this, but both his brother and sister ascribed Otto's self-willed and stubborn behaviour to his resentment at having to return to his parents. The young Traven had already detached himself from his surroundings and was living within his own sense of who he was rather than accepting that imposed upon him by the blind chance of birth. 'He never felt at home with us,' said Margarethe.

She and Ernst described Otto in terms which were uncannily appropriate for the maturing Traven. Without any knowledge of the man that we had studied and hunted, they depicted their brother as a self-possessed boy, a 'loner', who had been very particular about his dress and about protecting what was his. He was always on his own, often reading; he was, said Ernst, 'a strange peculiar boy who lived only in his own world, a world in which there was no room for anyone else'. When Luis Spota had asked Maria de la Luz Martinez about the man she lived with, Señor Traven Torsvan, she had replied: 'He is a very strange man, not very sociable. He does not have many friends and does not talk to anybody.' Herr Feige's words described his brother Otto as he had been around the year 1900; Señora Martinez spoke of the same man forty-five years later.

Stanislav in *The Death Ship* made himself into an orphan by simply telling people that he was, adding the embroidery that he 'had been so mistreated and so cruelly beaten every day by his foster-parents that he had jumped into the sea to end his life'. Traven made himself an orphan by telling the American consul in London that he had run away to sea at the age of ten, by claiming in the *B.T. News Reports* that he had fended for himself since he was seven. From Margarethe, I learned that it was as the young Otto Feige that he had first bestowed upon himself this romantic fantasy. Some time after his grandfather's death, the grandmother Wienecke came to live with the family, and continued to favour the precious Otto, causing jealousy among the other children. Otto was in his mid-teens when the old lady died and he was greatly affected. As far as he was concerned his true parents were now both dead and he declared himself an orphan.

I was able to trace the dates and places of birth of Otto's brothers and sisters, and they chart the movements of Adolf and Hormina Feige over the first fourteen years of their marriage. When the second child, Willi, was born at the end of 1884 they were living in Adolf's home town of Finsterwalde. Some time during the next four years, probably taking Otto with them, they moved to Grünberg (now Zielona Gora), a sizeable town twenty-five miles south of Swiebodzin. The next three children were born in Grünberg: Gertrud in May 1888, Max in June 1890, and Erna in July 1892. Then, when Otto was ten or eleven, the family returned to Schwiebus, where Hormina gave birth to Margarethe in December 1893, and to Ernst nearly two years later. Margarethe remembered clearly where the family had lived in Schwiebus and when I showed her a map of the town, pointed to the street without hesitation. The house was north of the market square, opposite the Cath-

olic Hospital. It was owned by a shoemaker called Sinnert, who
lived either next door or in part of the same dwelling, and who,
Frau Henze remembered, used to tell stories to the younger
Feiges.

By this time Otto was a star pupil at the local school. He
wanted to continue his studies past the usual leaving age and
to take up theology, with the intention of becoming a pastor.
The town council of Schwiebus offered to pay for the tuition
of this outstanding scholar if his parents would play their part
by providing for his board and lodging. It was a great opportunity for a boy of humble family, and a flattering recognition
of his intelligence and achievement. His own estimate of himself
as someone out of the ordinary would be confirmed by being
singled out for favour by the whole town. But the young Traven
was not to be allowed this distinction. The chance to assert his
individuality was removed before his hand could close upon
it. His parents had six other children and, deciding that they
could not afford to support this one any longer, insisted that
he take up an apprenticeship, during which his master would
provide him with food and clothing. The trade they chose was
almost comically suitable for Traven: he was to become a locksmith, with the firm of Meiers. 'When he was about to leave
grammar school, his parents wanted to give Stanislav as an
apprentice for four years to a master tailor ... he ran away from
home.'

Otto did not run away. He served his time as a locksmith,
holding within himself, perhaps, his anger at this latest and
most insulting rejection by his natural parents. From now on
they had lost all right to claim him as their son. Stanislav hated
his parents for trying to make an honest tailor of a boy who
wished to go to sea; Traven surely hated his for fashioning a
locksmith from a scholarly theologian. As we have seen, his
knowledge of the Bible and his simple, direct Christianity
remained with him and revealed themselves in many of his
works both as Marut and as Traven. Here, also, may lie the
explanation of that reference in *Der Ziegelbrenner* to a forcibly
abbreviated study of theology. He had not, as he hinted, been
dismissed from theological college for asking precociously challenging questions (nor was he Charles Trefny, thrown out for
posing as a doctor); the sad and humiliating truth was that he

did not get so far as the gates of a theological college, because his parents could not or would not afford it.

Adolf Feige, although a potter by trade, also worked in Schwiebus as a caretaker and trained as a factory foreman. In 1898 he moved his family again, this time just a few miles from Schwiebus to Stäpel, a tiny hamlet, where there was a factory which made fuel briquettes out of brown coal or similar surface deposits. Two years later a colleague from this factory moved 250 miles west to Wallensen in Lower Saxony, and sent word back that there was good work to be had at the Humboldt factory there. Wallensen is in an isolated area, surrounded by hills and missed by all the main roads, but Humboldt's, who also manufactured coal briquettes out of brown coal, had a farflung reputation as kindly and paternal employers. The factory provided a pension scheme, health insurance, cheap rents and free fuel to its employees – enticing benefits to a forty-year-old potter turned factory foreman who was struggling to earn a hard and meagre living. Adolf journeyed west at his colleague's suggestion and, in the summer of 1900, his family followed, breaking their train journey by staying overnight with a relation in Berlin. Their first home in Wallensen was in the upper storeys inside the steep pitched roof of Obertor, 24, a fine timbered house of 1738 in the heart of the village.

Otto and Willi, who was also apprenticed at Meiers, remained behind in Schwiebus. Otto finished his time and worked in the town for a while until he joined the army. It is hard to imagine the young man who was soon to be the archfoe of the military and the scourge of the warmongers volunteering, so he was probably conscripted on his twentieth birthday in February 1902 and would then have served until 1904. He was called to the colours of the Seventh Jäger Battalion, a battalion of foot soldiers originally composed of hunters and foresters. The six hundred men of the Seventh, mostly conscripts, were known as the Bückeburger Jäger, as they were based in Bückeburg, in a long, bleak, red-brick barracks, which still stands. Bückeburg lies about thirty-five miles north-west of Wallensen and it is reasonable to assume that Otto was summoned unwillingly from Schwiebus to join up where he was registered with his family. Margarethe remembered being proud of her elder brother when – home on leave – he cut a dash around Wallensen in his dark green uniform, apparently setting the village girls' hearts a-fluttering. Otto, who was always vain, was fussy about his uniform and used to cuff young Ernst when he played with it. Margarethe was old enough to be allowed to clean the buttons for him. Unfortunately, many German military records were destroyed in 1944–5, and I was unable to turn up any account of how the recruit Otto Feige conducted himself during his two years as a soldier. When he was discharged, he would have been put on the reserve list and, if he had stayed in the area and not changed his name, would have been drafted into the Twentieth Jäger, the reserve battalion, during the First World War. By then he had taken himself away, set light to his past and arisen from the ashes as Ret Marut. While his former comrades in the Twentieth Jäger served on the Western Front in September 1917, he was in Munich, waving his fist at the war in the first issue of *Der Ziegelbrenner*.

In 1904, after his release from the army, Otto came back to live with his family in Wallensen and moved all his things into the better of the family's two living-rooms. He worked and slept in there. The politics of Marut and Traven were already taking shape. Otto had come out of the army a convinced socialist and planned a campaign in the village. He kept placards and leaflets in his room and, from outside the door, the rest of the family could hear him rehearsing his speeches. It was these preliminaries for his political debut which caused his departure from home. His mother, upset enough by Otto camping in her front room, was worried by the prospect of her eldest son becoming a political agitator in their small village. The people around lived quietly in modest circumstances; they were small farmers, poor farm hands or workers at Humboldt's, and both parents feared that Otto's activities would stir up trouble for the Feiges in the community. There was a row at home and Otto left, never to return. His parents had brought him into the world a bastard, had failed to nurture him themselves, had torn him unhappily from the arms of his grandparents, dashed the cup of opportunity from his lips and now stamped on his politics. He had not become inured to this treatment. From now on he would avoid the possibility of further injury by becoming someone else. He would do without parents or invent his own. He would be who he wanted to be.

Otto was not much spoken of in his absence within the family but his reputation echoed down the years, so that when I met three of his nieces, they all knew of Otto the socialist and opponent of the Kaiser, who had caused turmoil among the Feiges. The fear that having a radical in the family might cause trouble at work had lingered for years after Otto had last darkened the door. The nieces were Willi's daughter, Gertrude Constabel,* who still lived in Wallensen, and two daughters of Otto's sister Gertrud, Erna Hamann and Gertraud Fromme, who both lived in Hanover. The three shared a family likeness and Frau Constabel and Frau Hamann bore a striking resemblance to photographs of the elderly Traven in Mexico.

Otto's mother was remembered as a clever woman, who acted as scribe for other inhabitants of the village who could not read or write. As with many names in this family, there was some confusion over the spelling of her Christian and surnames: she was known as Hermina rather than Hormina in later years, and her mother's maiden name was remembered as Bullack, not Bullarz. Whatever the spellings, the mention of her name provoked a burst of laughter from Traven's three nieces, for Hormina had become a family joke. She was, it transpired, a great gad-about. She travelled to her in-laws in Finsterwalde, to see her brother in Berlin, several times back to Schwiebus and, locally, to Hameln and Hanover. For a time, she was an active member of the Queen Louisa's Union (a sort of Women's Institute), which enabled her to do plenty of visiting, have coffee with the vicar's wife, and so on. She shared one enthusiasm with her eldest son, for she produced plays with the local children and took them to perform in the surrounding villages. She knitted, crocheted and enjoyed dressing up in her best clothes, but apparently did very little else. She would sit and say: 'We must do this,' or, 'We must do that,' meaning that her husband should get up and do it. The words 'We must do ... ' were a joke still current in the family, a memory of idle grandmother Hormina, who was never seen to do anything but sit and sew and look out of the window.

Traven's father, Adolf, was obviously something of a saint. He worked as a supervisor at Humboldt's and came home to do all the washing, ironing, cooking and cleaning. He even

* Frau Constabel died in 1979.

scrubbed the front steps, I was told. When he was on shift work
and returned at two in the afternoon, he used the extra hours
to cultivate the garden. And if there were spare minutes in the
day, he made shoes for the children out of old clothes and rub-
ber tyres. He was an easy-going man, less stern than his wife
and fond of children. The descriptions by his grandchildren included phrases like 'put-upon' and 'down-trodden', and one
anecdote might serve as a metaphor for his place in the household. Adolf used to enjoy sitting in a wicker chair outside the
front door, reading. In those days beggars regularly passed the
house and Adolf's daughter would often put out a bowl of soup
for them. One day Adolf spotted a beggar approaching and
got up and went inside, not wanting to sit and watch the beggar
consume a bowl of soup. The beggar, who had hoped for some
money, turned his nose up at the soup and poured it into the
folded umbrella which always stood by the front door. A day
or so later, Adolf came out to squeeze in a stroll between the
round of domestic chores and, seeing that it was raining, opened
the umbrella over his head, douching himself with cold lentil
soup.

From the photographs Traven looked more like his mother
than his father, and he shared with her a wanderlust and a
capacity to make the world accommodate itself to him. She sat
motionless while the household busied itself round her; he
remained out of sight while others attended obediently to his
written demands. She casually mentioned tasks which others
leapt to accomplish; he grumpily laid down conditions, which
others willingly complied with. She lived with a man who saw
to all the boring labours of the home; he lived with or hid
behind a succession of women who handled the practicalities
of his business affairs.

At first glance Traven was unlike his father in character: the
one a humble potter, living meekly in henpecked domesticity;
the other a bossy citizen of the world. But they shared a dapper-
ness in dress, notable energy, a capacity for hard grind, and
deafness in old age. Adolf was unable to assert himself to effect,
and so in many ways was Traven, at least in person. All his
orders and instructions, all his dogmatism and intransigence
were transmitted on the page. At the typewriter he was a
lion: uncompromising in his correspondence, swingeing in his

journalism, fulminating in his novels, bloodthirsty in his calls for retribution. In person he was often a mouse, reduced to sulking when he did not have his way. His political speeches in Wallensen remained within the four walls of the front room because, even as a man in his mid-twenties, he was overruled by his parents. In Munich the darkening of the hall for his lecture was not to conceal his identity but to save his face. His anarchism allowed him to avoid office, to cheer mainly from the sidelines when the revolution came, rather than speak out or strike in the van. He may have wished to be a man of action, inside he may have thought that he was one. But it was only on paper that he roared full-throatedly.

Of Otto's brothers and sisters, only Willi, nearly three years younger, was in any way close to him. They were nearest in age, they were the cleverest of the siblings and they were together as locksmiths in Schwiebus. After Otto had left, Willi worked at Humboldt's until he served in a lowly capacity in the army during the First World War. I detected a brotherly similarity in a taste for pretence. Some photographs of Willi in uniform showed him posing in the back seat of a chauffeur-driven car and at the controls of an aeroplane. After the war Willi invented a system for sorting sand and gravel and went into business with an army friend. Willi was not unlike Otto in temperament. He was no businessman – he provided the flair and invention for the company – and would often lie dreaming on a nearby hill, if necessary being summoned to the factory by the raising of a special flag. He had little contact with his brothers and sisters, although they lived in the same village. He played the piano and he liked to read, particularly Jack London. His second wife told me that Willi believed Otto must have died, otherwise he would have tried to make contact with him at some stage. He told her that Otto was the only one of his family that he was fond of. They were similar because they were 'both outsiders'.

Willi lived close at hand but apart from his family; the rest, with the exception of Ernst, clustered round the parents. Gertrud married a tailor named Hage and lived nearly all the rest of her life in Wallensen. The next child, Max, was also sent as apprentice to Meiers in Schwiebus, returning to work at Humboldt's and live two doors away from his parents. Erna,

ten years younger than Otto, suffered from an illness of the
brain and died at the age of nineteen. Margarethe stayed in
Wallensen and married Henze, a maintenance and storage
manager at the all-embracing Humboldt's. The youngest,
Ernst, broke away and worked as a waiter in London before
the First World War and in Ireland after it, later settling in
Hamburg as a taxi-driver. Eventually he, too, was drawn back
to Wallensen.

Neither the parents nor any of these brothers and sisters ever
saw Otto again after he left home. His disappearance did not
take the family by surprise, for he was such an unusual and
self-willed young man that it was clear to them that he would
not remain as a village locksmith. He went probably in 1904
or 1905 and a year or so later sent a girl to stay in Wallensen.
She was called Elsa (Ernst thought her second name was
Muste) and she came from Dresden, where her parents owned
a mill. She was in love with Otto but her father was opposed
to their marrying, and so Otto had suggested that she escape
the difficult time she was having at home by staying with his
family in Wallensen. Otto put in no appearance himself and
after about four weeks Elsa went away, crying as she left – possibly, thought Frau Henze, because the relationship with Otto
was over. It occurred to me that Elsa, who was an actress, might
actually have been Elfriede Zielke under another name, but
Frau Henze did not recognise a photograph of Elfriede and it
is most likely that this girl was someone quite separate. Elsa,
whether by accident or as an excuse to return, left a case behind
at the Feiges' house but she never came back to collect it.

After the visit of Elsa there was silence from Otto. Like Stanislav, 'he lost all and every desire to send word home that he
was still alive'. It was not until more than fifteen years had
passed, after the First World War, that the Feiges heard from
Otto for the last time. He wrote from London to say that he
was in trouble with the British authorities and that they were
going to throw him out. He must have written this letter soon
after his confession to the police in London, in an attempt to
prepare the ground in case there were enquiries about him in
Germany. There seems no other reason for him to have broken
his long, determined silence. He may have wished to remind
his family of his existence, so that they would back up his

account of who he said he was. If that was his aim, it was probably unnecessary as a means of preventing his return to Germany. It was certainly unsuccessful.

Late one Sunday afternoon, the young Margarethe came home at the Feiges' house on the outskirts of Wallensen to hear the sound of sobbing. She went to see what was the matter and found her mother crying in the lavatory. Between sobs Hormina managed to tell her daughter what had happened. The police had called at the house earlier in the day and asked for Otto. The mother, knowing about Otto's radical politics and that he had been held by the authorities in England, was desperately afraid of bringing trouble on the family. So she told the police that the man they sought was nothing to do with them; she had no son called Otto. The police went away and Hormina sat down and wept at what she had done. That was the last anyone in Wallensen ever heard of Otto Feige, until we arrived with news of B. Traven more than fifty years later.

Traven never knew it, of course; but with a haunting irony he, who denied his parents, denied his name and denied his country, was in turn denied by his own mother. Hormina shed tears at her own betrayal and at the loss of her son. And Traven may not have been impervious to the thought of the sadness his disappearance caused.

A shelf with little compartments was filled with letters for patrons. Bundles of letters, many of them from a mother, a wife, or a sweetheart, were piled up, covered with thick dust. The men to whom they were addressed might be dead, or working deep in the jungles clearing new oil fields, or on a tramp in the China Sea, or helping the Bolsheviks build up a workers' empire, with no time to think that the letter writers back home might be crying their eyes out over a lost sheep.

The Treasure of the Sierra Madre

I knew, now, why we had been able to trace Hermann Albert Otto Max Feige when the American officials and the German police had failed to find him fifty years before. On the one occasion in Traven's life when he told the truth about himself, his mother had lied and denied his existence.

26 A Visit from the Senora

When we returned from Germany, I edited in the new footage, delayed the final dub no longer, and made the film ready for transmission in the autumn. On the flight back from Hanover, Robinson had suggested changing the title from 'The Search for Traven' to 'B. Traven: A Mystery Solved'. I had agreed. If it sounded smug, it was a true reflection of the way we felt. At every stage the evidence itself had improved upon our speculation.

We could still tease ourselves with the thought that a shadow might lie across the birth. He was born Hermann Albert Otto Max Wienecke and it was three months later that Adolf Feige turned up to claim him. Thus, while Hormina was his mother, we cannot be absolutely sure that Adolf was his father. He might have been rescuing her after she had strayed with another – he did after all have a kindly and self-sacrificing nature. If we allow our minds to run along these lines, we might remember that the young Prince Wilhelm used to go black-cock shooting at Gorlitz in Silesia. It was from there in 1879 that he made a visit to the Schleswig-Holstein-Augustenberg family at Primkenau and fell in love with Dona, his wife-to-be. Gorlitz was eighty miles from Schwiebus and Primkenau only fifty. If Willy's taste ran to heavily built, small-town girls, that was not so far. But this has to remain a tease.

Traven did succeed in tricking us all, the police included, over his departure from London. He did not sail on the *Hegre*. An American researcher, Richard Mezo, secured from the Norwegian Directorate of Seamen the London muster roll for April 1924. Ret Marut of California was engaged as 'kullemper',

299

coal-trimmer, on the *Hegre* on April 17th, but a line was drawn
through his name. The police knew that he had signed on this
ship, he may even have reported it himself, so the Special
Branch told the Home Office and the Home Office told the
American Embassy and the American Embassy told the State
Department and the State Department told the FBI that Marut
was sailing from London on board the *Hegre*. And they were
all wrong.

Navn. (*Name.*)	Hjemsted. (*Domicile.*)	Fodselsaar og-dag. (*Year and date of Birth.*)
Khristian Jörgensen	*Khristiansand S*	2/1 – 87
Frederick George Offord	*Van London*	4/5 – 1900
Terence Barton	*Wichlow*	22/2 – 06
~~Abt Musuti~~	*~~Californiis~~*	

Marut–Traven did not arrive to join the *Hegre* at Morocco
Wharf, and she sailed without him. He made alternative
arrangements for leaving England. I have searched passenger
and crew lists of ships leaving London and other British ports
for Mexico around that time and have so far found no trace
of him. Perhaps he returned to Rotterdam and sailed to
Tampico, either direct or with a further change, from there.

The question remains – why did Traven hide? No simple
answer will serve. There is no mathematical solution to the
puzzle set by the complex layers and inconsistencies and the
sheer strangeness of the human personality, and Traven's was
as strange as most. The mystery cannot be explained away. But
by rummaging through a life, by excavating its foundations,
some clues emerge and they help us to make some sense of what
we cannot fully understand. Though he struggled against it,
Traven could not avoid his own history and like anyone else
carried with him the luggage of his beginnings. His character
and his philosophy were shaped by this burden.

How could he – a misbegotten child, torn from his beloved
grandparents, prevented from following his destiny – allow a
significance to birth and parentage? He had been let down in

this regard, not even granted the commonplace of legitimacy. To place a value on random inheritance and accidental labels was to accuse himself of a deficiency, to accept that he was at a disadvantage with others. To Traven, a system of values which relegated him to the second rank was a system which was wrong. Instead, he denied the importance and even the meaning of such labels, and eventually tore off the ones he had been given, adopting some of his own choosing. It was almost as if he believed that the use of names was a cunning scheme devised by the world just to catch him out and uncover the humiliations of his childhood, a test which only he would fail. Records and official forms were the examination papers set to rob him of his dignity. Martin Trinidad, the rebel school-teacher in *The Rebellion of the Hanged*, knew how to restore Traven to equal terms with the world.

The first thing we must do is attack the registry and burn the papers, all the papers with seals and signatures – deeds, birth and death certificates, tax records, everything ... Then nobody will know who he is, what he's called, who was his father, and what his father had ... What do we want with birth certificates?

Traven was pleased with his own cleverness at dodging questions, tricking officials and confusing the files, but by abandoning his true identity he compounded his difficulties in these matters and kept the wounds of his childhood ever sore. The world went on asking for, taking note of and using names and he countered with a tangle of lies, deceits and complications. His skirmishes with the authorities fanned his anger and sharpened his tongue. *The Death Ship* is full of mockery of, and resentment for, the uniformed classes: 'Kings and presidents don't rule the world; the brass button is the real ruler.' But, with the blind unreasonableness of the obsessed, he hated officials for disbelieving him and for insisting on proof of what he said, when all the time he was telling them lies. He was furious because they saw through him. Not always, of course, but when he was trying to leave Europe and reach America, a crucial period in his life, they spotted him as he tried to put his head down and pass swiftly through the crowd.

Traven learned to disassociate himself from his surroundings from his earliest years, developing the internal life which was to nourish him as a writer. The egoism was already in evidence. He felt betrayed by his family and his circumstances and grew up a loner, living apart and within himself. The individualistic philosophy of Max Stirner might have been composed with him in mind, and he seized upon it. It provided him with a justification for measuring the world against his own wants and enabled him to combine this with his yearning to help his fellow human beings. The Stirnerite philosophy of Der Ziegelbrenner grew naturally from the mind of the young Otto Feige:

THE NOBLEST, PUREST AND MOST SIGNIFICANT HUMAN LOVE IS THAT TO ONESELF! I want to be free! I myself want to be able to be glad! I am the one who wants to enjoy all the beautiful things on earth. I am the one who wants to be happy. But my freedom is secure only if all other people round me are free. I can be happy *only* if all other people round me are happy ... And therefore it is my own well-being, only my own self, for which I oppose all danger threatening my freedom and my happiness.

His wish to love and serve others and his need to protect himself were expressed in his writing by a naïve idealism, born of his simple hopes, and a mocking irony, born of his disappointment that man's feeble endeavours achieved so little and were so easily corrupted. Searching for simplicity and purity, he identified with the Indians of Mexico. They, like him, lived apart from the baseness of the prevailing civilisation and, also like him, they carried within them the hopes of humanity.

Traven moved to the perimeter of life in childhood and observed the activity from there for the remainder of his years. The self-contained child became the anonymous writer, staying on the edge of the throng in order to avoid hurt, to retain the clarity of his vision and, possibly, to preserve his illusions about himself. He was not the power out in the sun that he was behind his desk, where he could describe and pronounce upon the world without having to face it. John Huston has the key to one aspect of Traven, when he says that he was a proud man who needed a disguise in which to visit society – hence the persona of Hal Croves. Traven the writer believed himself to be, and was, an extraordinary man; Traven the physical person was, and knew himself to be, a quite ordinary person, unable to impose himself on the world as a man with the voice of B. Traven should. His vanity jibbed at this and he devised strategies to protect himself: dealing with outsiders through his female agents, venturing out himself only as Hal Croves, translator. At the time he made *The Treasure of the Sierra Madre*, Huston was married to Evelyn Keyes, who described her meetings with Croves in her autobiography. They confirm Huston's opinion that Croves cut an unimpressive figure.

On one occasion she and Huston went marlin fishing with Croves. After several hours Huston wanted to get up and stretch himself and asked Croves, who had not wanted to fish, if he would hold the rod for him. Croves did so under protest. A moment later a huge marlin struck and Croves helplessly let go of the rod, allowing it and the fish to disappear behind the boat. Huston struggled to control his irritation, while Croves apologised humbly over and over. When the filming began Croves, who was seen to take himself very seriously, again emerged in faintly ludicrous guise. He fell for the tall wife of one of the Mexican film crew and started wearing lifts in his shoes to add a few inches to his height. According to Evelyn Keyes, Huston made cruel fun of the diminutive Hal Croves, affecting to ask his advice in front of the whole crew, posing him unlikely filming problems and pretending to listen to his answers. Yet Croves later told his wife how influential he had been at the filming, and he probably believed that he had been.

It is no surprise that he felt comfortable with the Mexican Indians, for they were uncompetitive and with them he was unchallenged. Their culture and his whiteness removed the need for him to assert himself. Like a child who gets on more easily with adults than with his peers, or an adult comfortable only in the company of children, Traven moved contentedly among the Indians on his long expeditions, able to be himself. The adopted family of his last years brought him similar security. He was loved, his wishes were acceded to, no questions were asked, he brought his own rules, obligations and morality

with him and his individuality remained untouched. As he had
written in his poem *Khundar*, 'Where I stand with both my feet,
that is my country and my kingdom.' He, in turn, had loved
his stepdaughters as his own and found peace in a family at
last. In the previous three-quarters of a century, he had abandoned his parents, abandoned his brothers and sisters and abandoned his child. Yet, as the dedication to *The Bridge in the Jungle*
shows, he had not been able to cast overboard all memories
of what a son should feel for his mother.

> To the mothers
> > of every nation
> > of every people
> > of every race
> > of every colour
> > of every creed
> > of all animals and birds
> > of all creatures alive
> > > on earth

Hormina must have been included.

'But, in God's name, who are you actually?' Professor bent
close to the teacher's ear and whispered a word into it. Aloud
he said, with an open laugh, 'Don't repeat it even if you are
asked. We speak it only in special, very special circumstances
... what we were has changed to what we are.'

                                          General from the Jungle

Ever since our discoveries in Germany, I had wondered how
much Señora Lujan knew of her husband's real name and
family. She knew nothing of his brother and sister being alive,
but had the elderly Traven ever bent close to her ear and
whispered the truth? I was to have an opportunity to try to
find out, for the Señora let me know that she was coming to
England after visiting the Frankfurt Book Fair in the autumn
of 1978.

At the beginning of October I received a telephone call from a Scotsman, who exhibited a proprietorial air towards Señora Lujan and informed me that she was definitely coming to Europe at the end of the month. I asked if he could make sure that she got in touch with me when she arrived. By the end of October I had heard nothing and assumed that the Señora had omitted England from her trip to Europe.

In the meantime, we had arranged a transmission for the film, linking it to a showing of John Huston's film of *The Treasure of the Sierra Madre*. This was not to be until December, so the film would not have gone out by the time that the Señora arrived, if she did, during the autumn. This presented me with a problem. What we had found out about Traven was only a footnote in the history of literature, but it was a footnote that no one else had discovered. I was afraid that if I told the Señora the full story and showed her the film before it went out, she would behave as if she had known everything all along, possibly announcing it publicly and upstaging our modest scoop. I had no wish to harm or embarrass the Señora, let alone betray her in any way. There was nothing in the film to hurt her and no challenge to her rightful authority, for we concluded that her husband was the sole author of the B. Traven books. I decided that I would not send her a script ahead of time but would make sure that she received one on the day the film went out, so that she would be aware of my discoveries before they were open to all. If she came to London, I would see her and explain what I was doing.

The Scotsman rang again on November 13th to say that Señora Lujan was arriving in London the following day and he demanded that I show her the film. I had never heard of this man and asked him if he would get the Señora to ring me, it was her I wanted to talk to. I told him that the film was still in the laboratories. (It was actually having a new soundtrack copied but it would have been quite possible to show it.) The Scotsman, who had a bossy and unpleasing air, began to huff and puff and the call ended on unfriendly terms. Next day, Geoff Botterill, the film editor, rang to tell me that the outside laboratory where BBC films are processed had received a phone call from a Scotsman, who claimed to be from an outside production company, demanding to see the Traven film. Geoff Botterill had himself been rung by the same man.

After missing each other several times, the Señora and I eventually spoke on the telephone and arranged to meet, when, I said, I would tell her why I did not want her to see the film. I felt uncomfortable pussyfooting around in this way, but I argued to myself that she had not told us all she had known in Mexico, so I had some justification for withholding my discoveries for a time. I felt less uncomfortable when, ten minutes after the call, she rang again to say that her friend the Scotsman was a friend of the Managing Director of BBC Television. Would that help her to see the film? I replied, no.

The Señora and I met that evening at Television Centre. She was wearing a new light-coloured raincoat, looking as elegant as I remembered her, and she greeted me with a kiss on each cheek. As we drove to my house she told me about the sightseeing she had been doing, how at the British Museum she had moved no further than the manuscript room, where she had gazed in fascination at the autographs of the great men and women of letters. She was in London, she said, with a Hollywood scriptwriter who was writing a film about the life of her husband. They had been to Brixton prison to see where he was locked up but had not been allowed to go inside. She said her husband had told her that he did not mind being in prison, as long as he had a pencil and paper to write with. She gave a wide smile as if to say: 'See, what details I know about my husband's life.'

We reached my house in five minutes. My wife and daughters were excited to meet 'B. Traven's wife', as they knew her, and she in turn was full of charm and kindness. We had a drink and there was talk of Mexico, school, food and fashions. I took out the photographs I had brought home for the Señora. There were some we had taken of her in Mexico, one of the court record book reporting her husband's arrest and one of the Lloyd's List noting the departure of the *Hegre*, although I explained that it now seemed that Marut had not travelled on this ship. The Señora had also been to Lloyd's to enquire about shipwrecks in 1924. Her sudden interest in Brixton and Lloyd's, matters of which we had heard nothing on our first visit to Mexico, indicated that she had obtained her knowledge of these episodes not from her husband but, like us, from the American documents.

Although the photographs I showed her contained no new information, anyone but the Señora might have reacted more noticeably. She had the capacity to accept any new fact or question with a mask of matter-of-factness, a most effective device for guarding her knowledge and camouflaging the gaps in it. I was left pondering. I also had the full-face and profile police mug shots, which I knew that she had not seen before, and I now handed them to her. She responded with a delicious little ploy. She looked at the photographs, gave a brief laugh and said: 'Do you know, I think that I still have that hat somewhere at home?' Whether she really had the hat or not was quite secondary to the point she was making, that I could produce nothing which would surprise her. She was the sole landlord of all things in the house of Traven. It was the elaborate care she took to encompass everything about her husband that made me doubt that she knew all she pretended to. Her persistent doubling back to retrieve every last relic made her stories less rather than more convincing.

The Señora asked me why she could not see the film and what was in it. I said that I wished to preserve the film's embargo and hoped that it would make an impression when it went out. I assured her that it endorsed the fact that her husband was the writer and that it contained nothing to challenge her standing as the widow of B. Traven. A previous researcher had made ungentlemanly suggestions about the Señora in the manuscript of a book that he was trying to publish and she was trying to stop. It was a man I had spoken to on the telephone but never met and I set her mind at rest that neither he nor any of his allegations had any place in our film.

We talked more generally about Traven's books and his life and in a casual, almost absent-minded way the Señora seeded the conversation with some pointed remarks. 'My husband's birth place, I am sure, was in the United States. Yes, I am certain he was an American.' A few moments later: 'Of course, he hated all papers and forms and he never had a birth certificate. He never had a passport except when he got one in Mexico – because they gave it to him on his word, you see.' And then, even more off-handedly: 'You know all those things that he

told the police in London, all those names Arnolds and Barker
and Feige and so on, Baumann checked all those out and they
are not true, you know. He just made them up. He had to tell
the police these things. And, you know, saying that he was born
in that town Schieb ... Schwiebus, was that it? Something like
that. Well, it was checked and he made it up. So you see,
he was not born in Germany. He had to lie about these
things.'

What game was this? I carefully gave no response to this
groundbait, letting it float untouched through the conversation
as if I had not noticed it. Was she trying to draw me out because
she was unsure? Was she trying to divert me in case Schwiebus
and Feige were the truth? After all, her wedding certificate said
she had married a man called Traven Torsvan and the will,
in which she was named as sole heir, was made by a man called
Traven Torsvan Croves. She may have feared, unnecessarily,
that her position was in jeopardy. I did not lie to her about
what I had found out but, on that occasion, I was far from frank.
She had not been, and was not being, frank with me, and I
believe we both realised that we were testing each other. It was
not a tense or antagonistic evening, however. After our drinks
the Señora said a warm farewell to my daughters, and my wife
and I took her off to dinner.

Over the meal she told my wife that she and Traven had
originally planned to get married in London in the early 1950s,
but she was uncertain at the time, as they had not been together
long, and she knew that he did not really believe in marriage
and children. She wanted to be sure that she was doing right
by the two daughters of her first marriage. She laughed as she
related how Traven had told her that if she did not marry him
then, he would never ask her again so that, if they were ever
to marry, she would have to come to him on her knees. Lest
we suspected her of such an indignity, the Señora confided that
this had not been necessary.

The last decade of his life was surely a happy time. He was
surrounded by a loving family, relaxed and insulated from the
world as he had never been before, save in those first few years
in his grandparents' house. It was the Señora who had given
him this domesticity and rest in the evening of his life, and she
was now the standard-bearer for his work. If she held things

back, dissembled and tried to wheedle information from the likes of me, it was no more than Traven-hunters deserved. None of them would ever be the equal of her husband and at all costs, she must protect the great man and his great books.

We dropped the Señora off at her hotel, kissed goodbye and made promises to meet soon in London or Mexico. But the visit was not quite over. The next day the Scotsman was busy again, ringing the Managing Director, ringing my office, threatening to go to the press, if the Señora did not see the film. I suspected that he was angry because he had promised the Señora more than he could deliver and was trying to save face. I rang the Scotsman to explain that I had made my peace with the Señora and that my relations were with her and not with him. He blustered: he would 'have my guts for garters'; according to 'some of the lawyers' he had spoken to, he could blow the matter wide open; I did not know who I was dealing with (I still don't); if I ever crossed his path again he would 'screw [me] into the ground'. In the course of all this he let slip that Señora Lujan had asked him to allow the matter to rest, otherwise ... My Traven story was ending with someone being threatened for keeping a secret!

A month later I arranged through the British Embassy in Mexico City for a complete transcript of the film to be delivered by hand to Señora Lujan on the morning of December 19th, the day that the film was being transmitted. When the 19th came I sent transcripts to all the other participants. The film went out and while the world continued to turn, the BBC came to a halt. The failing Curse had lost all timing and a strike over pay began the day after transmission. I awaited a response from the Señora. In the weeks after Christmas, most of the other recipients sent their comments on the script, but from Rio Mississippi no word came. I thought that she would quickly ask for more details of what we had discovered and for the addresses of her husband's brother and sister. This time her curiosity would surely be such that she would be drawn into asking, instead of telling about Traven. I was wrong. The silence continued and I checked with the British Embassy that the script had been delivered. It had. Then at the end of March I received my reply, a picture postcard of Chiapas Indians sent from Mexico City.

Dear Will,
        Thank you for the script. Have been enjoying Chiapas.
Best regards to you and your three beautiful girls.

                                        ROSA ELENA

Señora Lujan had decided to keep some secrets of her own.

TRAVEN IN EUROPE

DANZIG 1911
MOHRUNGEN 1911

HOLLAND

R. Elbe

BERLIN 1910, 1921

HANOVER

PINNE

ROTTERDAM 1923

POTSDAM
MAGDEBURG
1904

POZNAN

WARSAW

BÜCKEBERG
1902

SCHWIEBUS 1882 1893

ESSEN 1907

WALLENSEN
1904

GRÜNBERG 1888

DÜSSELDORF 1912

FINSTERWALDE

POLAND

COLOGNE 1920

OHRDRUF 1908

GÖRLITZ

CRIMMITSCHAU 1909

KRONBERG

SUHL 1908

R. Oder

PRAGUE

GERMANY

R. Rhine

AUSTRIA-HUNGARY

R. Danube

MUNICH 1915

VIENNA 1919

KEY
● Towns Visited By Traven
╌ ╌ Boundaries pre-1918

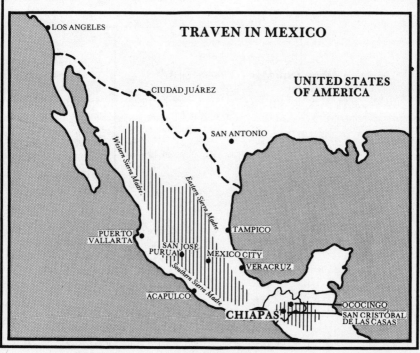

LOS ANGELES

TRAVEN IN MEXICO

**UNITED STATES
OF AMERICA**

CIUDAD JUÁREZ

SAN ANTONIO

Western Sierra Madre

Eastern Sierra Madre

PUERTO
VALLARTA

TAMPICO

SAN JOSÉ
PURUA

MEXICO CITY

VERACRUZ

Southern Sierra Madre

ACAPULCO

CHIAPAS

OCOCINGO
SAN CRISTÓBAL
DE LAS CASAS

The Family of B. Traven

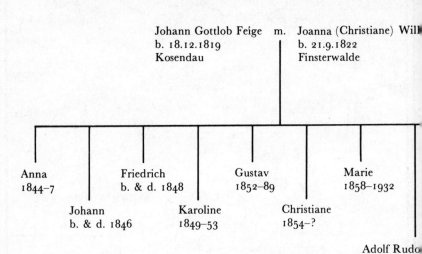

Johann Gottlob Feige   m.   Joanna (Christiane) Will
b. 18.12.1819   b. 21.9.1822
Kosendau   Finsterwalde

Anna   Friedrich   Gustav   Marie
1844–7   b. & d. 1848   1852–89   1858–1932

        Johann   Karoline   Christiane
        b. & d. 1846   1849–53   1854–?

                                                      Adolf Rudo
                                                      b. 23.5.186
                                                      d. 16.12.19

Hermann Albert *Otto* Max – Elfriede Zielke   Catherine Hermina
b. 23.2.1882 Schwiebus   *Gertrud* Ella
d. 26.3.1969 Mexico City   b. 18.5.1888 Grünber
                                                 d. 1.6.1951 Hanover*
                      Irene Zielke
                      b. 20.3.1912 Danzig

                      m. Rosa Elena Lujan   Erna Wolfgang Ge
                                                1911– 1920–

                      Adolf Friedrich *Wilhelm*   m. i ?
                      b. 5.12.1884 Finsterwalde   ii Maria
                      d. 26.5.1950 Hildesheim*   (Braba

                            Gertrude (Constabel)   Willi
                            1909–79   1914–

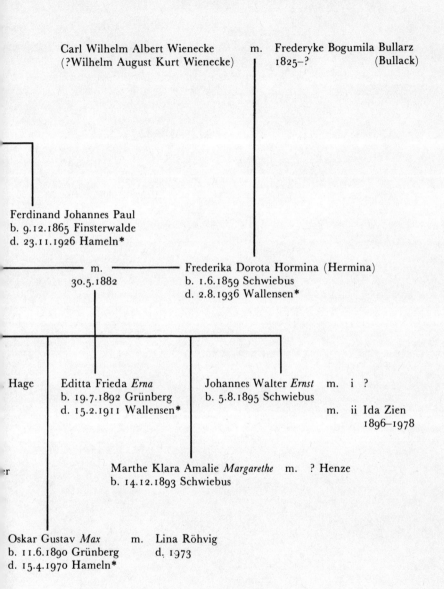

Carl Wilhelm Albert Wienecke   m.   Frederyke Bogumila Bullarz
(?Wilhelm August Kurt Wienecke)   1825–?   (Bullack)

Ferdinand Johannes Paul
b. 9.12.1865 Finsterwalde
d. 23.11.1926 Hameln*

        m.   Frederika Dorota Hormina (Hermina)
     30.5.1882   b. 1.6.1859 Schwiebus
             d. 2.8.1936 Wallensen*

Hage   Editta Frieda *Erna*   Johannes Walter *Ernst*   m.   i   ?
        b. 19.7.1892 Grünberg   b. 5.8.1895 Schwiebus
        d. 15.2.1911 Wallensen*   m.   ii   Ida Zien
                                                1896–1978

r   Marthe Klara Amalie *Margarethe*   m.   ? Henze
     b. 14.12.1893 Schwiebus

Oskar Gustav *Max*   m.   Lina Röhvig
b. 11.6.1890 Grünberg   d. 1973
d. 15.4.1970 Hameln*

                                      * Buried in Thüste or Wallensen

Appendix One

Identities Ascribed to B. Traven:

Jack London
Ambrose Bierce
American millionaire
Black American fugitive
Frans Blom
Professor Frank Tannenbaum
A leper
President Adolfo Lopez Mateos
Esperanza Lopez Mateos
August Bibelje
Jacob Torice
President Elias Calles
Chief editor of a German publishers
Cap'n Bilbo
Arthur Breisky
A group of writers in Honduras
A group of leftist Hollywood scriptwriters

Appendix Two

Some Dates in the Life of Traven

1882	Feb. 23rd	b. Schwiebus as Otto Wienecke
	May 6th	Son (Wilhelm) born to Crown Prince Wilhelm (later Wilhelm II)
	May 20th	becomes Otto Feige on parents' marriage
c. 1882–8		Lived with grandparents in Schwiebus
c. 1888–		
1900		With parents in Grünberg, Schwiebus and Stäpel
c. 1896		Confirmed
1896/7		Apprenticed to locksmith
c. 1900		Remains in Schwiebus when family move to Wallensen
c. 1902		In Magdeburg. Photograph taken there
1902–4		Army service in Bückeburg with Seventh Jäger Battalion
1904		Lives with family in Wallensen
1907	May	Parents' Silver Wedding: Otto already disappeared from home
1907		First record of Ret Marut: as actor in Essen
1908		Marut registers with police in Ohrdruf
1909		Acting in Crimmitschau
1910		In Berlin
1911		Acting in Pomerania, East and West Prussia, Posen and Silesia. Arrives Danzig
1912		Acting in Danzig. Daughter Irene Zielke b. March
		To Düsseldorf Theatre
		Police card states Marut is citizen of

1912		England – later changed to America *c.* 1915
		Marut's first published story
1914		Marut applies for US passport in Barmen – according to his later claim
	April	First known portrait of Marut by F.W. Seiwert
1915		Meets Irene Mermet
		Applies to San Francisco for copy of birth certificate
		Settles in Munich
1916		*An das Fräulein von S* ... by Richard Maurhut published in Munich
1917	Feb.	United States breaks off relations with Germany
	March	Marut applies for US passport in Munich
	April	United States and Germany at war Marut refused passport
	Sept.	First issue of *Der Ziegelbrenner* published
1918	Nov.	Eisner government in Munich: the Bavarian Republic Kaiser deposed
1919	Feb.	Eisner assassinated
	April	Republic of Councils (Räterepublik) in Munich. Marut is censor of press and on Commission to establish Revolutionary Tribunal
	May	Freikorps capture Munich; Räterepublik ended. Marut captured and escapes (?). Flees to Vienna
	June	Irene Mermet arrested and released Irene and Marut in Berlin?
1920	Jan.	*Der Ziegelbrenner* published from Vienna
	April	*Der Ziegelbrenner* published from Nippes, near Cologne
1921	June	Marut in Berlin

1921	Dec.	Last issue of *Der Ziegelbrenner* illustrated by F.W. Seiwert
1922		? in Switzerland and Holland
1923		Leaves Germany
	July	Arrives in Canada and turned away
	Aug.	Arrives in Britain
	Nov.	Arrested in London
	Dec.	Sent to Brixton Prison
	?	Irene Mermet engages lawyer for Marut and sends him money via Charles Hallinan
1924	Feb.	Marut released. Living in Commercial Road
		Writes to parents in Germany
1924	March	Applies for US citizenship in London
	April	Leaves London on board ship. Marut never heard of again.
	June/July	Arrives Tampico
1925	June	*Vorwärts* in Berlin begins serialisation of *The Cotton-Pickers*
		B. Traven writing from P.O. Boxes 972 and 1208 Tampico, Tamaulipas, Mexico
		Irene Mermet to Mexico
1926		*The Death Ship* published in Germany by Büchergilde Gutenberg
		With Irene Mermet in Tampico
		Traven Torsvan on scientific expedition to Chiapas
		Irene returns to United States
1927	April	Erich Mühsam's call to Der Ziegelbrenner
		Torsvan attends summer school of National University of Mexico
		The Treasure of the Sierra Madre published in Germany
1928		In Chiapas and crosses into Guatemala
		Land of Spring published in Germany
		In Mexico City at Hotel Panuco and

1928		with Maria de la Luz Martinez at Isabel la Catolica 17. P.O. Box 1480
1929		Expedition to Yucatan
		The Bridge in the Jungle and *The White Rose* published
		Visits United States?
1930		Expedition to Chiapas
		Buys Cashew Park in Acapulco
		Addresses: P.O. Box 49 Acapulco: P.O. Box 378 Mexico City
1931		*The Carreta* and *Government* published
1933		*The March to Caobaland* published
		Bernard Smith works on English manuscript from B.T.
1934		First English-language publication of B.T. book: *The Death Ship* in London and New York
1935		Corresponds with Herbert Klein
1936		*The Troza* and *The Rebellion of the Hanged* published
		Bernard Smith visits Mexico
1939	Aug.	Esperanza Lopez Mateos writes to Knopf
1940		*General from the Jungle* published
1942		Identity card for Traven Torsvan issued in Acapulco
		Esperanza Lopez Mateos becomes B. Traven's representative
1943		Mina Klein writes to buy *The Death Ship* from P.O. Box 2520 Mexico City
1945		Now using P.O. Box 18 Mexico City
1946		John Huston corresponds with B. Traven
1947		John Huston meets Hal Croves in Mexico City. First appearance of Croves.
		Croves on location of *The Treasure of the Sierra Madre*

1948		Croves writes from San Antonio and Mexico City
	July	Spota challenges Torsvan in Acapulco
	Aug.	Spota's article in *Mañana*
		Hal Croves comes to stay with Gabriel Figueroa
1949		Torsvan leaves Cashew Park
1951		*B.T. Mitteilungen* (*B.T. News Reports*) begin
		Esperanza Lopez Mateos dies
		Croves meets James Wong Howe and Sanora Babb Howe
1952		First mention of R.E. Lujan in connection with Traven works
1954		Croves at filming of *The Rebellion of the Hanged* in Chiapas
		Knopf instructed to send correspondence to R.E. Lujan, P.O. Box 2701, Mexico City
1956		Irene Mermet dies in United States
1957		Torsvan/Croves marries Rosa Elena Lujan in San Antonio
1958		Croves living at Calle Durango 353, Mexico City
1959		Torsvan also called Croves visits Germany for première of the film of *The Death Ship*
1960		*Aslan Norval* published
1963		*Stern* reporter Heidemann interviews Señora Lujan
1964		Croves moves to Rio Mississippi 61, Mexico City
1966		Judy Stone interviews Hal Croves
1968		Paul and Lupita Kohner visit Rio Mississippi 61
1969	March 26th	Torsvan/Croves dies

Appendix Three

Some of the Names Traven Used

Arnolds
Barker
Hal Croves
Traven Torsvan
Traves Torsvan
Traven Torsvan Torsvan
Traven Torsvan Croves
B.T. Torsvan
Ret Marut
Rex Marut
Robert Marut
Fred Maruth
Fred Mareth
Red Marut

Richard Maurhut
Albert Otto Max Wienecke
Adolf Rudolf Feige
Kraus
Martinez
Fred Gaudet
Lainger
Goetz Öhly
Anton Räderscheidt
Robert Bek-Gran
Arthur Terlelm
Wilhelm Scheider
Heinrich Otto Becker

Appendix Four

Some Occupations Pursued or Claimed

Writer
Actor
Stage director
Mechanic
Engineer
Bookseller
Photographer
Theatrical agent
Drama teacher
Merchant seaman
Sailor/cook

Explorer
Translator
Language teacher
Farmer
Fruit farmer
Tutor
Baker
Businessman
Soldier
Locksmith

Some Nationalities

English
American
Swedish
Norwegian

Lithuanian
German
Mexican

Appendix Five

Some Descriptions

(Sometimes he would have submitted his own description, with his capacity for deliberate as well as accidental confusion.)

1. Passport application, 1917 – Marut

Age: 35
Height: 5'7"
Eyes: blue-grey
Hair: brown
Complexion: fair
Chin: oval
Face: oval
Nose: broad
Forehead: medium

2. Home Office Criminal Record, 1923 – Marut

Age: 41
Height: 5'5½" (no shoes)
Eyes: blue
Hair: grey
Complexion: fresh
No distinctive marks or peculiarities

3. Description given by German authorities, 1924, to US Embassy, Berlin – Marut

Height: 1·65–1·68 m
Dark hair with large bald spot
Slim
Smooth-shaven
Healthy appearance
Good teeth
Slim hands, well-maintained nails
Fast gait
Well-dressed

4. Passport application made in London, 1924 – Marut

Age: 42
Height: 5′7″
Eyes: blue
Hair: dark brown/grey
Complexion: fair

5. Gaming Licence, 1929 – Torsvan

Height:	1·70 m.
Colour:	White
Eyes:	Blue
Hair:	Light brown
Forehead:	Normal
Mouth:	Normal
Beard:	Clean-shaven
Chin:	Rounded
Peculiarities:	None

6. Immigration Card, 1930 – Torsvan

Height:	1·68 m.
Colour:	White
Eyes:	Blue
Hair:	Fair/red (Rubesco)
Chin:	Normal, no beard
Eyebrows:	As hair
Moustache:	Clean-shaven
Nose:	Straight
Peculiarities:	None

7. Mexican Citizenship, 1951 – Torsvan

Height:	1·68 m.
Colour:	White
Eyes:	Blue
Hair:	Grey (Gris)
Beard:	–
Peculiarities:	None
Born:	Chicago, May 3rd, 1890
	Farmer

8. Mexican Passport, 1956 – Torsvan

Height: 1·68 m.
Colour: White
Eyes: Blue
Hair: Grey (Cano)
Peculiarities: None

Select Bibliography

The Books of B. Traven
First German and English language editions

Novels
Das Totenschiff, Büchergilde Gutenberg, Berlin, 1926
The Death Ship, trans. Erich Sutton, Chatto & Windus, London, 1934. Alfred A. Knopf, New York, 1934

Der Wobbly, Buchmeister-Verlag, Berlin, Leipzig, 1926
as *Die Baumwollpflücker*, Buchmeister-Verlag, Berlin, Leipzig, 1929
The Cotton-Pickers, trans. Eleanor Brockett, Robert Hale, London, 1956

Der Schatz der Sierra Madre, Büchergilde Gutenberg, Berlin, 1927
The Treasure of the Sierra Madre, trans. Basil Creighton, Chatto & Windus, London, 1934

Die Brücke im Dschungel, Büchergilde Gutenberg, Berlin, 1927
The Bridge in the Jungle, Alfred A. Knopf, New York, 1938

Die weisse Rose, Büchergilde Gutenberg, Berlin, 1929
The White Rose, Robert Hale, London, 1965

Der Karren, Büchergilde Gutenberg, Berlin, 1931
The Carreta, trans. Basil Creighton, Chatto & Windus, London, 1936

Regierung, Büchergilde Gutenberg, Berlin, 1931
Government, trans. Basil Creighton, Chatto & Windus, London, 1935

Der Marsch ins Reich der Caoba, Büchergilde Gutenberg, Zürich, Vienna, Prague, 1933
March to Caobaland, Robert Hale, London, 1960

Die Troza, Büchergilde Gutenberg, Zürich, Vienna, Prague, 1936

Die Rebellion der Gehenkten, Büchergilde Gutenberg, Zürich, Vienna, Prague, 1936

The Rebellion of the Hanged, trans. Charles Duff, Robert Hale, London, 1952. Alfred A. Knopf, New York, 1952

Ein General kommt aus dem Dschungel, Allert de Lange, Amsterdam, 1940
General from the Jungle, trans. Desmond I. Vesey, Robert Hale, London, 1954

Aslan Norval, Kurt Desch, Vienna, Munich, Basle, 1960

Non-fiction
Land des Frühlings, Büchergilde Gutenberg, Berlin, 1928

Short Stories
Der Busch, Büchergilde Gutenberg, Berlin, 1928. Some further stories were added to this collection in 1930

The first collection of Traven short stories in English was *Stories by the Man Nobody Knows*, Regency Books, Evanston, Illinois, 1961.

In Britain, the most recent editions of Traven are *The Treasures of B. Traven* (*The Death Ship*, *The Treasure of the Sierra Madre*, *The Bridge in the Jungle*), Jonathan Cape, 1980, and *The Cotton-Pickers* and *The Kidnapped Saint and Other Stories*, published in 1979 by Allison & Busby.

Works about B. Traven

Books
CHANKIN, DONALD O., *Anonymity and Death, The Fiction of B. Traven*, Pennsylvania State University Press, 1975
STONE, JUDY, *The Mystery of B. Traven*, William Kaufmann, Los Altos, California, 1977

For a fuller bibliography of Traven's writing and works about him, I recommend *B. Traven: An Introduction* by Michael Baumann, University of New Mexico, 1976. This is an indispensable book in English for anyone interested in Traven. The most complete bibliography is E. R. Hagemann's 'A Checklist of the Works of B. Traven and the Critical Estimates and Biographi-

cal Essays on Him, Together With a Brief Biography', in Papers
of the Bibliographical Society of America 53, 1959.

The other essential work on Traven is Rolf Recknagel's *B.
Traven: Beiträge zur Biografie*, Klaus Guhl, Berlin, 1977. (The
second edition, Verlag Reclam, Leipzig, 1971, contains an
admirable bibliography and filmography.) Recknagel's introduction to a collection of some of the early writings of Ret
Marut contains some additional material, *B. Traven – Ret
Marut, Das Fruehwerk*, Guhl, Berlin, 1977. Guhl also publish a
complete facsimile of *Der Ziegelbrenner*.

Articles on Traven:

BERMAN, PAUL, 'B. Traven, I Presume', *Michigan Quarterly
Review*, Ann Arbor, Winter 1978

HEIDEMANN, GERD, 'Wer ist der Mann, der Traven heisst?',
Stern, Hamburg, May 7th, 1967

JANNACH, HUBERT, 'B. Traven – An American or German
Author?', *German Quarterly* No. 36, 1963

JOHNSON, WILLIAM W., 'Who is Bruno Traven?', *Life*, New York,
March 10th, 1947
'The Traven Case', *New York Times Book Review*, New
York, March 10th, 1947
'A Noted Novelist Dies in Obscurity', *Los Angeles Times
Calendar*, Los Angeles, April 13th, 1969

KLEIN, MINA C., and KLEIN, ARTHUR, introduction to and translation of Ret Marut's 'In the Freest State in the World'
in *The Kidnapped Saint and Other Stories*, Lawrence Hill,
New York and Westport, 1975

LUJAN, ROSA ELENA, 'Remembering Traven', introduction to
The Kidnapped Saint and Other Stories, Lawrence Hill,
New York and Westport, 1975

MILLER, CHARLES H., 'B. Traven, American Author', *Texas
Quarterly* (6), Austin, 1963
Introduction to *The Night Visitor and Other Stories* by B.
Traven, Hill and Wang, New York, 1966

RASKIN, JONAH, 'In Search of Traven' in *The Radical Reader*, ed.
Stephen Knight and Michael Wilding, Wild and
Woolly, Sydney, 1977

SCHMID, MAX, 'Der Geheimnisvolle B. Traven' in *Tages-Anzeiger*,
Zürich, Nov. 1963–Jan. 1964

SMITH, BERNARD, 'B(ashful). Traven', *New York Times Book Review*, New York, November 22nd, 1970

SPOTA, LUIS, '*Mañana* descubre la identidad de B. Traven', *Mañana*, Mexico City, August 7th, 1948

SUAREZ, LUIS, 'y Presenta al mundo a B. Traven', *Siempre*, Mexico City, October 19th, 1966

'*Siempre* desentrana, al fin, la misteriosa actividad de Traven en la selva de Chiapas', *Siempre*, Mexico City, May 7th, 1969

WOODCOCK, GEORGE, 'On the Track of B. Traven', *The Times Literary Supplement*, London, August 27th, 1976

Other Useful Works

Unless otherwise stated, the place of publication is London

On F.W. Seiwert

BOHNEN, ULI, *Franz W. Seiwert: Leben und Werk*, Kölnischer Kunstverein, Cologne, 1978

On the filming of 'The Treasure of the Sierra Madre'

KEYES, EVELYN, *Scarlett O'Hara's Younger Sister*, W.H. Allen, 1978

KOHNER, FREDERICK, *The Magician of Sunset Boulevard*, Morgan Press, Palos Verdes, California, 1977

PRATLEY, GERALD, *The Cinema of John Huston*, Tantivy Press, 1977

On Germany and the Kaiser

BALFOUR, MICHAEL, *The Kaiser and his Times*, Cresset Press, 1964

BENNETT, DAPHNE, *Vicky, Princess Royal of England and German Princess*, Harvill Press, 1971

CRAIG, GORDON A., *Germany 1866–1945*, Oxford University Press, 1978

GRUNBERGER, RICHARD, *Red Rising in Bavaria*, Arthur Barker, 1973

LISTOWEL, JUDITH, *A Hapsburg Tragedy*, Ascent Books, 1978

MITCHELL, ALLAN, *Revolution in Bavaria*, Princeton University Press, Princeton N.J., 1965

PALMER, ALAN, *The Kaiser*, Weidenfeld and Nicolson, 1978

WATT, RICHARD M., *The Kings Depart*, Weidenfeld and Nicolson, 1969

WHITTLE, TYLER, *The Last Kaiser*, Heinemann, 1977

WILLIAM II, *My Early Life*, Methuen, 1926

General

BUNYAN, TONY, *The Political Police in Britain*, Julian Friedmann, 1976

CORDAN, WOLFGANG, *Secret of the Forest*, Gollancz, 1963

Index

Note: italic numbers refer to quotations